Recommender Algorithms

2026 Practitioner's Guide

Rauf Aliev

Contents

1 Foundational and Heuristic-Driven Algorithms **17**

1.1 Content-Based Filtering 17

1.1.1 The Vector Space Model (VSM): A Foundational Framework 17

1.1.2 TF-IDF: A Classic VSM Weighting Scheme 21

1.1.3 Embedding-based Similarity: A Latent Approach to VSM 22

1.1.4 Limitations of Content-Based Filtering 32

1.1.5 Alternative Word2Vec Architecture: CBOW 33

1.1.6 Handling Rare and Unknown Features: Subword Embeddings (FastText) 34

1.2 Rule-Based and Heuristic Systems 34

1.2.1 Classic Rule-Based Systems 35

1.2.2 Heuristic-Driven Algorithms 35

1.2.2.1 Top Popular (Most Popular) 36

1.2.3 Association Rule Mining 36

1.2.3.1 Frequent Itemset Mining Algorithms 37

1.2.3.1.1 Apriori: The Classic Approach 37

1.2.3.1.2 FP-Growth: A More Efficient Alternative 39

1.2.3.1.3 Eclat: A Vertical Approach 40

1.2.3.2 Rule Generation and Key Metrics 43

1.2.3.3 Practical Considerations 44

1.2.3.4 Use Cases & Production Readiness 44

2 Interaction-Driven Recommendation Algorithms **47**

2.1 Core Properties of Recommendation Data 47

2.1.1 Types of Ratings Feedback 47

2.1.2 The Long-Tail Property 48

2.2 Recommendation Tasks 48

2.3 Classic & Neighborhood-Based Models 48

2.3.1 ItemKNN (Item-based k-Nearest Neighbors) 49

2.3.2 SAR (Simple Algorithm for Recommendations) 56

2.3.3 UserKNN (User-based k-Nearest Neighbors) 63

2.3.4 Comparing User-Based and Item-Based Approaches 69

2.3.5 SlopeOne 70

2.3.6 Attribute-Aware k-Nearest Neighbors 73

2.4 Latent Factor Models (Matrix Factorization) . . . 75
2.4.1 Classic Singular Value Decomposition (SVD) . . . 78
2.4.2 FunkSVD (Biased Matrix Factorization) . . . 80
2.4.3 Probabilistic Matrix Factorization (PMF) . . . 85
2.4.4 Weighted Regularized Matrix Factorization (WRMF) . . . 90
2.4.5 Pairwise Ranking Objective: BPR (Bayesian Personalized Ranking) . . . 99
2.4.6 SVD++ . . . 102
2.4.7 TimeSVD++ (Time-aware SVD++) . . . 109
2.4.8 Item-based Latent Models: SLIM & FISM . . . 112
2.4.9 Non-Negative Matrix Factorization (NonNegMF) . . . 123
2.4.10 Collaborative Metric Learning (CML) . . . 126
2.5 Deep Learning Hybrids & Representation Learning . . . 130
2.5.1 Neural Collaborative Filtering (NCF) Framework and NeuMF . . . 131
2.5.2 Factorization Machine-based: DeepFM & xDeepFM . . . 136
2.5.3 Autoencoder-based: DAE & VAE . . . 140
2.5.4 A Modern Baseline for CF: SimpleX . . . 146
2.5.5 EASE (Embarrassingly Shallow Autoencoders) . . . 149
2.6 Sequential & Session-Based Models . . . 150
2.6.1 RNN-based: GRU4Rec . . . 150
2.6.2 CNN-based: NextItNet . . . 153
2.6.3 Attention/Transformer-based: SASRec & BERT4Rec . . . 156
2.6.4 With Contrastive Learning: CL4SRec . . . 159
2.6.5 Generative Adversarial Networks (GANs): IRGAN . . . 163
2.6.6 Diffusion for CF: DiffRec . . . 166
2.6.7 GFlowNets: GFN4Rec . . . 169
2.6.8 Normalizing Flows: IDNP . . . 172

3 Context-Aware Recommendation Algorithms **177**
3.1 Factorization Machine Family . . . 177
3.1.1 Factorization Machines (FM) . . . 177
3.1.2 AMF (Attentional Factorization Machine) . . . 179
3.2 Cross-Network Models . . . 180
3.2.1 Wide & Deep . . . 180
3.2.2 Mathematical & Engineering Foundations of Wide & Deep . . . 181
3.3 Tree-Based Models for CTR Prediction . . . 183
3.3.1 LightGBM (Light Gradient Boosting Machine) . . . 184

4 Text-Driven Recommendation Algorithms **191**
4.1 Review-Based Models . . . 191
4.1.1 DeepCoNN (Deep Cooperative Neural Networks) . . . 191
4.1.2 NARRE (Neural Attentional Rating Regression with Review-level Explanations) 192
4.2 Large Language Model (LLM)-Based Paradigms . . . 193
4.2.1 Retrieval-based: Dense Retrieval & Cross-Encoders . . . 193

4.2.2 Generative / Instruction-Tuned . . . 194
4.2.3 RAG & Feature Extraction . . . 195
4.2.4 LLM Agents & Tool Use . . . 195
4.3 Conversational Recommender Systems . . . 196
4.3.1 Dialogue-based Preference Elicitation . . . 196
4.3.2 Natural Language Explanation & Critique . . . 197

5 Multimodal Recommendation Algorithms **199**
5.1 Contrastive Learning for Multimodal Alignment . . . 199
5.1.1 CLIP (Contrastive Language-Image Pre-Training) . . . 199
5.1.2 ALBEF (Align Before Fuse) . . . 200
5.2 Generative Multimodal Models . . . 201
5.2.1 Multimodal VAEs . . . 201
5.2.2 Multimodal Diffusion . . . 201

6 Knowledge-Aware Recommendation Algorithms **205**
6.1 Graph Neural Networks for CF: NGCF & LightGCN . . . 205
6.1.1 NGCF (Neural Graph Collaborative Filtering) . . . 205
6.1.2 LightGCN (Light Graph Convolution Network) . . . 206
6.1.3 Self-Supervised Graph Learning for CF: SGL . . . 208
6.2 Embedding-based & Path-based Models . . . 211

7 Specialized Recommendation Tasks **213**
7.1 Debiasing & Fairness . . . 213
7.2 Cross-Domain Recommendation . . . 213
7.3 Meta-Learning for Cold Start . . . 213

8 New Algorithmic Paradigms in Recommender Systems **215**
8.1 Reinforcement Learning (RL) for RecSys . . . 215
8.1.1 Core Idea . . . 215
8.1.2 Key Concepts & Algorithms . . . 215
8.1.2.1 Multi-Armed Bandits (MAB) & Contextual Bandits . . . 215
8.1.2.2 Deep Reinforcement Learning (e.g., DQN, Actor-Critic) . . . 216
8.2 Causal Inference in Recommender Systems . . . 216
8.2.1 Core Idea . . . 216
8.2.2 Key Concepts & Algorithms . . . 216
8.2.2.1 Uplift Modeling . . . 216
8.3 Explainable AI (XAI) for RecSys . . . 217
8.3.1 Core Idea . . . 217
8.3.2 Key Concepts & Algorithms . . . 217
8.3.2.1 Graph-Based Explanations . . . 217
8.3.2.2 Feature-Based Explanations . . . 218

9 Evaluating Recommender Systems **219**
9.1 Metrics for Rating Prediction . . . 219
9.1.1 Root Mean Squared Error (RMSE) . . . 219
9.1.2 Mean Absolute Error (MAE) . . . 221
9.2 Metrics for Top-N Ranking . . . 222
9.2.1 Precision@k and Recall@k . . . 222
9.2.2 Mean Average Precision (MAP@k) . . . 223
9.2.3 Normalized Discounted Cumulative Gain (nDCG@k) . . . 225
9.3 Beyond-Accuracy Metrics . . . 227
9.3.1 Diversity . . . 227
9.4 Metrics for Classification Tasks in Recommendation . . . 229
9.4.1 Confusion Matrix . . . 229
9.4.2 Matthews Correlation Coefficient (MCC) . . . 231
9.4.3 Log Loss (Binary Cross-Entropy) . . . 232
9.4.4 ROC Curve and AUC Score . . . 233
9.4.5 F-beta Score . . . 235
9.4.6 Cohen's Kappa . . . 237
9.4.7 Brier Score . . . 238

Abstract

This book serves as an essential practitioner's guide to the world of recommender algorithms as it stands in early 2026. We begin with the indispensable baselines—from classic neighborhood models to powerful matrix factorization—and build toward the sophisticated deep learning architectures that power today's largest platforms, including hybrids for CTR prediction and state-of-the-art sequential models.

A core theme of this guide is the practical integration of the latest technological breakthroughs. We dedicate significant attention to the transformative impact of Large Language Models (LLMs), offering architectural blueprints for leveraging them as powerful semantic feature extractors, building reliable Retrieval-Augmented Generation (RAG) pipelines, and designing the next wave of generative and conversational recommender agents. Furthermore, we explore the critical role of multimodal models like CLIP for solving visual cold-start problems and provide insights into specialized areas like debiasing and fairness.

This is more than a survey; it is a toolkit for the modern engineer. Each section balances conceptual depth with pragmatic advice on implementation, scalability, and production readiness, making it the definitive resource for professionals tasked with creating value through personalization.

Introduction

In the modern digital ecosystem, users are confronted with a virtually infinite selection of items, from products and movies to news articles and music. This phenomenon, often termed "information overload," presents a significant challenge for both consumers and platforms. Recommender systems have emerged as a critical technology to address this challenge, serving as personalized information filters that guide users toward relevant content, thereby enhancing user experience, engagement, and commerce.

The field of recommendation algorithms has undergone a remarkable evolution. Early systems were built on simple statistical methods that leveraged direct user-item interactions. These foundational techniques, known as collaborative filtering, gave way to more sophisticated latent factor models, which sought to uncover the hidden dimensions of user preference by decomposing the user-item interaction matrix. The deep learning revolution subsequently ushered in a new era, with neural networks enabling the modeling of complex, non-linear relationships that were previously intractable.

This progression continued with the development of specialized architectures to capture the sequential dynamics of user behavior, borrowing heavily from advances in natural language processing. Concurrently, a new perspective emerged that modeled the recommendation problem as a graph, applying Graph Neural Networks to capture high-order relationships between users and items. Most recently, the landscape is being reshaped by the advent of large-scale generative models, including Generative Adversarial Networks, Diffusion Models, and, most notably, Large Language Models (LLMs), which are redefining the boundaries of what recommender systems can achieve.

This book aims to provide a structured, high-level, and practical overview of this algorithmic landscape. We organize our survey into several principal sections based on the primary data modality and methodological approach each class of algorithms leverages:

1. **Foundational and Heuristic-Driven Algorithms.** Models that rely on intrinsic item attributes (Content-Based) or manually defined heuristics (Rule-Based) to generate recommendations, offering interpretability and effectiveness for cold-start scenarios.

2. **Interaction-Driven Recommendation Algorithms.** The core of collaborative filtering, where models rely exclusively on user-item interaction data (e.g., ratings, clicks, purchases).

3. **Context-Aware Recommendation Algorithms.** Advanced models that leverage explicit side features and contextual information, crucial for industrial applications like CTR prediction.

4. **Text-Driven Recommendation Algorithms.** Models that incorporate unstructured text, such as user reviews or item descriptions, and are increasingly powered by LLMs.

5. **Multimodal Recommendation Algorithms.** Models that fuse information from multiple sources, such as text and images, to create a holistic understanding of items and preferences.

6. **Knowledge-Aware Recommendation Algorithms.** Advanced models that leverage structured knowledge from external sources like knowledge graphs.

7. **Specialized Recommendation Tasks.** A look at crucial sub-fields like ensuring fairness, mitigating bias, and addressing the cold-start problem.

8. **New Algorithmic Paradigms.** An exploration of emerging paradigms that extend beyond traditional recommendation, focusing on long-term value, causality, and transparency.

9. **Evaluating Recommender Systems.** A practical guide to the metrics and methodologies used to measure the performance and quality of recommender systems.

For each algorithm, we provide a concise explanation of its core concept, key differentiators, primary use cases, and practical considerations for implementation, along with a link to its seminal paper. Our objective is to equip engineers and researchers with a comprehensive map to navigate the field, understand its historical trajectory, and make informed decisions when designing and deploying the next generation of recommender systems.

Structure and Prerequisites

This book is structured to guide you progressively from foundational concepts to the state-of-the-art, with a focus on practical understanding and implementation. Below is an overview of the book's organization and the knowledge recommended to get the most out of it.

How This Book Is Organized

We have organized the content into thematic sections that build upon one another, guiding you progressively from foundational concepts to the state-of-the-art. This structure is based on the primary data modality and algorithmic approach each family of models utilizes.

- **Section 1: Foundational and Heuristic-Driven Algorithms.** We begin with the essential building blocks of recommendation. This includes content-based filtering methods like TF-IDF and the Vector Space Model, alongside simple yet crucial rule-based systems such as "Top Popular". These models serve as powerful baselines and are often vital components in more complex hybrid systems.

- **Section 2: Interaction-Driven Recommendation Algorithms.** As the largest and most comprehensive section, this chapter forms the core of both classic and modern collaborative filtering. We journey from traditional neighborhood-based methods (ItemKNN, UserKNN) to the powerful latent-factor models of matrix factorization (SVD, BPR, WRMF). From there, we transition into the deep learning era, covering hybrid architectures (NCF, NeuMF), sophisticated sequential models that learn from user behavior over time (GRU4Rec, SASRec, BERT4Rec), and conclude with cutting-edge generative paradigms like IRGAN and DiffRec.

- **Sections 3 & 4: Text-Driven and Multimodal Algorithms.** Here, we explore how to leverage richer, unstructured data to enhance recommendations. We cover models that learn from user reviews and item descriptions, followed by a deep dive into the transformative impact of Large Language Models (LLMs) in roles ranging from feature extraction to fully generative and conversational agents. We then expand into the visual domain, discussing how multimodal models like CLIP create a shared understanding between text and images to effectively solve cold-start problems.

- **Advanced Topics: Context, Knowledge, and Specialized Tasks.** The final sections cover advanced topics critical for building robust, real-world systems. We discuss context-aware models that are the workhorses of industrial CTR prediction (Wide & Deep, LightGBM) and knowledge-aware models that leverage the rich structure of external knowledge graphs. We conclude with a focused look at specialized but essential sub-fields, including debiasing, fairness, and meta-learning strategies for tackling cold-start scenarios.

- **Appendix.** For readers keen on implementation, the appendix provides detailed, line-by-line explanations of the code presented in the tutorials, clarifying the role of each function and library.

Essential Mathematical Basics for Understanding Latent Matrix Models

We assume that the reader is already familiar with all of the following, but for the sake of completeness and consistency of presentation, we provide a very brief introduction to the mathematical foundations that will be frequently referenced in the later chapters of the book.

Matrix Representation in Recommendations

A matrix is a structured grid of numbers, often used in recommendation systems to represent interactions between users and items. Specifically:

- Rows correspond to users (e.g., individuals in a dataset).
- Columns correspond to items (e.g., movies, products).
- Each cell contains an interaction value, such as a rating (e.g., 5 stars) or a binary indicator (1 for interaction, 0 otherwise).

When most cells are empty—because users interact with only a small subset of items—the matrix is described as sparse. Latent matrix models aim to predict these missing values by uncovering patterns within the observed data.

Example — A small matrix R with 3 users and 4 items might appear as:

$$R = \begin{pmatrix} 5 & ? & 3 & ? \\ ? & 4 & ? & 2 \\ 1 & ? & 5 & ? \end{pmatrix}$$

Here, "?" denotes unknown values to be predicted.

Vectors and Dot Products

A vector is a sequence of numbers, such as a row or column extracted from a matrix. In latent matrix models, users and items are represented by *latent vectors*—compact lists of numbers capturing hidden characteristics (e.g., a user's preference for action or romance genres, inferred from data).

The dot product measures the similarity between two vectors by computing a single scalar value. For vectors $\vec{u} = (u_1, u_2, \ldots, u_k)$ and $\vec{i} = (i_1, i_2, \ldots, i_k)$, the dot product is defined as:

$$\vec{u} \cdot \vec{i} = u_1 i_1 + u_2 i_2 + \cdots + u_k i_k$$

In recommendation systems, the dot product between a user's latent vector and an item's latent vector predicts the expected rating, with a higher value indicating a stronger predicted preference.

Example — A user's latent vector (0.8 for action, 0.2 for romance) and an item's vector (0.9 for action, 0.1 for romance) yield a dot product of $0.8 \times 0.9 + 0.2 \times 0.1 = 0.74$, suggesting a likely positive match.

Matrix Factorization (Decomposition)

Matrix factorization involves decomposing a large user-item matrix R into two smaller matrices, U (containing user latent vectors) and V (containing item latent vectors), such that their product approximates R:

$$R \approx U \times V^T$$

Here, V^T denotes the transpose of V, aligning item vectors as columns. The term *latent* refers to the hidden factors (e.g., genres, styles) that these vectors represent, learned directly from the data.

This decomposition is efficient because it reduces dimensionality. For a matrix R with m users and n items, U is $m \times k$ and V is $n \times k$, where k (the number of latent factors) is small (e.g., 10–100). This approach addresses sparsity by predicting missing entries based on learned patterns.

Loss Functions and Optimization

Latent matrix models optimize U and V by minimizing a loss function, which quantifies the discrepancy between predicted and actual ratings. A common choice is the Mean Squared Error (MSE), defined for actual ratings r and predicted ratings $\hat{r}$ as:

$$\text{MSE} = \frac{1}{N} \sum (r - \hat{r})^2$$

Optimization techniques, such as gradient descent, iteratively adjust U and V to reduce this error. Gradient descent starts with random U and V and updates them in small steps to approach the minimum loss, analogous to finding the lowest point in a landscape.

Some models, like ALS, use an alternating approach, where U is fixed to optimize V, then V is fixed to optimize U, repeating until convergence.

Regularization

To prevent overfitting—where models memorize noise rather than generalizing patterns—regularization is employed. This technique penalizes overly large values in U and V, encouraging simpler solutions.

A standard regularization method is L2 regularization, which adds a penalty term to the loss function:

$$\lambda(|\vec{u}|^2 + |\vec{i}|^2)$$

Here, λ controls the strength of the penalty, and $|\vec{u}|^2$ and $|\vec{i}|^2$ represent the squared magnitudes of the user and item vectors, respectively. This ensures the model focuses on meaningful patterns.

Overview of Recommender Algorithms

Foundational and Heuristic-Driven Algorithms

Vector Space Model (VSM) — A foundational framework for content-based filtering that represents items and user preferences as vectors in a high-dimensional feature space, where similarity is calculated based on vector proximity. (see page 17)

TF-IDF — A classic weighting scheme for the Vector Space Model (VSM) that calculates feature weights based on a term's frequency within an item and its inverse frequency across the entire catalog, making it an effective baseline for recommending new items with descriptive metadata. (see page 21)

Embedding-based Similarity (Word2Vec) — This latent approach to VSM uses models like Word2Vec to learn dense feature embeddings based on co-occurrence, capturing semantic relationships that TF-IDF misses. The model is trained to predict context features that appear alongside a given feature, creating a vector space where similar features are mapped closely together. (see page 22)

CBOW (Continuous Bag-of-Words) — As an alternative to Word2Vec's Skip-gram, the CBOW model learns feature embeddings by predicting a central feature from the average of its surrounding context features, offering a more computationally efficient approach that performs well for frequent features. (see page 33)

FastText — Extending Word2Vec, FastText addresses the out-of-vocabulary problem by learning embeddings for character n-grams rather than entire features, allowing it to construct meaningful vectors for rare or previously unseen features by combining the representations of their constituent parts. (see page 34)

Classic Rule-Based Systems — These systems use manually defined, domain-specific logical rules (e.g., "if-then") to generate recommendations based on business knowledge rather than statistical learning, offering complete transparency and control but lacking personalization and scalability. (see page 35)

Top Popular — This simple heuristic-driven algorithm recommends items based on their overall popularity across all users, typically measured by the total number of interactions, serving as a common non-personalized baseline that is effective for the cold-start problem. (see page 36)

Apriori — the classic algorithm for association data mining. It works iteratively by first identifying individual items that meet a minimum support threshold (i.e., appear frequently). It then uses these frequent items to generate candidate pairs, tests their frequency, and continues this level-by-level process for triplets, quadruplets, and so on. Its efficiency comes from the **Apriori Principle**: if an itemset is frequent, all of its subsets must also be frequent, which allows the algorithm to prune a vast number of candidates early on. However, its primary drawback is the need to make multiple passes over the database and the potential to generate a massive number of candidate sets, making it slow for large datasets. (see page 37)

FP-Growth — more efficient alternative that avoids the costly candidate generation step of Apriori. It works by first compressing the entire transactional database into a compact tree structure known as an FP-tree. This tree stores the itemset information in a way that allows the algorithm to mine frequent itemsets directly from this structure with just two passes over the data. This makes it significantly faster and more memory-efficient, especially for large datasets. (see page 39)

Eclat — takes a different approach by using a **vertical data layout**. Instead of listing items for each transaction (horizontal format), it creates a list of transaction IDs for each item. It then finds frequent itemsets by simply intersecting these transaction ID lists. (see page 40)

Interaction-Driven Recommendation Algorithms

ItemKNN — A classic neighborhood-based collaborative filtering model that recommends items similar to those a user has previously interacted with. It computes item-to-item similarity based on the interaction patterns of all users, making it more scalable than user-based approaches when the number of users greatly exceeds the number of items. (see page 49)

SAR (Simple Algorithm for Recommendations) — A fast and scalable item-based model optimized for implicit feedback that builds an item similarity matrix based on co-occurrence counts rather than more complex metrics like cosine similarity, making it a simple yet powerful baseline. (see page 56)

UserKNN — In contrast to ItemKNN, this model finds users with similar interaction histories to a target user and recommends items that those "neighboring" users liked. This approach often generates more diverse and serendipitous recommendations but is less scalable as the user base grows. (see page 63)

SlopeOne — An extremely simple item-based algorithm that predicts ratings based on the pre-computed average rating *deviation* between pairs of items. It has no iterative training phase and can be updated incrementally as new ratings arrive, making it lightweight and fast. (see page 70)

Attribute-Aware k-NN — An extension of k-NN that combines both collaborative signals (user interactions) and content-based signals (item attributes) into a hybrid similarity metric, which is particularly effective for alleviating the item cold-start problem. (see page 73)

FunkSVD (Biased Matrix Factorization) — A breakthrough matrix factorization model that predicts ratings as the sum of a global average, user and item biases, and the dot product of user and item latent vectors. Unlike true SVD, it is an optimization-based model that works on sparse data and learns its parameters via methods like Stochastic Gradient Descent. (see page 80)

PMF (Probabilistic Matrix Factorization) — A probabilistic version of matrix factorization that treats latent factors as probability distributions and assumes ratings are drawn from a Gaussian distribution centered at the user-item dot product, providing a principled Bayesian approach to regularization. (see page 85)

WRMF (Weighted Regularized Matrix Factorization) — A matrix factorization model specifically designed for implicit feedback, which treats all unobserved items as negative examples but assigns them a much lower confidence weight than positive interactions. It is typically optimized with an efficient Alternating Least Squares (ALS) algorithm. (see page 90)

BPR (Bayesian Personalized Ranking) — A foundational model that reframes recommendation from rating prediction to a pairwise ranking task. It is trained to ensure that for any user, a positive (interacted-with) item has a higher prediction score than a negative (unobserved) item, making it ideal for optimizing ranked lists from implicit feedback. (see page 99)

SVD++ — An extension of FunkSVD (Biased MF) that incorporates implicit feedback to enrich the user's latent representation. A user's preference is modeled not just by their explicit latent vector but also by an aggregated vector representing all the items they have interacted with, regardless of the rating. (see page 102)

TimeSVD++ — An extension of SVD++ that incorporates temporal dynamics by modeling user biases, item biases, and user factors as functions of time, allowing it to capture the dynamic nature of preferences and item popularity. (see page 109)

SLIM & FISM — These models directly learn a sparse item-to-item similarity matrix from implicit data. SLIM uses a sparse linear model with L1/L2 regularization to create an efficient and interpretable matrix, while FISM factorizes the similarity matrix into two smaller embedding matrices to better capture latent relationships and handle extreme data sparsity. (see page 112)

Non-Negative Matrix Factorization (NonNegMF) — A variant of matrix factorization that constrains the user and item latent factors to be non-negative, resulting in an additive, parts-based representation that is often more interpretable than standard matrix factorization. (see page 123)

CML (Collaborative Metric Learning) — Reframes collaborative filtering as a metric learning problem, learning a shared embedding space where the Euclidean distance between a user and item reflects their compatibility. It uses a pairwise loss to pull positive user-item pairs closer together than negative pairs, serving as a powerful alternative to BPR for ranking tasks. (see page 126)

NCF (Neural Collaborative Filtering) & NeuMF — NCF is a framework that generalizes matrix factorization by replacing the dot product with a flexible multi-layer perceptron (MLP) to capture complex, non-linear user-item interactions. Its flagship model, NeuMF, fuses a linear matrix factorization path with a non-linear MLP path to combine the strengths of both approaches for state-of-the-art performance on implicit feedback tasks. (see page 131)

DeepFM & xDeepFM — These are hybrid architectures for CTR prediction that combine a "wide" component for memorizing low-order feature interactions with a "deep" component for generalizing to high-order interactions. DeepFM uses a Factorization Machine for the wide part, while xDeepFM enhances this with a Compressed Interaction Network (CIN) to learn explicit, high-order feature interactions in a more controlled manner. (see page 136)

Autoencoder-based (DAE & VAE) — This approach frames recommendation as a reconstruction task, training a neural network to compress a user's entire interaction history into a low-dimensional vector and then reconstruct it. Denoising Autoencoders (DAEs) learn robust representations from corrupted inputs, while Variational Autoencoders (VAEs) offer a probabilistic, generative approach that is particularly effective for modeling the uncertainty in implicit feedback data. (see page 140)

SimpleX — A simple yet powerful bi-encoder baseline for collaborative filtering that achieves state-of-the-art performance through a contrastive learning objective (InfoNCE). It learns to pull positive user-item pairs together in an embedding space while pushing them apart from in-batch negative items, enhanced by consistency regularization for more robust training. (see page 146)

EASE (Embarrassingly Shallow Autoencoders) — A non-neural, linear autoencoder that learns an item-item similarity matrix to reconstruct user interaction histories. Its key differentiator is a closed-form analytical solution that eliminates the need for iterative training, making it an extremely strong, simple, and reproducible baseline for implicit feedback tasks. (see page 149)

GRU4Rec — A pioneering sequential model that applies a Gated Recurrent Unit (GRU), a type of RNN, to session-based recommendation. It processes a sequence of user interactions one by one, maintaining an evolving hidden state that captures the user's current intent to predict the next item they will interact with. (see page 150)

NextItNet — An alternative sequential model that uses stacked layers of dilated 1D convolutions to efficiently identify patterns and long-range dependencies in user interaction histories. Unlike RNNs, its convolutional architecture can process all parts of a sequence in parallel, making training significantly faster and more scalable for very long sequences. (see page 153)

SASRec & BERT4Rec — These models apply the Transformer architecture's self-attention mechanism to sequential recommendation. SASRec is unidirectional, using masked self-attention to predict the next item based only on past actions. In contrast, BERT4Rec is bidirectional and is trained to predict masked items using both past and future context, allowing it to learn a richer, more holistic representation of user interests. (see page 156)

CL4SRec (Contrastive Learning for Sequential Recommendation) — A framework that enhances sequential models like SASRec by adding an auxiliary contrastive learning objective. It trains the model to recognize that two different augmented views of the same user sequence should have similar representations, forcing it to learn more robust and generalizable user profiles, especially in sparse data scenarios. (see page 159)

IRGAN — Adapts the Generative Adversarial Network (GAN) framework to recommendation by training a Generator (the recommender) to produce plausible user-item pairs and a Discriminator to distinguish them from real interactions. This adversarial game forces the Generator to learn a more robust model of user preferences, effectively performing a type of hard negative mining. (see page 163)

DiffRec — A generative model that adapts Denoising Diffusion Probabilistic Models (DDPMs) to recommendation. It learns the distribution of user preferences by training a neural network to reverse a fixed process of gradually adding noise to user interaction profiles, enabling the generation of high-quality and diverse recommendations from pure noise. (see page 166)

GFN4Rec — Frames recommendation as a sequential list-building task using Generative Flow Networks (GFlowNets). The model learns a policy to construct a slate of items step-by-step, where the probability of generating a list is proportional to a predefined reward, inherently promoting both relevance and diversity in the final set of recommendations. (see page 169)

IDNP (Interest Dynamics Neural Process) — Leverages the principles of Normalizing Flows, a class of generative models that learn a data distribution through a series of invertible transformations. This allows it to model a user's preference as a complex probability distribution over time, capturing uncertainty and making it particularly promising for few-shot or cold-start sequential recommendation tasks. (see page 172)

Text-Driven Recommendation Algorithms

DeepCoNN — A foundational review-based model that uses two parallel Convolutional Neural Networks (CNNs) to learn latent representations directly from raw text. One CNN processes all reviews written *by* a user to form a user vector, while the other processes all reviews written *for* an item to form an item vector, which are then combined to predict a rating. (see page 191)

NARRE — An extension of DeepCoNN that incorporates a dual attention mechanism to identify and assign higher weights to the most useful and informative reviews when constructing user and item representations. This not only improves accuracy by filtering out noise but also provides a natural pathway to explainability by highlighting the most influential reviews. (see page 192)

LLM-based Retrieval (Dense Retrieval & Cross-Encoders) — This is a standard two-stage architecture for large-scale systems. First, a fast bi-encoder independently creates embeddings for a user query and all items to retrieve a set of candidates from a massive catalog. Second, a slower but more accurate cross-encoder re-ranks these candidates by processing the user query and each item *together* to produce a precise relevance score. (see page 193)

LLM-based Generative / Instruction-Tuned — This approach reframes recommendation as a text generation task where an instruction-tuned LLM is given a prompt with a user's history and a task (e.g., "Recommend 5 sci-fi movies and explain why"). The model leverages its vast world knowledge and zero-shot reasoning ability to generate a coherent, natural language response containing both recommendations and justifications. (see page 194)

LLM-based RAG & Feature Extraction — This paradigm uses an LLM as a powerful component to enhance other systems. It can act as a sophisticated feature extractor, creating high-quality semantic embeddings from text to feed into any downstream model. Alternatively, in a Retrieval-Augmented Generation (RAG) setup, it grounds a generative LLM with externally retrieved, up-to-date information to ensure its recommendations are factually accurate and to mitigate hallucinations. (see page 195)

LLM Agents & Tool Use — An advanced paradigm where the LLM acts as a reasoning engine that can autonomously plan and use external tools (e.g., APIs, databases, other recommender models). It decomposes a complex user request into a series of sub-tasks and tool calls to fulfill multi-step, sophisticated goals beyond what a single model can achieve. (see page 195)

Conversational RecSys (Dialogue-based) — This approach creates an interactive, multi-turn dialogue to actively elicit a user's preferences, especially in cold-start scenarios. The system acts like a guided assistant, asking clarifying questions to progressively narrow down options and understand the user's true, often ambiguous, intent. (see page 196)

Multimodal Recommendation Algorithms

CLIP (Contrastive Language-Image Pre-Training) — A foundational model that learns a shared embedding space for images and text by training on a massive dataset of (image, caption) pairs with a contrastive objective. Its powerful zero-shot transfer capability allows it to understand visual concepts described in text without explicit fine-tuning, making it an extremely effective tool for generating semantic embeddings from item images to solve the visual cold-start problem. (see page 199)

ALBEF (Align Before Fuse) — A multimodal architecture that first aligns image and text features from unimodal encoders using a contrastive loss, and *then* fuses them using a cross-modal encoder. Its multi-task training objective allows it to learn finer-grained interactions between visual regions and words, making it a state-of-the-art model for complex multimodal reasoning tasks. (see page 200)

Multimodal VAEs — Extends the Variational Autoencoder framework to learn a joint latent probability distribution across multiple modalities (e.g., image and text). Its probabilistic nature makes it excellent at handling missing modalities and enables cross-modal generation, such as creating a likely text description for a given product image. (see page 201)

Multimodal Diffusion — Applies the denoising diffusion process to multimodal data, learning the joint distribution by training a model to reverse the process of gradually adding noise to data from multiple modalities simultaneously. This paradigm is capable of generating exceptionally high-quality and realistic multimodal content, representing the cutting edge of generative modeling. (see page 201)

Context-Aware Recommendation Algorithms

Factorization Machines (FM) — A powerful model for context-aware recommendation that extends matrix factorization to handle any real-valued feature vector. Its key innovation is efficiently modeling all pairwise feature interactions using factorized parameters, which allows it to estimate interaction strengths for feature combinations it has never seen in the training data, thus solving the data sparsity problem. (see page 177)

AMF (Attentional Factorization Machine) — An extension of Factorization Machines that incorporates an attention mechanism to learn the importance of different pairwise feature interactions. This allows the model to focus on the most predictive combinations while filtering out noise, improving both accuracy and interpretability for CTR prediction tasks. (see page 179)

Wide & Deep — A pioneering hybrid architecture from Google that jointly trains a "wide" linear component for memorizing frequent feature co-occurrences and a "deep" neural network for generalizing to unseen feature combinations. This unified approach allows the model to be both powerful and efficient, making it a foundational architecture for large-scale industrial CTR prediction. (see page 180)

LightGBM — A high-performance gradient boosting framework that uses an ensemble of decision trees to predict CTR based on a wide array of user, item, and contextual features. Its primary differentiators are its speed and efficiency, which are achieved through leaf-wise tree growth and native handling of categorical features, making it a workhorse for industrial ranking tasks on tabular data. (see page 184)

Knowledge-Aware Recommendation Algorithms

NGCF (Neural Graph Collaborative Filtering) — A pioneering model that applies a standard Graph Neural Network (GNN) to the user-item interaction graph. It learns embeddings by iteratively aggregating features from a node's neighborhood, including feature transformation matrices and non-linear activations, to capture high-order connectivity patterns. (see page 205)

LightGCN — A radical simplification of NGCF that achieves superior performance by removing the feature transformation matrices and non-linear activations, leaving only the core GNN component of neighborhood aggregation. It learns user and item embeddings by simply taking the weighted sum of their neighbors' embeddings from the previous layer, proving that for CF, effectively modeling the graph structure is key. (see page 206)

SGL (Self-supervised Graph Learning) — A training paradigm applied on top of GNN-based recommenders like LightGCN to improve embedding quality. It introduces an auxiliary contrastive learning task, training the model to recognize that a node's representation should be similar across two different augmented views of the graph, which forces it to learn more robust and generalizable representations, especially in sparse data scenarios. (see page 208)

New Algorithmic Paradigms

Reinforcement Learning (RL) for RecSys — This paradigm frames recommendation as a sequential decision problem where an "agent" (the system) learns a "policy" to recommend items that maximize a long-term reward, such as user engagement over an entire session. It shifts the focus from predicting a single accurate interaction to optimizing the entire sequence of recommendations for long-term value. (see page 215)

Causal Inference in RecSys — This approach moves beyond correlation to understand causation, aiming to recommend items that will actually *persuade* a user to interact, rather than just recommending items they were likely to choose anyway. Techniques like Uplift Modeling identify "persuadable" users to maximize the true incremental impact of the recommendations. (see page 216)

Explainable AI (XAI) for RecSys — This field focuses on making the recommendation process transparent and trustworthy by answering the question "Why was this recommended to me?". Methods include generating explanations by finding paths in a knowledge graph or highlighting the most influential user/item features that led to the recommendation. (see page 217)

1 Foundational and Heuristic-Driven Algorithms

Before the dominance of collaborative filtering, the recommendation landscape was shaped by foundational approaches that remain relevant today as powerful baselines, components of hybrid systems, and transparent business logic engines. These algorithms operate not on user interaction patterns but on intrinsic item attributes (Content-Based) or manually defined heuristics (Rule-Based). They are highly interpretable, easy to implement, and effectively address the cold-start problem for new items.

1.1 Content-Based Filtering

Content-based filtering recommends items similar to those a user has liked in the past, **based on the attributes of the items themselves**. It operates on the principle: "Show me more of what I like," by building a user profile from their interactions (e.g., likes, ratings, or views) and matching it to item features. This approach is independent of other users' data, making it robust against data sparsity and effective for recommending niche items or new items with descriptive metadata. However, it may over-specialize, recommending only highly similar items, and relies heavily on high-quality metadata.

> **How it works...** Imagine you've watched and loved the movie *Blade Runner*. A content-based system would analyze its attributes: `Genre: Sci-Fi`, `Theme: Cyberpunk`, `Director: Ridley Scott`. It would then search its catalog for other items with similar attributes, such as *Alien* (also directed by Ridley Scott) or *Ghost in the Shell* (also sci-fi and cyberpunk), and recommend them to you. The user's taste is built as a profile based on the content of items they've previously enjoyed.

1.1.1 The Vector Space Model (VSM): A Foundational Framework

Key concept — The Vector Space Model (VSM) is the foundational framework for content-based filtering. It represents items and user preferences as vectors in a high-dimensional space where each dimension corresponds to a specific feature (e.g., a genre, a brand, a keyword). Similarity between items, or between an item and a user, is then calculated as the proximity of their vectors in this space.

Key differentiator — VSM is not a single algorithm but a flexible **model** that provides the theoretical underpinning for many content-based techniques. It separates the abstract idea of vector representation from the specific implementation of how vector weights are calculated (e.g., TF-IDF or binary), making it a versatile and fundamental concept.

Use cases — As a general framework, it's the basis for recommending articles, products, or media based on metadata. It is particularly effective for explaining the mechanics of content-based filtering and for building systems in cold-start scenarios where item attributes are available but interaction data is sparse.

When to Consider — Understanding VSM is the first step in building any content-based recommender. It provides the essential blueprint for representing content numerically, upon which specific weighting schemes and similarity metrics are built.

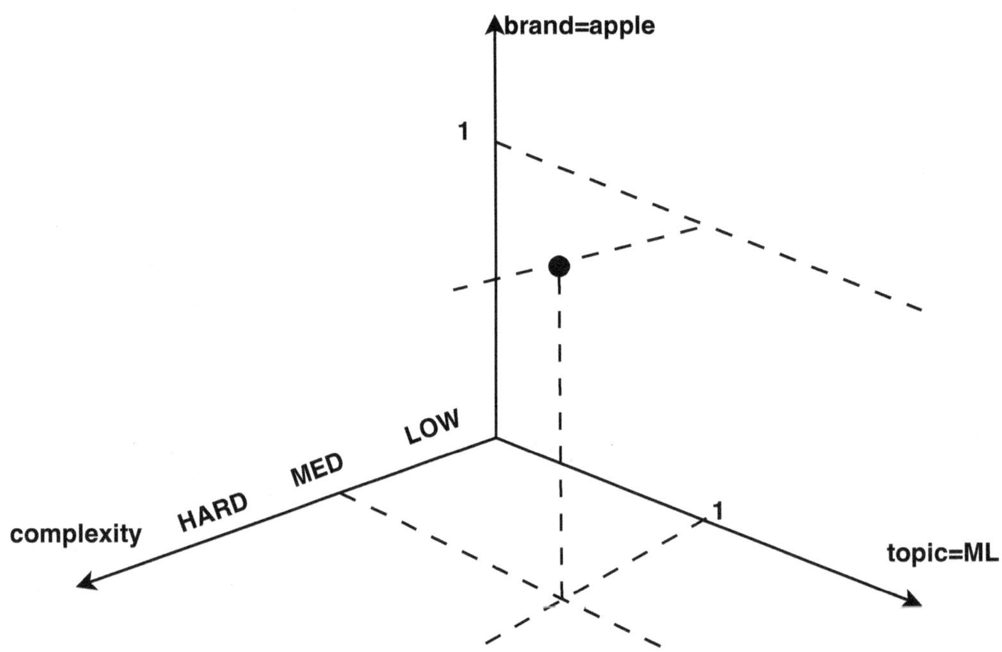

Seminal Papers:

- Salton, G., Wong, A., & Yang, C. S. (1975). *A Vector Space Model for Automatic Indexing.* https://dl.acm.org/doi/10.1145/361219.361220.

Useful links:

- Vector Space Model, Wikipedia article [https://en.wikipedia.org/wiki/Vector_space_model]

Mathematical Foundations of VSM

The Vector Space Model is an algebraic framework that allows us to perform geometric and mathematical operations on items by representing them as numerical vectors.

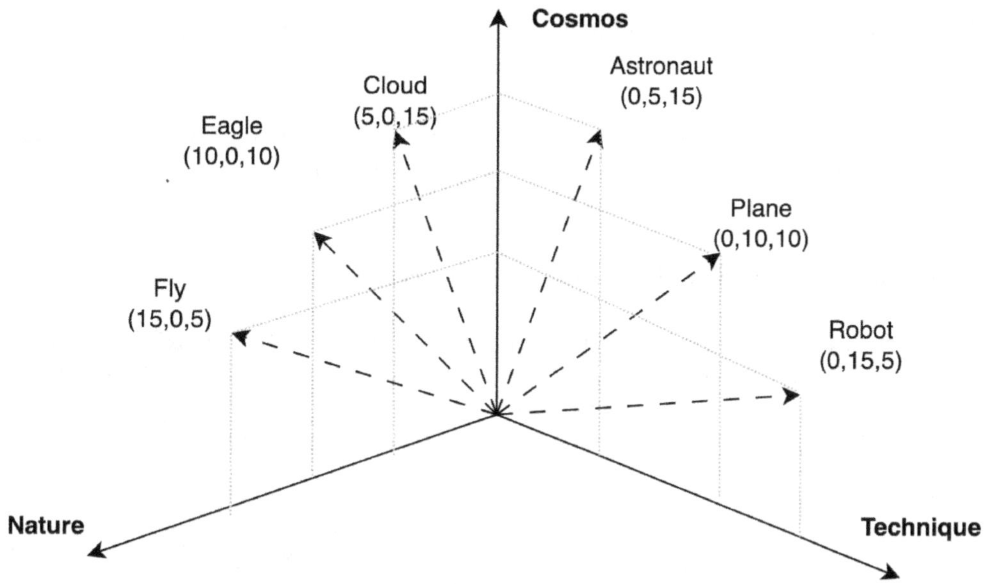

To generalize from its origins in text analysis, we map:

- A "document" is an **item** in the catalog.
- A "term" is a **feature** (e.g., `genre='sci-fi'`, `brand='Apple'`, `topic='machine-learning'`).
- The "corpus" is the entire **catalog of items.**

Part A: Representing Items as Vectors

The first step is to define the dimensions of the vector space by creating a "vocabulary" of all unique features across the entire catalog, $F = \{f_1, f_2, \ldots, f_n\}$. Each item i is then represented as an n-dimensional vector $\vec{i}$:

$$\vec{i} = (w_{1,i}, w_{2,i}, \ldots, w_{n,i})$$

The value $w_{k,i}$ is a **weight** that signifies the importance of feature f_k in item i.

Part B: Feature Weighting Schemes

The VSM framework supports various methods for calculating the weight $w_{k,i}$. The choice of scheme is crucial for performance. Common schemes include:

- **Binary:** A simple scheme where $w_{k,i} = 1$ if feature f_k is present in item i, and 0 otherwise.
- **Term Frequency (TF):** The weight is the count or normalized frequency of the feature in the item.
- **TF-IDF:** The most common and effective scheme, which assigns a high weight to features that are important to a specific item but rare across the entire catalog. We will detail its calculation in the next section.

Part C: Measuring Similarity with Cosine Similarity

Once items are represented as vectors, their similarity is measured by their proximity. **Cosine Similarity** is the standard metric, measuring the cosine of the angle between two vectors. It is robust to differences in the number of features (vector magnitude) and effectively captures similarity. For two item vectors, $\vec{A}$ and $\vec{B}$:

$$\text{similarity}(\vec{A}, \vec{B}) = \cos(\theta) = \frac{\vec{A} \cdot \vec{B}}{|\vec{A}||\vec{B}|} = \frac{\sum_{k=1}^{n} A_k B_k}{\sqrt{\sum_{k=1}^{n} A_k^2}\sqrt{\sum_{k=1}^{n} B_k^2}}$$

A score near **1** indicates high similarity, while a score near **0** indicates dissimilarity.

Part D: Creating User Profiles for Recommendation

VSM can be extended to recommend items to a user by creating a vector representation for that user's preferences. A user's profile vector, $\vec{u}$, is computed by aggregating the vectors of the items they have positively interacted with (e.g., rated highly, purchased). A common method is to calculate the average of these item vectors:

$$\vec{u} = \frac{1}{|I_u|} \sum_{i \in I_u} \vec{i}$$

where I_u is the set of items the user liked. Recommendations are then generated by calculating the cosine similarity between the user's profile vector $\vec{u}$ and all unseen item vectors.

If a user u is new, the set I_u is empty, and you cannot compute a profile vector for them (so called a user cold-start problem).

1.1.2 TF-IDF: A Classic VSM Weighting Scheme

Key concept — This classic approach provides a specific method for calculating the feature weights within the Vector Space Model. **TF-IDF (Term Frequency-Inverse Document Frequency)** converts an item's features into a numerical vector, assigning scores that reflect each feature's importance to the item relative to the entire catalog.

Key differentiator — Its simplicity, interpretability, and effectiveness as a baseline. Unlike collaborative filtering, it can recommend brand-new items as long as they have descriptive features, solving the item cold-start problem. However, it assumes feature independence, which may miss semantic relationships (e.g., "sci-fi" and "space opera" being related).

Use cases — Recommending articles based on topics, suggesting products based on specifications, or finding similar movies based on genres and directors. It's ideal for domains with rich metadata.

When to Consider — Use TF-IDF as a first-pass content-based recommender or a strong baseline. It excels when you need a fast, simple, and explainable model that relies purely on item features, especially with diverse descriptive features.

Mathematical Foundations

This approach provides a precise formula for the feature weights, $w_{k,i}$, used in the Vector Space Model.

Part A: Calculating the TF-IDF Score

The TF-IDF score reflects a feature's importance to an item within the catalog and combines two components:

(1) **Term Frequency (TF):** Measures how relevant a feature f is to an item i. For non-text features, it's typically binary (1 if present, 0 otherwise) or a weighted relevance score. A common normalized form is:

$$\text{tf}(f, i) = \frac{\text{count or relevance of feature } f \text{ in item } i}{\text{total number of features in item } i}$$

(2) **Inverse Document Frequency (IDF):** Measures the feature's rarity across the entire catalog I, giving higher weight to rare features and lower weight to common ones. To avoid division by zero, smoothing is applied:

$$\text{idf}(f, I) = \log\left(\frac{|I| + 1}{\text{Number of items with feature } f + 1}\right)$$

The final **TF-IDF score** for a feature is the product of these two values, representing its weight in the item's vector:

$$\text{score}(f, i, I) = \text{tf}(f, i) \times \text{idf}(f, I)$$

Because any single item only has a small subset of all possible features, these vectors are typically very sparse.

Part B: Making a Recommendation

(1) For each item in the catalog, construct its vector using the TF-IDF scores of its features.

(2) Take a target item (e.g., the last item a user interacted with).

(3) Calculate the Cosine Similarity between its TF-IDF vector and all other items' vectors.

(4) Recommend the items with the highest similarity scores.

1.1.3 Embedding-based Similarity: A Latent Approach to VSM

These models learn dense embeddings using the distributional hypothesis: "features that appear in similar contexts (e.g., co-occurring in the same items) have related meanings." In recommendation systems, this hypothesis extends to non-text domains like item tags, where features such as "sci-fi" and "cyberpunk" co-occurring in movies suggest semantic similarity. By learning latent representations, these embeddings capture underlying relationships not explicitly defined in metadata, making them a powerful approach to content-based filtering. A neural network learns these embeddings via a pretext task.

Imagine training a model like a game of word association, but for features—given "sci-fi", predict "cyberpunk" but not "romance". This contrasts with the Vector Space Model (VSM) described earlier, which relies on deterministic vector weights from explicit statistics (e.g., TF-IDF). Here, the probabilistic nature of embedding models, such as Skip-gram, enables them to capture subtler semantic nuances through learning.

To avoid confusion with VSM, it's important to understand the training mechanism. The described approach, Skip-gram with Negative Sampling, reframes the prediction task as a series of independent binary classification problems. For each positive feature pair, the model learns to distinguish it from several randomly chosen "negative" pairs. This is achieved using the sigmoid function, which outputs a probability for each individual pair, a process fundamentally different from VSM's algebraic framework. This contrasts with an alternative training method for Word2Vec, Hierarchical Softmax, which does use a Softmax layer to model a probability distribution over the entire feature vocabulary.

The process of using embeddings for recommendations can be broken down into two distinct stages: first, we **train** a model like Skip-gram to learn high-quality vector representations for our features; second, we **use** those representations to calculate similarity and generate a ranked list of recommendations.

Stage 1: Training (Creating a "Map" of Features with Skip-gram)

The first stage is dedicated to building the core components: the feature embeddings. The goal is not to create recommendations directly, but to learn a meaningful "map" where features with similar meanings are located close to each other. The Skip-gram model is an excellent tool for this map-making process.

The objective is to learn a dense vector for each unique feature. The **Skip-gram with Negative Sampling** architecture trains the model to predict context features that co-occur with a center feature, while distinguishing "wrong" combinations. For example, in a movie database, if "sci-fi" is the center feature for *Blade Runner*, context features might include "cyberpunk" or "dystopian", while "romance" (a negative sample) should score low.

In the Skip-gram with Negative Sampling model, used for learning feature embeddings, two key terms come up: **center feature** and **context feature**. These are crucial for understanding how the model learns relationships between features (like tags, words, or attributes) based on their co-occurrence in items (like movies, books, or products).

- **Center Feature** (f_c): This is the feature the model focuses on at a given moment during training. For example, in a movie database, the center feature might be the tag "sci-fi" from a movie's description. The model systematically iterates through all features in the dataset, selecting one at a time as the center feature to ensure comprehensive learning. The model is trying to figure out which other features (like "cyberpunk" or "action") tend to appear alongside "sci-fi" in the same movie. Understanding means the model learns to predict these related features by adjusting numerical vectors (embeddings) so that features appearing together have similar vectors. For example, if "sci-fi" and "cyberpunk" often show up in the same movies, their vectors become closer in a mathematical "space," capturing their relationship.

- **Context Feature** (f_o): These are the other features that appear alongside the center feature in the same item. For instance, if "sci-fi" is the center feature for a movie like *Blade Runner*, context features might include "cyberpunk," "dystopian," or "futuristic" because they're also tags for that movie. The model learns to predict these context features based on the center feature, figuring out which ones naturally go together.

The model's objective is to learn to predict "context features" f_o that co-occur with a "center feature" f_c. It's trained to give high similarity scores to true co-occurring pairs (e.g., `('sci-fi', 'cyberpunk')`) and low scores to random "negative" pairs (e.g., `('sci-fi', 'romance')`).

The objective function for a true pair (f_c, f_o) is:

$$\mathcal{J} = \log \sigma(v'_{f_o} \cdot v_{f_c}) + \sum_{i=1}^{k} \mathbb{E}_{f_i \sim P_n(f)}[\log \sigma(-v'_{f_i} \cdot v_{f_c})]$$

Let's break it down:

- $\mathcal{J}$ is the overall objective function for this training example—we aim to maximize it. In practice, optimization algorithms minimize the negative of this expression, $\mathcal{L} = -\mathcal{J}$.
- The first term, $\log \sigma(v'_{f_o} \cdot v_{f_c})$, focuses on the true pair, pushing the model to give them a high similarity score.
- The second term, $\sum_{i=1}^{k} \mathbb{E}_{f_i \sim P_n(f)}[\log \sigma(-v'_{f_i} \cdot v_{f_c})]$, handles the "negative" examples. It pushes the model to give low similarity scores to k randomly sampled features that do not belong with the center feature.
- v_f and v'_f are two vector representations for a feature f.
- $\sigma(\cdot)$ is the sigmoid function, $\sigma(x) = 1/(1 + e^{-x})$.

Key Hyperparameters The embedding dimension (e.g., 50–300), the number of negative samples k (e.g., 5–20), and the noise distribution $P_n(f)$ significantly affect performance. For item features, the definition of context is also crucial; in our case, we consider all co-occurring features within the same item to be part of the context. The noise distribution $P_n(f)$ is often set as the unigram distribution raised to the 0.75 power, as proposed in the original Word2Vec paper.

At the end of this training stage, the job of Skip-gram is done. The final output is not a list of recommendations, but a high-quality "dictionary" where each feature in our catalog is mapped to a dense vector embedding.

After training, the vectors v_f become the feature embeddings.

Note on Applicability While this approach is designed for content-based recommendation using item features (e.g., tags or attributes), it can be adapted for collaborative filtering by treating items themselves as "features" and user interaction lists (e.g., rated movies) as "contexts," as shown in the accompanying tutorial code. This creates item embeddings akin to item2vec, blending content-based and collaborative approaches.

References:

- Mikolov, T., Sutskever, I., Chen, K., Corrado, G., & Dean, J. (2013). Distributed Representations of Words and Phrases and their Compositionality. Advances in Neural Information Processing Systems (NIPS). https://arxiv.org/abs/1310.4546

Caveat — Skip-gram with Negative Sampling is efficient but sensitive to noisy data. An alternative, hierarchical softmax, may be considered for smaller datasets or when computational resources are limited, as it avoids sampling negatives but requires a tree structure.

Stage 2: Usage (Generating a Ranked Recommendation List)

Once the "map" of feature embeddings is created, we can use it to plot a route—that is, to generate an ordered list of recommendations for a user. This is a separate, multi-step process that uses the embeddings learned in Stage 1.

Create Item Vectors from Feature Embeddings

Since an item's features are typically an unordered set (e.g., the tags "sci-fi" and "action" are equivalent to "action" and "sci-fi"), the most direct approach is to aggregate their feature embeddings. The simplest and most common aggregation method is **averaging**. The item's vector $\vec{x}_i$ is computed as the element-wise average of the vectors of all its features. This creates a vector representing the item's semantic center of gravity.

$$\vec{x}_i = \frac{1}{N} \sum_{k=1}^{N} v_{f_k}$$

This approach is computationally efficient and correctly treats the features as a "bag of features," ignoring any arbitrary order.

Calculating Similarity

Once all items are represented as dense vectors, we can determine the order of recommendations by measuring proximity. We take a target item vector (e.g., the last item a user liked) and compute the **Cosine Similarity** between its vector and the vectors of all other items in the catalog.

$$\text{similarity}(\vec{x}_i, \vec{x}_j) = \frac{\vec{x}_i \cdot \vec{x}_j}{|\vec{x}_i||\vec{x}_j|}$$

Ranking and Recommending

The final recommendation list is generated by sorting all items in descending order based on their cosine similarity scores. The items with the highest scores are the top recommendations, presented to the user.

This can be done for a target item or for a user's profile vector, which can be created by averaging the vectors of all items they have positively interacted with.

Feature embeddings (Step 1) capture the semantics of individual attributes, enabling fine-grained similarity between tags. Item embeddings (Step 2) build on this by representing entire items, either by aggregating feature embeddings or learning a holistic vector. This shift from feature-level to item-level representations allows recommendations based on overall item similarity (e.g., recommending Alien for liking Blade Runner), offering a more context-aware approach suitable for content-based systems.

Reference:

- Le, Q., & Mikolov, T. (2014). Distributed Representations of Sentences and Documents. International Conference on Machine Learning (ICML). https://arxiv.org/abs/1405.4053

Tutorial #1: Content-Based Similarity with Feature Embeddings

> The tutorial sections in this guide are entirely optional, though they can be extremely valuable for building intuition and a deeper understanding of the algorithms in practice. They assume, however, a basic familiarity with the libraries and frameworks being used. If you are interested in exploring why a particular method, function, or framework class is invoked at a specific point in the code, we encourage you to consult the Appendix, where we provide detailed, line-by-line commentary for selected algorithms from the Tutorial sections.

This tutorial implements the content-based embedding model as described in the theoretical section. Instead of using user interaction data, we will learn embeddings for **item features** (movie genres) to find items with similar content.

The core idea is:

(1) Treat each movie's list of genres as a "sentence."

(2) Use a Skip-gram model to learn dense vector embeddings for each genre.

(3) Represent each movie by averaging the embeddings of its genres.

(4) Recommend movies by finding those with the highest Cosine Similarity.

For the line-by-line explanations of the code samples, please see the Appendix.

Step 1: Prepare Data from Movie Genres

First, we load the `u.item` file from the MovieLens 100k dataset. This file contains movie titles and their associated genres, which will serve as our content features.

```
import torch
import torch.nn as nn
import torch.optim as optim
import numpy as np
import pandas as pd
from torch.utils.data import Dataset, DataLoader
from collections import defaultdict

#  Data Loading and Preparation

movie_df = pd.read_csv(
    'ml-100k/u.item', sep='|', encoding='latin-1', header=None,
    names=['movie_id', 'title'] + list(range(22))
)

# Extract genres for each movie
genre_cols = movie_df.columns[-19:]
movie_genres = {}
for index, row in movie_df.iterrows():
    genres = [
        genre_cols[i] for i, val in enumerate(row[genre_cols]) if val
    ]
    if genres: # Only include movies with at least one genre
        movie_genres[row['movie_id']] = genres

#  Vocabulary and Pair Generation

all_genres = sorted(list(set(
    g for genres in movie_genres.values() for g in genres
)))
genre_to_idx = {genre: i for i, genre in enumerate(all_genres)}
vocab_size = len(all_genres)
print(f"Found {len(movie_genres)} movies and {vocab_size} genres.")

# Generate positive pairs from co-occurring genres in the same movie
positive_pairs = []
for genres in movie_genres.values():
    if len(genres) >= 2:
```

```
        indices = [genre_to_idx[g] for g in genres]
        for i in range(len(indices)):
            for j in range(len(indices)):
                if i != j:
                    positive_pairs.append((indices[i], indices[j]))
print(f"Generated {len(positive_pairs)} positive genre pairs.")

# Create negative sampling distribution from genre frequency
genre_freq = defaultdict(int)
for genres in movie_genres.values():
    for g in genres: genre_freq[g] += 1

freq_list = [genre_freq[g] for g in all_genres]
prob = np.array(freq_list) ** 0.75
prob /= prob.sum()
prob_tensor = torch.from_numpy(prob).float()

# Setup DataLoader for training
class GenrePairsDataset(Dataset):
    def __len__(self): return len(positive_pairs)
    def __getitem__(self, idx): return torch.tensor(positive_pairs[idx])

dataloader = DataLoader(GenrePairsDataset(), batch_size=1024, shuffle=True)
```

Step 2: Define the SkipGramNS Model

The model architecture uses PyTorch's `nn.Embedding` layers to store the genre vectors. Its `forward` method implements the Skip-gram with Negative Sampling loss function, which trains the model to give high scores to co-occurring genres and low scores to random pairs.

```
class SkipGramNS(nn.Module):
    def __init__(self, vocab_size, embed_dim):
        super().__init__()
        self.in_embed = nn.Embedding(vocab_size, embed_dim)
        self.out_embed = nn.Embedding(vocab_size, embed_dim)
        self.in_embed.weight.data.uniform_(-1, 1) # Init weights
        self.out_embed.weight.data.uniform_(-1, 1)

    def forward(self, centers, contexts, negatives):
        v_c = self.in_embed(centers)
        v_o = self.out_embed(contexts)
        pos_dot = (v_c * v_o).sum(1)
```

```
        pos_loss = torch.log(torch.sigmoid(pos_dot))

        v_neg = self.out_embed(negatives)
        v_c_unsq = v_c.unsqueeze(2)
        neg_dot = torch.bmm(v_neg, v_c_unsq).squeeze(2)
        neg_loss = torch.log(torch.sigmoid(-neg_dot)).sum(1)

        loss = - (pos_loss + neg_loss).mean()
        return loss
```

Step 3: Train the Model to Learn Genre Embeddings

The training loop feeds batches of positive genre pairs to the model. For each pair, it also draws `k` negative samples. The optimizer then adjusts the embedding weights to minimize the loss, gradually teaching the model the relationships between genres.

To understand why we use Adam: Recall the mathematical objective from the Skip-gram with Negative Sampling (NS). The objective function for each training example is:

$$\mathcal{J} = \log \sigma(v'_{f_o} \cdot v_{f_c}) + \sum_{i=1}^{k} \mathbb{E}_{f_i \sim P_n(f)}[\log \sigma(-v'_{f_i} \cdot v_{f_c})]$$

In practice, we minimize the loss $\mathcal{L} = -\mathcal{J}$ using gradient descent. Adam is an adaptive variant of Stochastic Gradient Descent (SGD) that adjusts the learning rate for each parameter based on the history of gradients, making it more efficient and stable for training embedding models like this one. It helps converge faster than plain SGD, especially with noisy data from negative sampling, by incorporating momentum and adaptive scaling (as described in the Adam paper by Kingma & Ba, 2014).

For negative sampling, we use `torch.multinomial` to draw k negative samples per positive pair from the precomputed probability distribution (`prob_tensor`). This distribution is the unigram frequency raised to the 0.75 power $P_n(f) \propto \text{freq}(f)^{0.75}$, as recommended in the original Word2Vec paper (Mikolov et al., 2013). `torch.multinomial` efficiently samples from this categorical distribution without replacement, simulating the expectation $\mathbb{E}_{f_i \sim P_n(f)}$ in the objective function. For very large vocabularies (e.g., thousands of unique items), this can be computationally expensive due to repeated sampling; optimizations like subsampling frequent items (to reduce noise from common words/movies) or hierarchical softmax (as an alternative to NS) may improve efficiency in such cases.

```
device = torch.device("cuda" if torch.cuda.is_available() else "cpu")
model = SkipGramNS(vocab_size, embed_dim=30).to(device)
optimizer = optim.Adam(model.parameters(), lr=0.01)
k, epochs = 5, 20
```

```
print("\nStarting training for genre embeddings...")
for epoch in range(epochs):
    total_loss = 0
    for batch in dataloader:
        centers, contexts = batch[:, 0].to(device), batch[:, 1].to(device)
        # Draw k negative samples for each positive pair
        negs = torch.multinomial(prob_tensor, len(centers) * k, True)
        negs = negs.view(len(centers), k).to(device)

        loss = model(centers, contexts, negs)
        optimizer.zero_grad()
        loss.backward()
        optimizer.step()
        total_loss += loss.item()
    print(f"Epoch {epoch+1}: Loss = {total_loss/len(dataloader):.4f}")

# Extract the learned genre embeddings for use in recommendation
genre_embeddings = model.in_embed.weight.data.cpu().numpy()
```

Step 4: Generate Content-Based Recommendations

With the genre embeddings learned, we can now build our recommender. We represent each movie by averaging the embedding vectors of its genres. Recommendations are then generated by calculating the cosine similarity between these aggregated movie vectors.

```
# Create a vector for each movie by averaging its genre embeddings
movie_vectors = {}
for movie_id, genres in movie_genres.items():
    if genres:
        genre_indices = [genre_to_idx[g] for g in genres]
        movie_vectors[movie_id] = genre_embeddings[genre_indices].mean(0)

# Convert to a matrix and list for efficient similarity calculation
movie_ids_list = list(movie_vectors.keys())
movie_matrix = np.array([movie_vectors[mid] for mid in movie_ids_list])

def get_similar_movies(target_title, top_n=5):
    target_row = movie_df[movie_df['title'] == target_title]
    if target_row.empty:
        print(f"Movie '{target_title}' not found.")
        return
```

```
    target_id = target_row['movie_id'].iloc[0]
    target_idx = movie_ids_list.index(target_id)
    target_vec = movie_matrix[target_idx]

    # Calculate cosine similarity between the target and all others
    sims = (movie_matrix @ target_vec) / (
        np.linalg.norm(movie_matrix, axis=1) * np.linalg.norm(target_vec)
    )

    # Get top N indices, excluding the first one (the item itself)
    sim_indices = np.argsort(sims)[::-1][1:top_n+1]

    print(f"\nMovies similar to '{target_title}':")
    for idx in sim_indices:
        sim_id = movie_ids_list[idx]
        sim_title = movie_df[movie_df['movie_id']==sim_id]['title'].iloc[0]
        score = sims[idx]
        print(f"- {sim_title}: Sim = {score:.4f}")

get_similar_movies('Toy Story (1995)', top_n=5)
get_similar_movies('Star Wars (1977)', top_n=5)
```

Output:

```
 Step 1: Preparing Data

Found 1682 movies with genres and 19 unique genres.
Generated 3350 positive genre pairs.
 Step 2: Training Model

Using device: cpu
Epoch 5/20: Avg Loss = 3.3323
Epoch 10/20: Avg Loss = 2.5826
Epoch 15/20: Avg Loss = 2.4474
Epoch 20/20: Avg Loss = 2.3943
 Step 3: Generating Recommendations

Movies similar to 'Toy Story (1995)' (Genres: [6, 7, 8]):
- Aladdin and the King of Thieves (1996) (Genres: [6, 7, 8]): Sim = 1.0000
- Goofy Movie, A (1995) (Genres: [6, 7, 8, 17]): Sim = 0.9559
- Aladdin (1992) (Genres: [6, 7, 8, 15]): Sim = 0.9441
- Little Rascals, The (1994) (Genres: [7, 8]): Sim = 0.8897
```

```
- Mouse Hunt (1997) (Genres: [7, 8]): Sim = 0.8897

Movies similar to 'Star Wars (1977)' (Genres: [4, 5, 17, 18, 20]):
- Return of the Jedi (1983) (Genres: [4, 5, 17, 18, 20]): Sim = 1.0000
- Starship Troopers (1997) (Genres: [4, 5, 18, 20]): Sim = 0.9505
- Empire Strikes Back, The (1980) (Genres: [4, 5, 11, 17, 18, 20]): Sim = 0.9484
- African Queen, The (1951) (Genres: [4, 5, 17, 20]): Sim = 0.9408
- Last of the Mohicans, The (1992) (Genres: [4, 17, 20]): Sim = 0.9117

Movies similar to 'Scream (1996)' (Genres: [14, 19]):
- Village of the Damned (1995) (Genres: [14, 19]): Sim = 1.0000
- Scream (1996) (Genres: [14, 19]): Sim = 1.0000
- Believers, The (1987) (Genres: [14, 19]): Sim = 1.0000
- Nightwatch (1997) (Genres: [14, 19]): Sim = 1.0000
- Loch Ness (1995) (Genres: [14, 19]): Sim = 1.0000
```

Note on Similarity Scores of 1.0:

As seen in the recommendations for 'Scream (1996)', several movies have a perfect similarity score of 1.0. This is not an error but a direct consequence of our methodology. Since we represent each movie solely by averaging its genre embeddings, any two movies that share the exact same set of genres will have identical vector representations. The cosine similarity between identical vectors is always 1.0. This highlights a limitation of using a small, discrete set of features; to achieve more nuanced recommendations, one could incorporate additional content features like keywords, tags, or director/actor information.

1.1.4 Limitations of Content-Based Filtering

- **Limited Serendipity.** Since it recommends items similar to what a user already likes, it can struggle to introduce novel and diverse content. This can lead to an over-specialization of recommendations.

- **Requires Rich Metadata.** The performance of content-based methods is entirely dependent on the quality and richness of the item features. Items with sparse or no metadata cannot be accurately represented and are difficult to recommend.

- **Inability to Leverage Collaborative Information.** These methods are "deaf" to the wisdom of the crowd. They cannot capture preferences that emerge from user-item interaction patterns, such as learning that users who like item A also tend to like item C, even if A and C have no features in common.

Production Ready?

- **Content-Based Filtering: Absolutely Production-Ready.** These techniques are robust, scalable, and widely deployed. TF-IDF is a cornerstone of information retrieval and serves as a powerful baseline in many production systems. Semantic models using Word2Vec/Doc2Vec are also common for enriching item representations.

TF-IDF, Cosine Similarity:

- **scikit-learn** : The definitive library for these tasks. It provides highly optimized and easy-to-use implementations of `TfidfVectorizer` and `cosine_similarity`.

Word2Vec, Doc2Vec:

- **Gensim** : The standard, go-to library for training and using Word2Vec and Doc2Vec models.
- **spaCy** : A powerful NLP library that provides pre-trained word embeddings and easy access to document vectors.

1.1.5 Alternative Word2Vec Architecture: CBOW

As an alternative to the Skip-gram model, the **Continuous Bag-of-Words (CBOW)** architecture offers a different but related approach to learning feature embeddings. While Skip-gram predicts context features from a central feature, CBOW does the reverse: it predicts the central feature based on the sum or average of its surrounding context feature embeddings.

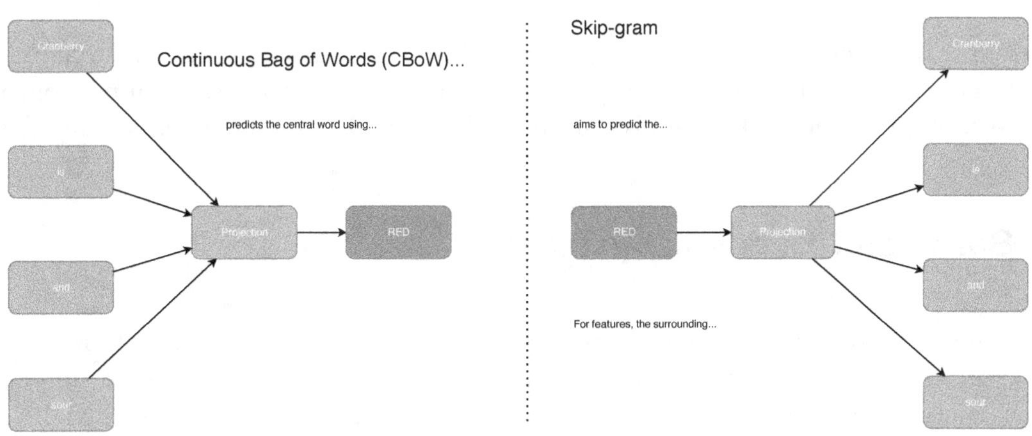

Key concept — CBOW is more computationally efficient and tends to perform better for frequent features. For a given set of context features (e.g., `['cyberpunk', 'dystopian']` for a movie), the model is trained to predict the most likely center feature ('sci-fi'). This approach smooths over the distributional information from the entire context, making it faster to train.

When to Consider — Use CBOW when training speed is a priority and your dataset has a sufficient number of examples for your key features. It serves as an efficient alternative to Skip-gram for learning dense feature representations.

1.1.6 Handling Rare and Unknown Features: Subword Embeddings (FastText)

A significant limitation of standard Word2Vec models (both Skip-gram and CBOW) is their inability to handle out-of-vocabulary (OOV) features—items that were not seen during training. The **FastText** model solves this by learning embeddings for **character n-grams**, rather than entire features.

Key concept — FastText represents each feature as a bag of its constituent character n-grams. For example, the feature sci-fi might be broken down into n-grams like <sc, sci, ci-, i-f, -fi, fi> (where < and > denote the start and end of the feature). The model learns embeddings for these n-grams, and the final vector for a feature is the sum of its n-gram vectors.

> **It should be noted that this algorithm is more applicable to text processing than to objects with features, which are the basis of content-based methods. Therefore, it is presented here mainly for completeness and consistency.**

Key differentiator — This subword approach allows the model to construct a meaningful vector for a previously unseen feature by combining the vectors of its parts. For instance, if the model has seen "sci-fi" and "romance," it can generate a reasonable vector for the OOV feature "sci-mance" because it recognizes the component n-grams.

Use cases — This is extremely valuable for recommendation systems dealing with dynamic or niche catalogs where new item attributes (features) appear frequently. It provides a robust solution to the **feature cold-start problem** and generally improves the quality of embeddings for rare features.

1.2 Rule-Based and Heuristic Systems

Rule-based and heuristic systems represent the most transparent and direct approach to recommendation. They operate not on learned user-interaction patterns but on manually defined logic or simple, universal metrics. These methods are highly interpretable, easy to implement, and serve as crucial components for handling business constraints, promotions, and the cold-start problem where interaction data is absent.

However, this reliance on manually crafted logic is also their primary weakness. Such systems lack the ability to learn from data or adapt to changing user behavior automatically. As the number of rules and contextual factors grows, the system can become brittle and cumbersome to maintain, with conflicts between rules requiring complex, manual resolution. Furthermore, because they operate on explicit instructions rather than discovered patterns, they struggle to provide truly personalized or serendipitous recommendations, limiting their ability to uncover novel user interests that are not already encoded in the business logic.

1.2.1 Classic Rule-Based Systems

Key concept — Classic rule-based systems use manually defined, domain-specific **logical predicates** (often in an "if-then" structure) to generate recommendations. These rules are crafted based on business knowledge and do not involve statistical learning from user data; they are a direct implementation of business logic.

Key differentiator — Their complete transparency and control. The reason for a recommendation is never a black box; it's a direct consequence of a predefined rule (e.g., `IF user.location == "New York" AND context.season == "winter" THEN recommend item.category == "heavy coats"`). This makes them predictable, easy to debug, and simple to modify based on changing business needs.

Drawback — Their primary limitation is scalability in terms of maintenance. As the number of rules grows, managing them, resolving conflicts, and updating them becomes increasingly complex and brittle.

Use cases — Implementing business-critical promotions ("Top 10 Bestsellers in Your Region"), strategic recommendations (promoting high-margin items), or providing sensible defaults for new users (e.g., showing the most popular items on the homepage). They are often used as a foundational layer or a filtering mechanism in a hybrid system.

When to Consider — Use a rule-based system when recommendations need to be 100% transparent, controllable, and aligned with explicit business goals. They are also invaluable for handling the "coldest start" scenario (a brand new site with no users or interactions) and for creating non-personalized but useful features like "Most Popular" or "New Arrivals" lists.

1.2.2 Heuristic-Driven Algorithms

These algorithms are not personalized to individual users but instead rely on global aggregate metrics. They are simple, computationally efficient, and serve as powerful baselines.

1.2.2.1 Top Popular (Most Popular)

Key concept — This heuristic recommends items based on their overall popularity across all users. Popularity is typically measured by the total number of interactions (e.g., views, purchases, or ratings).

Mathematical Foundations

Let I be the set of all items in the catalog. For each item i in that set, we define a popularity score $P(i)$ as the total count of users who have interacted with it.

To calculate this, let U be the set of all users. The score $P(i)$ is the size of the set of users u who have interacted with item i. This is written formally as:

$$P(i) = |\{u \in U \mid \text{user } u \text{ interacted with item } i\}|$$

Here, the vertical bars $|\cdot|$ mean "the size of the set." So, the formula simply counts every user who has a record of interacting with that specific item. The recommendation list is then generated by sorting all items in descending order of their score $P(i)$ and taking the top N.

Use cases — It is the most common non-personalized recommendation strategy, often used as a fallback for new users or in "Top 10" lists on homepages. It effectively mitigates the cold-start problem by providing a sensible default.

1.2.3 Association Rule Mining

Association Rule Mining discovers "if-then" patterns from transactional data. In the context of recommendation, this translates to finding rules like `{item A} -> {item B}`, which means that users who interacted with item A are also likely to interact with item B. This is the fundamental logic behind ubiquitous e-commerce features like "Frequently Bought Together" and "Customers Who Viewed This Also Viewed".

Unlike collaborative filtering, which models user profiles, this method is item-centric and operates on a simple principle of co-occurrence. The process typically involves two major steps:

(1) **Frequent Itemset Mining:** First, identify all sets of items that frequently appear together in transactions. (2) **Rule Generation:** Second, generate reliable "if-then" rules from these frequent itemsets.

1.2.3.1 Frequent Itemset Mining Algorithms

The computational core of association rule mining is finding the frequent itemsets. Several algorithms have been developed for this task, each with different strategies and trade-offs.

1.2.3.1.1 Apriori: The Classic Approach The Apriori algorithm is a foundational method for frequent itemset mining, efficiently identifying all itemsets in a dataset that satisfy a minimum support threshold (`min_support`). It leverages the **Apriori Principle**: *if an itemset is frequent, then all of its subsets must also be frequent.* This principle allows the algorithm to prune a large number of candidate itemsets, making the search computationally feasible. Apriori works iteratively, first finding frequent individual items, then frequent pairs, triplets, and so on, pruning candidates at each step. Its primary bottleneck is the computationally expensive process of generating and testing a vast number of candidate itemsets, particularly for datasets with many unique items.

Key Concepts

- **Support**: The support of an itemset is the number (or proportion) of transactions in the dataset that contain that itemset. For an itemset X, Support(X) is the count of transactions containing X.
- **Confidence**: For an association rule A -¿ B, confidence measures the probability that transactions containing A also contain B. It is calculated as $Confidence(A- > B) = Support(A \cap B)/Support(A)$.
- **Frequent Itemset**: An itemset is frequent if its support is at least `min_support`.

Mathematical Foundations & Walkthrough

Apriori uses a level-wise, breadth-first search to find frequent itemsets. It operates in passes, where pass k identifies all frequent itemsets of size k, denoted L_k.

The Algorithm Step-by-Step

The algorithm follows a two-stage process at each pass:

1. **Join Step**: Generate candidate itemsets of size k, denoted C_k, by joining the set of frequent itemsets of size $k-1, L_(k-1)$, with itself. Two itemsets from $L_(k-1)$ are joined if they share the same first k-2 items when sorted lexicographically, and their last items differ. The differing item is appended to form a new candidate.
2. **Prune Step**: Apply the Apriori Principle to prune candidates in C_k whose $(k-1)$-subsets are not in $L_(k-1)$, as they cannot be frequent. Then, scan the database to compute the support of each remaining candidate. Discard candidates with support less than `min_support`.

This process repeats, incrementing k, until no new frequent itemsets are found (i.e., L_k is empty).

Example

To illustrate Apriori, consider a grocery store dataset with 5 transactions and a `min_support` of 2 transactions (i.e., itemsets must appear in at least 40% of transactions to be frequent).

Original Transactions:

- T1: {Milk, Bread, Butter}
- T2: {Milk, Bread}
- T3: {Milk, Butter}
- T4: {Bread, Butter}
- T5: {Milk}

Iteration 1 (k=1): Find Frequent 1-Itemsets

- **Scan Database**: Count the support of each individual item.
  - Support({Milk}) = 4
  - Support({Bread}) = 3
  - Support({Butter}) = 3
- **Prune**: All items have support ¿= min_support = 2.
- **Result (L_1)**: L_1 = { {Milk}, {Bread}, {Butter} }

Iteration 2 (k=2): Find Frequent 2-Itemsets

Join Step: Generate C_2 by joining L_1 with itself.

C_2 = { {Milk, Bread}, {Milk, Butter}, {Bread, Butter} }

Prune Step: All 1-item subsets are in L_1, so no candidates are pruned yet. Scan the database:

- Support({Milk, Bread}) = 2 (in T1, T2)
- Support({Milk, Butter}) = 2 (in T1, T3)
- Support({Bread, Butter}) = 2 (in T1, T4)

Result (L_2): L_2 = { {Milk, Bread}, {Milk, Butter}, {Bread, Butter} }

Iteration 3 (k=3): Find Frequent 3-Itemsets

Join Step: Join L_2 with itself. Joining {Milk, Bread} and {Milk, Butter} (sharing {Milk}) yields {Milk, Bread, Butter}.

- C_3 = { {Milk, Bread, Butter} }

Prune Step: Check 2-item subsets of {Milk, Bread, Butter} (i.e., {Milk, Bread}, {Milk, Butter}, {Bread, Butter}). All are in L_2, so keep the candidate. Scan the database:

- Support({Milk, Bread, Butter}) = 1 (in T1)
- Since Support ¡ min_support = 2, this itemset is not frequent.

Result (L_3): L_3 = {}

The algorithm terminates because L_3 is empty, indicating no further frequent itemsets can be found. The final set of frequent itemsets is $L_1 \cap L_2$.

Generating Association Rules

From the frequent itemsets, we can derive association rules. For example, consider the rule {Bread} → {Milk}:

- Support({Bread, Milk}) = 2
- Support({Bread}) = 3
- Confidence({Bread} → {Milk}) = Support({Bread, Milk}) / Support({Bread}) = 2/3 ≈ 66.67%

If a minimum confidence threshold (e.g., 60%) is set, this rule would be retained.

Scalability and Limitations

Apriori's candidate generation can lead to a combinatorial explosion, as the number of potential itemsets grows exponentially with the number of unique items. This makes it computationally expensive for large datasets or when mining large frequent itemsets. Additionally, multiple database scans are required, which can be slow for large datasets. Alternatives like FP-Growth, which uses a tree-based structure to avoid explicit candidate generation, offer improved performance for such cases.

1.2.3.1.2 FP-Growth: A More Efficient Alternative The FP-Growth (Frequent Pattern Growth) algorithm is a highly popular and often more efficient alternative. Its main advantage is that it completely avoids the expensive candidate generation step of Apriori. It achieves this by first compressing the transactional database into a compact tree structure called an FP-tree. It then mines this tree directly to extract frequent itemsets. For large datasets, this approach is typically much faster and requires less memory.

The diagram below illustrates the FP-Growth (Frequent Pattern Growth) algorithm. The process begins with a transaction table on the left, listing items purchased (e.g., {a, c, d, f, g, i, m, p}) alongside their transaction IDs. These transactions are transformed into an "Item bought ORDERED" format, prioritizing items by frequency.

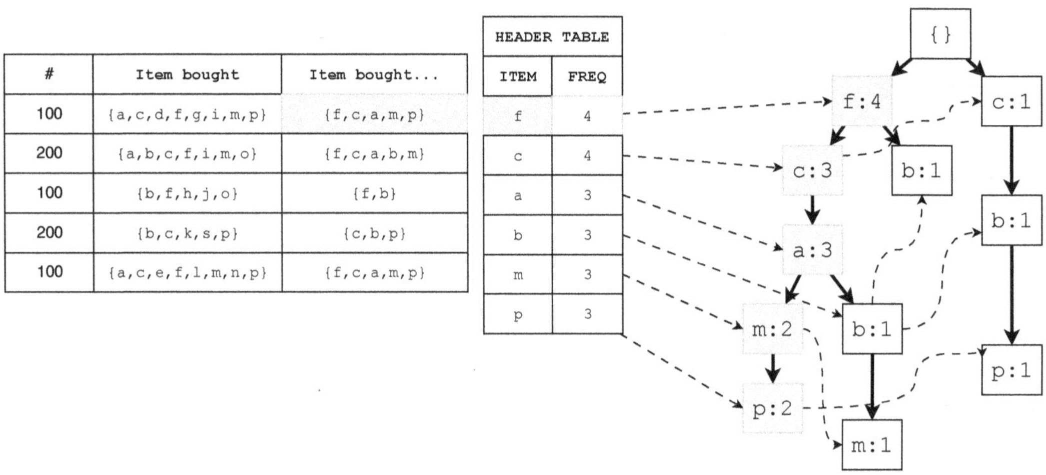

The Header Table on the right lists items (e.g., f, c, a, b, m, p) along with their frequencies (e.g., f: 4, c: 4). This table guides the construction of an FP-Tree (Frequent Pattern Tree), a compact structure that stores the dataset. The tree is built by inserting items node by node, with nodes representing items and links connecting frequent items. Dashed lines indicate paths for item linkage, while solid lines show the tree structure. For instance, the root node branches into 'f:4', which further splits into 'c:3' and 'a:3', reflecting the ordered frequent items.

The FP-Tree enables efficient mining of frequent patterns by traversing its nodes and using the header table to explore conditional pattern bases, ultimately identifying associations like {f, c} or {a, m} based on support thresholds.

1.2.3.1.3 Eclat: A Vertical Approach ECLAT stands for Equivalence Class Clustering and bottom-up Lattice Traversal. It was proposed as an efficient alternative to algorithms like Apriori, particularly for handling large datasets. While Apriori uses a breadth-first search and a horizontal data layout (where each transaction is listed with its items), Eclat adopts a vertical data layout and a depth-first search strategy. This shift allows Eclat to compute itemset supports more efficiently by leveraging set intersections, making it especially suitable for dense datasets (where many items appear across a high proportion of transactions).

Let's use a simple grocery store dataset with 5 transactions to illustrate. Assume min_sup = 2 (i.e., an itemset must appear in at least 2 transactions to be frequent).

Original Transactions (Horizontal Layout):

- T1: {Milk, Bread, Butter}
- T2: {Milk, Bread}
- T3: {Milk, Butter}
- T4: {Bread, Butter}
- T5: {Milk}

Step 1: Convert to Vertical Layout (TID-Lists):

- Milk: {T1, T2, T3, T5} (support = 4)
- Bread: {T1, T2, T4} (support = 3)
- Butter: {T1, T3, T4} (support = 3)

All 1-itemsets are frequent (support is greater or equal 2).

Step 2: Generate 2-Itemsets via Intersections:

- {Milk, Bread}: Intersect Milk's list {T1, T2, T3, T5} and Bread's {T1, T2, T4} → {T1, T2} (support = 2) → Frequent.
- {Milk, Butter}: Intersect {T1, T2, T3, T5} and {T3, T1, T4} → {T1, T3} (support = 2) → Frequent.
- {Bread, Butter}: Intersect {T1, T2, T4} and {T1, T3, T4} → {T1, T4} (support = 2) → Frequent.

Step 3: Generate 3-Itemsets (Recursive Depth-First):

Start with prefix "Milk" (equivalence class for extensions of {Milk}):

- Extend {Milk, Bread} with Butter: Intersect {T1, T2} (from {Milk, Bread}) and {T1, T3, T4} (Butter's list) → {T1} (support = 1) → Not frequent (below min_sup).
- Extend {Milk, Butter} with Bread: Similarly, {T1, T3} ∩ {T1, T2, T4} → {T1} (support = 1) → Not frequent.

Now, consider other branches (e.g., starting from "Bread"):

- Extend {Bread, Butter} with Milk: {T1, T4} $\cap$ {T1, T2, T3, T5} $\rightarrow$ {T1} (support = 1) $\rightarrow$ Not frequent.

Frequent Itemsets Found:

- 1-itemsets: {Milk}, {Bread}, {Butter}
- 2-itemsets: {Milk, Bread}, {Milk, Butter}, {Bread, Butter}
- No 3-itemsets.

Step 4: From Frequent Itemsets to Recommendations

The Eclat algorithm efficiently found the frequent itemsets. The next step is to generate **association rules** from them and measure their strength using a key metric: **Confidence.**

Confidence answers the question: "If a user buys item A, how likely are they to also buy item B?"

The formula is:

$$\text{Confidence}(A \rightarrow B) = \frac{\text{Support}(A \cup B)}{\text{Support}(A)}$$

Applying to the Grocery Example

Using the frequent itemsets and support counts you found, we can calculate the confidence for potential rules. Let's set a `min_confidence` threshold of **60%**.

Known Support Counts:

- `Support({Milk})` = 4
- `Support({Bread})` = 3
- `Support({Butter})` = 3
- `Support({Milk, Bread})` = 2
- `Support({Milk, Butter})` = 2
- `Support({Bread, Butter})` = 2

Rule Calculations:

- Bread → Milk: Confidence = 2/3 (Strong)
- Butter → Milk: Confidence = 2/3 (Strong)
- Bread → Butter: Confidence = 2/3 (Strong)
- Milk → Bread: Confidence = 2/4 (Weak)
- Milk → Butter: Confidence = 2/4 (Weak)
- Butter → Bread: Confidence = 2/3 (Strong)

Recommendation Logic

The system uses the strong rules (those above the 60% confidence threshold) to make recommendations.

- **Scenario:** A customer adds **Bread** to their cart.
- **Action:** The system checks the strong rules. It finds that Bread → Milk (66.7%) and Bread → Butter (66.7%) are valid. It then recommends **Milk** and **Butter** to the user.
- **Counter-example:** The rule Milk → Bread has a confidence of only 50%, which is below the threshold. Therefore, the system would *not* recommend Bread just because a user bought Milk.

1.2.3.2 Rule Generation and Key Metrics

Once the frequent itemsets have been identified, the next step is to generate strong association rules from them. The strength of a rule is measured by three key metrics derived from co-occurrence counts. To understand them, imagine a large collection of shopping baskets (transactions).

(1) Support — This metric indicates how frequently an itemset appears in the dataset. It is a measure of the itemset's general prevalence. A high support means the combination is common. For a rule $A \to B$, the support is the proportion of transactions that contain both A and B.

$$\text{Support}(A \to B) = \frac{\text{count}(A \cup B)}{\text{Total Transactions}}$$

(2) Confidence — This measures the predictive power of the rule, essentially its accuracy. It answers the question: "If a transaction contains item A, what is the probability that it will also contain item B?".

$$\text{Confidence}(A \to B) = \frac{\text{Support}(A \to B)}{\text{Support}(A)} = \frac{\text{count}(A \cup B)}{\text{count}(A)}$$

This is the proportion of transactions containing A that *also* contain B. A high confidence suggests a strong connection.

(3) Lift — This metric measures how much more likely items A and B are to be purchased together than if they were independent events. A lift greater than 1 indicates a positive correlation, meaning the items co-occur more often than by random chance. A lift of 1 suggests independence, and a lift less than 1 suggests a negative correlation.

$$\text{Lift}(A \to B) = \frac{\text{Confidence}(A \to B)}{\text{Support}(B)} = \frac{\text{count}(A \cup B)}{\text{count}(A) \cdot \text{count}(B)}$$

A lift of 2, for example, means that the presence of item A makes the purchase of item B twice as likely.

1.2.3.3 Practical Considerations

- **Algorithm Choice:** For most practical applications, **FP-Growth** is often preferred over Apriori due to its superior performance. **Eclat** is a strong contender on dense datasets.
- **Setting Thresholds:** The most challenging part is choosing the right `min_support` and `min_confidence` thresholds. If `min_support` is too high, you may miss valuable niche patterns. If it's too low, you may be overwhelmed with a massive number of trivial and uninteresting rules.
- **Actionable Rules:** The goal is to find not just statistically significant rules, but rules that are also actionable and interesting. **Lift** is a crucial metric here, as it helps filter out obvious rules (e.g., `{milk} -> {bread}`) and highlights more surprising and potentially valuable connections.

1.2.3.4 Use Cases & Production Readiness

Use Cases — The primary use case is generating "Frequently Bought Together" or "Customers who viewed this also viewed" recommendations in e-commerce. It excels at finding direct, actionable relationships between specific items.

Production Ready? — **Absolutely Production-Ready.** These heuristic and rule-based systems are not just baselines; they are critical, foundational components of virtually every commercial recommender system. They provide a necessary layer of editorial control, business logic, and predictability that complements and governs more complex machine learning models.

Python Frameworks

- `mlxtend`: This library provides robust, easy-to-use, and well-documented Python implementations of the Apriori, FP-Growth, and Eclat algorithms for mining association rules. It integrates seamlessly with **Pandas** DataFrames.
- **Apache Spark MLlib**: For very large-scale, distributed computation, Spark's machine learning library offers parallelized implementations of FP-Growth, making it possible to run association rule mining on massive datasets that would be intractable on a single machine.

2 Interaction-Driven Recommendation Algorithms

Interaction-driven recommendation algorithms **rely solely on user-item interaction data, such as ratings, clicks, or purchases, without incorporating additional content like text or images.** These algorithms, foundational to collaborative filtering, analyze patterns in user engagement to predict preferences. Their design and performance depend on the nature of the interaction data and the specific recommendation task they address.

2.1 Core Properties of Recommendation Data

The effectiveness of recommendation algorithms is shaped by two key properties of the interaction data.

2.1.1 Types of Ratings Feedback

The signals that fuel recommendation algorithms fall into two main categories based on how users express their preferences: explicit and implicit feedback.

Explicit feedback offers a clear, direct expression of a user's preference. This feedback is often numerical and structured, taking forms such as **interval-based ratings** on a discrete 5-star scale ($\{1, 2, 3, 4, 5\}$) , **ordinal ratings** that use ordered categories like {`"Strongly Disagree", "Neutral", "Strongly Agree"`} , or simple **binary ratings** like a thumbs-up or thumbs-down.

More commonly, systems rely on **implicit feedback**, which is inferred from user actions like clicks, views, or purchases. Although this data is abundant, it is also significantly noisier. A crucial subset of this is **Unary Ratings**, where systems only observe positive interactions, such as a purchase or a "like," without any corresponding negative signals. In this scenario, the absence of an interaction does not necessarily mean dislike—it could simply mean a lack of awareness. This ambiguity requires specialized algorithms, and models like BPR or WRMF are specifically tailored to learn from this type of one-class data.

2.1.2 The Long-Tail Property

Interaction data in real-world systems is highly skewed: a few popular items receive most interactions, while the vast majority (the "long tail") are rarely rated. This has significant implications:

- **Economic Importance:** Long-tail items often drive substantial profits, not just bestsellers.
- **Algorithmic Bias:** Algorithms may favor popular items due to their richer data, reducing recommendation diversity.
- **Evaluation Challenges:** Sparse interactions in the long tail complicate training and evaluating recommendations for these items.

2.2 Recommendation Tasks

The type of available feedback directly informs the primary task a recommender system is designed to solve. Recommendation algorithms are generally designed for two distinct tasks, each with different goals and evaluation metrics.

1. **Rating Prediction:** When the data consists of **explicit feedback**, the natural objective is to predict the **exact rating** a user would assign to an item (e.g., predicting a 4.2-star rating for a movie). Models like SVD, ALS, and k-NN approaches are optimized for this task and are evaluated using error-based metrics like **Root Mean Squared Error** (*RMSE*) and **Mean Absolute Error** (*MAE*), which measure how close predicted ratings are to actual ones.

1. **Item Ranking:** With **implicit feedback**, where clear negative preferences are absent, the goal shifts to generating an **ordered list** of items a user is most likely to interact with, prioritizing relative preference over absolute score accuracy. Algorithms like BPR, NCF, and SASRec are designed for this task and are evaluated using rank-based metrics such as *Precision@k* and *Recall@k*, which assess the quality of the top-k recommended items. Importantly, ranking models cannot be fairly evaluated with *RMSE*, as their scores are not meant to predict exact ratings but to ensure correct ordering.

2.3 Classic & Neighborhood-Based Models

These are foundational "memory-based" collaborative filtering approaches that recommend items based on similarities between users or items. They operate directly on the user-item interaction matrix, are simple, interpretable, and work well with sparse data but can struggle with scalability, coverage, and cold-start issues in very large or sparse datasets. They serve as powerful baselines for more complex models.

2.3.1 ItemKNN (Item-based k-Nearest Neighbors)

ItemKNN (Item-based K-Nearest Neighbors) recommends items similar to those the user has interacted with in the past, based on item similarity computed from user interactions (often using adjusted cosine similarity to account for user biases).

Key concept — It builds item similarity matrices, assuming users tend to like items similar to ones they've liked before.

Key Differentiator — More scalable than UserKNN for large item catalogs since item similarities change less frequently; offers transparency via "Because you watched X, you might like Y."

Use cases — Streaming services like Netflix for "similar to what you've watched," or Amazon's early item-based recommender for efficient, real-time suggestions. Consider it when your item set is stable, data is sparse, and you need efficient computation with reasonable accuracy and minimal training.

Hyperparameters

- **k (Number of Neighbors)**: This defines how many of the most similar items will be used to predict a rating for a target item. A small k might lead to recommendations that are highly relevant but less diverse, while a large k can increase diversity but may introduce noise from less similar items.

- **Similarity Metric**: This is the formula used to measure the similarity between pairs of items. Common choices include Cosine Similarity, Adjusted Cosine Similarity (which accounts for user rating scale biases), and Pearson Correlation. The best choice depends on the nature of your data (e.g., explicit vs. implicit feedback).

- **Minimum Support (min_support)**: This sets a threshold for the minimum number of users who must have rated both items in a pair for their similarity to be calculated. It helps ensure that similarity scores are statistically significant and not based on a small, noisy sample.

- **Shrinkage**: This is a regularization parameter used to dampen similarity scores for items with few co-ratings. It "shrinks" these less reliable scores toward zero, preventing noise from items with low support from dominating the recommendations.

Seminal Papers:

- Item-based collaborative filtering recommendation algorithms, Sarwar, Badrul and Karypis, George and Konstan, Joseph and Riedl, John., 2001\. https://dl.acm.org/doi/10.1145/371920.372071
- On the challenges of studying bias in Recommender Systems: A UserKNN case study. Savvina Daniil, Manel Slokom, Mirjam Cuper, Cynthia C.S. Liem, Jacco van Ossenbruggen, Laura Hollink. https://arxiv.org/abs/2409.08046

Production Ready?

- Item-based k-NN, in particular, is a proven, scalable, and effective algorithm that has been a cornerstone of production recommender systems for years. It is famously used by companies like Amazon for their "customers who bought this also bought" feature, demonstrating its real-world utility. While it remains a powerful tool, especially as a baseline or a component in a hybrid system, it can face challenges with data sparsity and, in the case of user-based variants, scalability issues as the number of users grows.

Mathematical Foundations

Part A: The Core Idea - Item Similarity

ItemKNN operates by first building a static, offline model of how similar items are to one another. The similarity is not based on item attributes (like genre or brand) but on how users have rated them collectively. The intuition is that if many users give similar ratings to two items, those items are likely similar in some meaningful way.

A common and effective metric is **Adjusted Cosine Similarity**. It improves upon standard cosine similarity by accounting for user rating biases (i.e., some users tend to give higher or lower ratings in general).

The similarity $sim(i, j)$ between item i and item j is calculated as:

$$sim(i, j) = \frac{\sum_{u \in U_{ij}} (r_{ui} - \bar{r}_u)(r_{uj} - \bar{r}_u)}{\sqrt{\sum_{u \in U_{ij}} (r_{ui} - \bar{r}_u)^2} \sqrt{\sum_{u \in U_{ij}} (r_{uj} - \bar{r}_u)^2}}$$

Where:

- U_{ij} is the set of all users who have rated **both** item i and item j.

- r_{ui} is the rating user u gave to item i.
- $\bar{r}_u$ is the average rating given by user u across all items they have rated.

By subtracting each user's average rating, we center the ratings, effectively comparing whether user u rated items i and j higher or lower than their personal average. This results in a more robust similarity score, ranging from -1 (dissimilar) to +1 (very similar).

Part B: The Prediction Model

Once the similarity matrix is built, predicting a rating $\hat{r}_{ui}$ for a user u on an unrated target item i is done by looking at the items the user *has* already rated. The prediction is a **weighted average** of the user's ratings on the neighbors of item i.

Specifically, we first identify the set of items that user u has rated, which are also the most similar to item i. This is the "k-nearest neighbors" set.

The prediction formula is:

$$\hat{r}_{ui} = \frac{\sum_{j \in N_i^k(u)} sim(i,j) \cdot r_{uj}}{\sum_{j \in N_i^k(u)} |sim(i,j)|}$$

Where:

- $N_i^k(u)$ is the set of the **k nearest neighbors** of item i that user u has rated.
- $sim(i,j)$ is the pre-calculated similarity between the target item i and a neighbor item j.
- r_{uj} is the actual rating user u gave to the neighbor item j.

The numerator sums the similarity-weighted ratings, while the denominator normalizes the score by the sum of the absolute similarity weights. This ensures the predicted rating falls within a logical range.

Part C: Improving Robustness - Shrinkage

A practical issue arises when the set of co-raters U_{ij} is very small. A similarity score based on just one or two users is not statistically reliable and can add noise to the predictions. To mitigate this, a **shrinkage parameter** (β) is introduced to discount similarity scores that have low support.

The adjusted similarity score $sim'(i,j)$ is calculated as:

$$sim'(i,j) = \frac{|U_{ij}|}{|U_{ij}| + \beta} \cdot sim(i,j)$$

This shrinkage factor works as follows:

- If the number of co-raters $|U_{ij}|$ is large, the fraction $\frac{|U_{ij}|}{|U_{ij}|+\beta}$ is close to 1, and the original similarity score is trusted.
- If $|U_{ij}|$ is small, the fraction is closer to 0, which "shrinks" the unreliable similarity score towards zero, reducing its impact on the final prediction.

Tutorial: Item-based k-NN From Scratch

> The tutorial sections in this guide are entirely optional, though they can be extremely valuable for building intuition and a deeper understanding of the algorithms in practice. They assume, however, a basic familiarity with the libraries and frameworks being used. If you are interested in exploring why a particular method, function, or framework class is invoked at a specific point in the code, we encourage you to consult the Appendix, where we provide detailed, line-by-line commentary for selected algorithms from the Tutorial sections.

This tutorial walks through a practical implementation of the Item-based k-Nearest Neighbors (ItemKNN) algorithm. We will build a recommender from scratch that mirrors the mathematical foundations described previously, focusing on calculating an item similarity matrix and using it to predict user ratings.

Step 1. Prepare Data

First, we need to represent our data as a user-item interaction matrix. For this example, we'll create a small, sparse matrix using NumPy, where rows represent users, columns represent items, and the values are ratings. A zero indicates that the user has not rated the item.

```
import numpy as np

# Create a sample user-item rating matrix
# Rows: Users, Columns: Items
# 0 indicates no rating
R = np.array([
    [5, 3, 0, 1, 4, 0],
    [4, 0, 0, 1, 3, 5],
    [1, 1, 5, 5, 0, 4],
    [0, 1, 4, 4, 0, 0],
    [2, 0, 3, 0, 5, 4],
])
```

This matrix R is the core input for our model. Each row is a user's rating history, which will be used to infer their preferences.

Step 2. Define the ItemKNNRecommender Class

Next, we'll encapsulate the algorithm's logic within a Python class. This class will store the model's parameters (like the number of neighbors k), the learned similarity matrix, and the training data. The main methods will be fit() to train the model and predict_for_user() to generate scores for a single user.

```
class ItemKNNRecommender:
    def __init__(self, k=2, min_support=1, shrinkage=2.0):
        self.k = k
        self.min_support = min_support
        self.shrinkage = shrinkage
        self.similarity_matrix_ = None
        self.train_data_ = None
        self.user_means_ = None

    def fit(self, R):
      # To be implemented in the next step
      pass

    def predict_for_user(self, user_ratings):
      # To be implemented later
      pass
```

This structure provides a clean blueprint for our recommender. The *init* method sets the key hyperparameters that control the model's behavior, such as k for the neighborhood size.

Step 3. Calculate Item-to-Item Similarity (The fit method)

This is the core training step where we build the item similarity matrix based on the mathematical foundations. We will implement the Adjusted Cosine Similarity to account for user rating biases. We also apply shrinkage to discount similarities calculated from only a few co-raters, making our model more robust.

```
    def fit(self, R):
        self.train_data_ = R
        num_items = R.shape[1]
        self.similarity_matrix_ = np.zeros((num_items, num_items))

        # Part A: Adjusted Cosine Similarity
        # Calculate the mean rating for each user
        # who has rated at least one item
        self.user_means_ = np.true_divide(R.sum(axis=1), (R!=0).sum(axis=1))
        # Replace NaN (from users with no ratings) with 0
```

```
        self.user_means_[np.isnan(self.user_means_)] = 0

        # Center the ratings by subtracting the user's mean
        R_centered = R - np.where(R != 0, self.user_means_[:, np.newaxis], 0)

        # Calculate cosine similarity on the centered matrix
        from sklearn.metrics.pairwise import cosine_similarity
        self.similarity_matrix_ = cosine_similarity(R_centered.T)

        # Part C: Applying Shrinkage and Min Support
        # Calculate co-rated counts
        mask = (self.train_data_ > 0).astype(float)
        co_rated_counts = mask.T @ mask

        # Apply min_support threshold
        if self.min_support > 0:
            self.similarity_matrix_[co_rated_counts < self.min_support] = 0

        # Apply shrinkage factor
        if self.shrinkage > 0:
            counts_shrinkage = (co_rated_counts + self.shrinkage)
            shrinkage_factor = co_rated_counts / counts_shrinkage
            self.similarity_matrix_ *= shrinkage_factor

        # An item cannot be its own neighbor
        np.fill_diagonal(self.similarity_matrix_, 0)

        return self
```

After the fit method is run, self.similarity_matrix_ contains the learned relationships between all pairs of items. This matrix is pre-computed and stored, allowing for efficient predictions later.

Step 4. Make Predictions (The predict_for_user method)

With the similarity matrix built, we can now predict a rating for any item a user hasn't seen. The prediction is a weighted average of the user's ratings on other items, where the weights are the similarities of those items to the target item. We only consider the top k most similar items (the "nearest neighbors") that the user has rated.

```
    # Continuing the ItemKNNRecommender class...

    def predict_for_user(self, user_ratings):
```

```
predictions = np.zeros_like(user_ratings, dtype=float)

# Find items the user has already rated
rated_inds = np.where(user_ratings > 0)[0]

# Iterate over all items to predict scores for unrated ones
for item2pdct in range(len(user_ratings)):
    if user_ratings[item2pdct] == 0:
        # Get similarities between the target item and
        # all items the user has rated
        sims2rtd_itms = self.similarity_matrix_[item2pdct, rated_inds]

        # Get the user's ratings for those items
        ratings_of_rated = user_ratings[rated_inds]

        # Select the top K nearest neighbors
        if self.k > 0 and len(sims2rtd_itms) > self.k:
            # Find indices of the top-k absolute similarities
            top_neighbors = np.argsort(-np.abs(sims2rtd_itms))[:self.k]

            # Filter down to only the top-k neighbors
            sims2rtd_itms = sims2rtd_itms[top_neighbors]
            ratings_of_rated = ratings_of_rated[top_neighbors]

        # Calculate the weighted average
        numerator = sims2rtd_itms @ ratings_of_rated
        denominator = np.sum(np.abs(sims2rtd_itms))

        if denominator > 1e-8: # Add a small epsilon to avoid division by 0
            predictions[item2pdct] = numerator / denominator

return predictions
```

This method implements the prediction formula directly. It iterates through potential items, finds the user's rated neighbors, and computes the final score.

Step 5. Putting It All Together

Finally, let's instantiate our recommender, train it on our data, and use it to generate a ranked list of recommendations for a target user. We'll generate predictions for the first user and show which unrated items the model recommends most highly.

```
# 1. Instantiate the recommender with hyperparameters
item_knn = ItemKNNRecommender(k=2, min_support=1, shrinkage=1.0)

# 2. Train the model on the rating data
item_knn.fit(R)

# 3. Get recommendations for a specific user (e.g., user 0)
target_user_ratings = R[0, :]
predicted_scores = item_knn.predict_for_user(target_user_ratings)

# 4. Generate the final ranked list
# Create a list of (item_id, score) for unrated items
unrated_items = np.where(target_user_ratings == 0)[0]
recommendations = sorted(
    zip(unrated_items, predicted_scores[unrated_items]),
    key=lambda x: x[1],
    reverse=True
)

print(f"Original ratings for User 0: {target_user_ratings}")
print(f"Predicted scores for User 0: {np.round(predicted_scores, 2)}")
print("\nTop recommendations for User 0:")
for item_id, score in recommendations:
    print(f"  Item {item_id}: Predicted Score = {score:.4f}")
```

The output shows the predicted scores for the items the user hasn't rated, with Item 2 being the top recommendation. This process demonstrates the end-to-end workflow of an ItemKNN model: training the similarity model and then using it to generate personalized, ranked recommendations.

2.3.2 SAR (Simple Algorithm for Recommendations)

Key concept — SAR (Simple Algorithm for Recommendations) is a fast, scalable, item-based algorithm based on **co-occurrence** counting. It builds an item similarity matrix by analyzing how frequently pairs of items appear in users' interaction histories. It then uses this matrix to recommend items that are similar to those a user has already interacted with.

Key differentiator — Its main distinction is its **simplicity and speed**, which are rooted in counting rather than more complex methods like matrix factorization or gradient descent. Unlike ItemKNN, which often uses adjusted cosine similarity for explicit ratings, SAR is optimized for **implicit feedback** (clicks, purchases) and uses metrics like Jaccard similarity or "lift" to measure the strength of association between items.

Use cases — SAR is excellent for quickly building powerful baseline models, especially in environments where implicit feedback data is dominant, such as e-commerce ("users who bought this also bought...") or streaming services ("users who watched this also watched...").

When to Consider — An engineer should consider SAR when a fast, scalable, and easily interpretable model is required. It is an excellent choice when you have a large item catalog and want to generate personalized recommendations from implicit signals without the overhead of deep learning.

Hyperparameters

- **`similarity_type`**: The metric used to calculate similarity. Common choices are `jaccard` and `lift`. Jaccard measures the intersection over the union, while lift measures how much more often the items co-occur than would be expected by chance.
- **`threshold`**: The minimum number of co-occurrences required for the similarity between two items to be considered non-zero. This helps filter out noisy and statistically insignificant relationships.
- **`normalize`**: A flag indicating whether the similarity matrix should be normalized. Normalization can help mitigate the popularity bias, preventing popular items from dominating recommendations.

Production Ready?

- **Absolutely.** SAR was developed at Microsoft Research as a practical, scalable algorithm for production environments. Its efficiency and simplicity make it a reliable choice for building baseline models or systems where speed and interpretability are paramount.

Seminal Paper/Resource:

While SAR does not have a classic academic "seminal paper" like many other algorithms, its implementation and principles are thoroughly documented in the official **Microsoft Recommenders** repository, which serves as the primary resource.

- Microsoft Recommenders Repository. https://github.com/recommenders-team/recommenders

Mathematical Foundations

The mathematical foundation of SAR is centered on building an item similarity matrix from co-occurrence statistics and then using that matrix to generate scores.

Part A: Building the Co-occurrence Matrix

The core of the algorithm is a co-occurrence matrix C, where each entry C_{ij} represents the number of users who have interacted with both item i and item j. This can be computed efficiently via matrix multiplication.

First, a binary user-item interaction matrix A of size $m \times n$ is created, where m is the number of users and n is the number of items. $A_{ui} = 1$ if user u has interacted with item i, and 0 otherwise.

The co-occurrence matrix C (of size $n \times n$) is computed as:

$$C = A^T A$$

An entry C_{ij} in the resulting matrix is the dot product of column i and column j from matrix A, which is exactly the number of users who interacted with both items. The diagonal entries C_{ii} contain the total number of interactions for each item i.

Part B: Calculating the Similarity Matrix

The similarity matrix S is derived by applying a chosen metric to the co-occurrence matrix C.

(1) **Jaccard Similarity:** This metric measures similarity as the size of the intersection divided by the size of the union. For two items i and j, it is the number of users who interacted with both, divided by the number of users who interacted with at least one of them.

$$S_{ij}^{\text{jaccard}} = \frac{C_{ij}}{C_{ii} + C_{jj} - C_{ij}}$$

(2) **Lift:** This metric measures how much more often items i and j appear together than would be expected if they were independent. It corrects for item popularity.

$$S_{ij}^{\text{lift}} = \frac{C_{ij}}{C_{ii} \cdot C_{jj}}$$

After calculation, a `threshold` is applied to set any similarity values based on insufficient co-occurrence counts to zero.

Part C: Generating Recommendations

To generate recommendations for a user u, their interaction history (vector a_u from matrix A) is multiplied by the similarity matrix S.

The prediction score $\hat{r}_{ui}$ for a user u and an unrated item i is calculated as the sum of similarities between item i and all items j the user has already interacted with:

$$\hat{r}_{ui} = \sum_{j \in I_u} S_{ij}$$

where I_u is the set of items user u has interacted with.

In matrix form, this can be expressed as:

$$\hat{R} = AS$$

The matrix $\hat{R}$ contains the prediction scores for all user-item pairs. To get the final recommendation list for a user, we simply take the corresponding row from $\hat{R}$, filter out items the user has already seen, and sort the rest by their scores in descending order.

Tutorial: SAR (Simple Algorithm for Recommendations) From Scratch

> The tutorial sections in this guide are entirely optional, though they can be extremely valuable for building intuition and a deeper understanding of the algorithms in practice. They assume, however, a basic familiarity with the libraries and frameworks being used. If you are interested in exploring why a particular method, function, or framework class is invoked at a specific point in the code, we encourage you to consult the Appendix, where we provide detailed, line-by-line commentary for selected algorithms from the Tutorial sections.

This tutorial walks through a practical implementation of the SAR (Simple Algorithm for Recommendations) algorithm. We will build a recommender from scratch that mirrors the mathematical foundations described previously, focusing on calculating an item co-occurrence matrix and using it to generate a ranked list of Top-N recommendations from implicit feedback.

Step 1. Prepare Implicit Feedback Data

First, we need to represent our data as a user-item interaction matrix. For this example, we'll create a small, binary matrix using NumPy, where rows represent users, columns represent items, and a value of `1` indicates an implicit interaction (like a click or purchase). A `0` indicates no interaction.

```
import numpy as np

# Create a sample user-item interaction matrix (implicit feedback)
# Rows: Users, Columns: Items
# 1 = interacted, 0 = no interaction
R = np.array([
    [1, 1, 0, 1, 0, 0],
    [1, 0, 0, 1, 1, 1],
```

```
    [0, 1, 1, 1, 0, 1],
    [0, 1, 1, 0, 0, 0],
    [1, 0, 1, 0, 1, 1],
])
```

This matrix R (which corresponds to matrix A in the mathematical foundations) is the core input for our model. SAR will learn which items are similar based on how often they appear together in users' interaction histories.

Step 2. Define the SARRecommender Class

Next, we'll encapsulate the algorithm's logic within a Python class. This class will store the model's hyperparameters (like the `threshold`), the learned similarity matrix, and the co-occurrence matrix. The main methods will be `fit()` to train the model and `predict()` to generate ranking scores.

```
class SARRecommender:
    def __init__(self, threshold=1):
        self.threshold = threshold
        self.similarity_matrix_ = None
        self.co_occurrence_matrix_ = None
        self.train_data_ = None

    def fit(self, R):
      # To be implemented in the next step
      pass

    def predict(self, R_input):
      # To be implemented later
      pass
```

This structure provides a clean blueprint. The `__init__` method sets the `threshold` hyperparameter, which controls the minimum number of co-occurrences needed to consider two items similar.

Step 3. Build the Co-occurrence and Similarity Matrices (The `fit` method)

This is the core training step where we implement Parts A and B of the mathematical foundations. We first build the item co-occurrence matrix `C` and then use it to compute the Jaccard similarity matrix `S`.

```
# Continuing the SARRecommender class...
    def fit(self, R):
        self.train_data_ = R
        num_items = R.shape[1]
```

```
        # Part A: Build the Co-occurrence Matrix
        # This is the practical implementation of C = A^T * A
        self.co_occurrence_matrix_ = self.train_data_.T @ self.train_data_

        # Part B: Calculate the Similarity Matrix (Jaccard)
        # Get the diagonal of C, which contains item interaction counts
        item_counts = np.diag(self.co_occurrence_matrix_)

        # Calculate the denominator for Jaccard similarity:
        # C_ii + C_jj - C_ij
        denominator = (item_counts[:, np.newaxis] + item_counts -
                       self.co_occurrence_matrix_)

        # To avoid division by zero
        denominator[denominator == 0] = 1e-8

        self.similarity_matrix_ = self.co_occurrence_matrix_ / denominator

        # Apply the co-occurrence threshold
        self.similarity_matrix_[
            self.co_occurrence_matrix_ < self.threshold
        ] = 0

        # An item cannot be its own neighbor
        np.fill_diagonal(self.similarity_matrix_, 0)

        return self
```

After the `fit` method runs, `self.similarity_matrix_` contains the learned relationships between all pairs of items based on Jaccard similarity. This matrix is pre-computed, allowing for efficient predictions.

Step 4. Generate Ranking Scores (The predict method)

With the similarity matrix built, generating scores is a single, efficient matrix multiplication, as described in Part C of the mathematical foundations. The predicted score matrix `R_scores` is the user-item interaction matrix `R` multiplied by the item-item similarity matrix `S`. We then filter out scores for items the user has already seen.

```
# Continuing the SARRecommender class...
    def predict(self, R_input):
        # Prediction is a matrix multiplication: R_hat = A @ S
        R_scores = R_input @ self.similarity_matrix_
```

```
        # Filter out scores for items the user has already seen
        return np.where(R_input > 0, 0, R_scores)
```

This method directly implements the SAR prediction formula. The output scores are not probabilities or ratings; they are values used to rank items for recommendation.

Step 5. Putting It All Together

Finally, let's instantiate our recommender, train it, and use it to generate a ranked list of recommendations for a target user.

```
# 1. Instantiate the recommender with a threshold
sar = SARRecommender(threshold=2)

# 2. Train the model on the implicit interaction data
sar.fit(R)

# 3. Generate the full matrix of ranking scores
R_scores = sar.predict(R)

# 4. Get recommendations for a specific user (e.g., user 0)
target_user_interactions = R[0, :]
scores_for_user = R_scores[0, :]

# 5. Generate the final ranked list for unseen items
unseen_items = np.where(target_user_interactions == 0)[0]
recommendations = sorted(
    zip(unseen_items, scores_for_user[unseen_items]),
    key=lambda x: x[1],
    reverse=True
)

print(f"User 0 interacted with: {np.where(target_user_interactions > 0)[0]}")
print(f"Scores for unseen items: {np.round(scores_for_user[unseen_items], 2)}")
print("\nTop recommendations for User 0:")
for item_id, score in recommendations:
    if score > 0:
        print(f"  Item {item_id}: Ranking Score = {score:.4f}")
```

The output shows the ranking scores for the items the user has not yet seen, with Item 2 being the top recommendation. This demonstrates the end-to-end workflow of the SAR model: training the similarity model and then using it to generate personalized, ranked recommendations.

2.3.3 UserKNN (User-based k-Nearest Neighbors)

UserKNN (User-based K-Nearest Neighbors) finds users similar to the target user based on their interaction histories (using similarity measures like cosine or Pearson correlation on rating vectors) and recommends items that those similar users liked.

Key concept — It assumes similar users have similar tastes, enabling predictions from "neighbors."

Key differentiator — : Focuses on user similarities, making it intuitive for scenarios where user preferences are stable and interpretability is key (e.g., explaining recommendations via "Users who liked X also liked Y").

Use cases — E-commerce sites for personalized suggestions based on similar shoppers, or early recommender systems like GroupLens. Consider it when you have a moderate number of users, ample interaction data, and want quick, explainable recommendations without deep learning overhead.

Seminal Papers:

- GroupLens: an open architecture for collaborative filtering of netnews. Resnick, Paul and Iacovou, Neophytos and Suchak, Mitesh and Bergstrom, Peter and Riedl, John. 1994\. https://dl.acm.org/doi/10.1145/192844.192905.
- On the challenges of studying bias in Recommender Systems: A UserKNN case study. Savvina Daniil, Manel Slokom, Mirjam Cuper, Cynthia C.S. Liem, Jacco van Ossenbruggen, Laura Hollink. https://arxiv.org/abs/2409.08046

Mathematical Foundations

The logic for UserKNN is a mirror image of ItemKNN. Instead of finding similar items, we find similar users. The process involves the same two major steps: calculating similarity and making a weighted prediction.

Part A: The Core Idea - User Similarity

Here, we measure the similarity between two users, u and v, based on the items they have both rated. The concept is directly analogous to the **Adjusted Cosine Similarity** used for items, but applied to user rating vectors (the rows of the rating matrix) instead of item vectors (the columns). This metric is more commonly known as the **Pearson Correlation Coefficient**.

The similarity $sim(u, v)$ between user u and user v is calculated as:

$$sim(u, v) = \frac{\sum_{i \in I_{uv}} (r_{ui} - \bar{r}_u)(r_{vi} - \bar{r}_v)}{\sqrt{\sum_{i \in I_{uv}} (r_{ui} - \bar{r}_u)^2} \sqrt{\sum_{i \in I_{uv}} (r_{vi} - \bar{r}_v)^2}}$$

Where:

- I_{uv} is the set of items rated by **both** user u and user v.
- r_{ui} is the rating user u gave to item i.
- $\bar{r}_u$ is the average rating given by user u.

Notice this formula's structure is identical to the one for item similarity. We are simply switching the roles of users and items—summing over a common set of items instead of a common set of users.

Part B: The Prediction Model

To predict the rating $\hat{r}_{ui}$ for a target user u on an item i, we find the *k-nearest neighbors* of user u who have already rated item i. The prediction is based on how these similar users rated that specific item.

However, simply averaging their raw ratings would be misleading, as each neighbor has their own rating scale. Instead, we calculate how much each neighbor's rating for item i **deviated from their personal average**. The final prediction is the target user's average rating, adjusted by the weighted average of these deviations.

The prediction formula is:

$$\hat{r}_{ui} = \bar{r}_u + \frac{\sum_{v \in N_u^k(i)} sim(u, v) \cdot (r_{vi} - \bar{r}_v)}{\sum_{v \in N_u^k(i)} |sim(u, v)|}$$

Where:

- $\bar{r}_u$ is the average rating of our target user u, which serves as a baseline.
- $N_u^k(i)$ is the set of the **k nearest neighbors** of user u who have also rated item i.

- $sim(u, v)$ is the similarity between user u and a neighbor v.
- $(r_{vi} - \bar{r}_v)$ is the crucial term: the rating deviation of neighbor v for item i.

In essence, we are answering the question: "Based on how much my neighbors liked or disliked this item relative to their own tastes, how much would I like or dislike it relative to my own?"

Tutorial: User-based k-NN From Scratch

> The tutorial sections in this guide are entirely optional, though they can be extremely valuable for building intuition and a deeper understanding of the algorithms in practice. They assume, however, a basic familiarity with the libraries and frameworks being used. If you are interested in exploring why a particular method, function, or framework class is invoked at a specific point in the code, we encourage you to consult the Appendix, where we provide detailed, line-by-line commentary for selected algorithms from the Tutorial sections.

This tutorial provides a step-by-step guide to implementing the User-based k-Nearest Neighbors (UserKNN) algorithm from scratch in Python. We will follow the mathematical principles outlined previously to build a recommender that first identifies similar users and then leverages their ratings to predict scores for a target user.

Step 1. Prepare Data

The first step is to represent our data in a user-item interaction matrix. For this tutorial, we will use a small, sparse NumPy array where rows correspond to users, columns to items, and the values are the ratings. A rating of 0 signifies that a user has not yet interacted with an item.

```
import numpy as np

# Create a sample user-item rating matrix
# Rows: Users, Columns: Items
# A value of 0 indicates that the item has not been rated.
R = np.array([
    [5, 3, 0, 1, 4, 0],
    [4, 0, 0, 1, 3, 5],
    [1, 1, 5, 5, 0, 4],
    [0, 1, 4, 4, 0, 0],
    [2, 0, 3, 0, 5, 4],
])
```

This matrix, R, serves as the fundamental input for our model. Each row represents a user's known preferences, which the algorithm will use to find "neighboring" users with similar tastes.

Step 2. Define the UserKNNRecommender Class

To organize our logic, we will create a UserKNNRecommender class. This class will store the model's hyperparameters (like k), the computed user-similarity matrix, and the training data. The primary methods will be fit() to train the model and predict() to generate scores for all users.

```
from sklearn.metrics.pairwise import cosine_similarity

class UserKNNRecommender:
    def __init__(self, k=20):
        self.k = k
        self.similarity_matrix = None
        self.train_data = None
        self.user_means = None
        self.R_predicted = None

    def fit(self, R):
      # This method will be implemented in the next step.
      pass

    def predict(self):
      # This method will be implemented later.
      pass
```

This class structure creates a clear blueprint for our recommender. The *init* method initializes the key hyperparameters that will govern the model's behavior, most notably k, which determines the size of each user's neighborhood.

Step 3. Calculate User-to-User Similarity (The fit method)

This step is the core of the training process, where we build the user-user similarity matrix according to the mathematical foundations. We will use Pearson Correlation, which is equivalent to Adjusted Cosine Similarity applied to user vectors. This involves first centering each user's ratings by subtracting their personal average rating and then computing the cosine similarity between these centered vectors. This process accounts for user rating biases (e.g., some users rate more generously than others).

```
# Continuing the UserKNNRecommender class...

def fit(self, R):
 self.train_data = R

 # Part A: Adjusted Cosine Similarity (Pearson Correlation)
 # Calculate the mean rating for each user.
```

```
    # np.true_divide handles division by zero for users with no ratings.
    self.user_means = np.true_divide(self.train_data.sum(axis=1),
                                     (self.train_data != 0).sum(axis=1))
    # Replace any resulting NaNs (from users with no ratings) with 0.
    self.user_means[np.isnan(self.user_means)] = 0

    # Center the ratings by subtracting the user's mean from
    # each of their non-zero ratings.
    R_centered = self.train_data - np.where(self.train_data != 0,
                                            self.user_means[:, np.newaxis], 0)

    # Calculate cosine similarity on the centered user-rating vectors.
    self.similarity_matrix = cosine_similarity(R_centered)

    # A user cannot be their own neighbor, so we set their self-similarity to 0.
    np.fill_diagonal(self.similarity_matrix, 0)

    return self
```

After executing the fit method, the self.similarity_matrix now holds the learned similarity scores for every pair of users. This matrix is pre-computed and stored, enabling the model to make predictions efficiently in the next step.

Step 4. Make Predictions (The predict method)

With the similarity matrix established, we can now predict ratings for items that a user has not yet seen. The prediction is calculated by identifying the k-nearest neighbors for a target user and then computing a weighted average of how those neighbors rated the target item. The final score is the target user's average rating adjusted by this weighted deviation, as described in the mathematical formula.

```
# Continuing the UserKNNRecommender class...

def predict(self):
    num_users, num_items = self.train_data.shape
    predictions = np.zeros_like(self.train_data, dtype=float)
    # Iterate over each user to make predictions
    for u in range(num_users):
        # Get indices of most similar users
        neighbor_indices = np.argsort(-self.similarity_matrix[u, :])
        # Predict scores for each unrated item
        for i in range(num_items):
            if self.train_data[u, i] != 0:
                continue
```

```
                numerator = 0
                denominator = 0
                neighbor_count = 0
                # Calculate weighted average from the k-nearest neighbors
                for neighbor_idx in neighbor_indices:
                    if neighbor_count >= self.k:
                        break
                    # Ensure the neighbor has rated the item
                    if self.train_data[neighbor_idx, i] > 0:
                        sim = self.similarity_matrix[u, neighbor_idx]
                        neighbor_rating = self.train_data[neighbor_idx, i]
                        neighbor_mean = self.user_means[neighbor_idx]
                        # Add the weighted rating deviation to the totals
                        numerator += sim * (neighbor_rating - neighbor_mean)
                        denominator += np.abs(sim)
                        neighbor_count += 1
                # Calculate the final prediction
                if denominator > 0:
                    pred = self.user_means[u] + (numerator / denominator)
                    # Clip the score to be within the valid rating range
                    predictions[u, i] = np.clip(pred, 1, 5)
                else:
                    # Use the user's average as a fallback
                    predictions[u, i] = self.user_means[u]
        # Combine original ratings with the new predictions
        self.R_predicted = np.where(
            self.train_data > 0,
            self.train_data,
            predictions
        )
        return self.R_predicted
```

This method directly implements the UserKNN prediction formula. It systematically calculates a score for every empty slot in the user-item matrix by leveraging the opinions of a user's most similar peers.

Step 5. Putting It All Together

Finally, let's see the recommender in action. We will instantiate the UserKNNRecommender class, train it on our sample data using the fit method, and then generate a full matrix of predicted ratings with the predict method. We will then examine the recommendations for a specific user.

```
# 1. Instantiate the recommender with a neighborhood size k=2.
user_knn = UserKNNRecommender(k=2)

# 2. Train the model on the rating data to build the similarity matrix.
user_knn.fit(R)

# 3. Generate the full matrix of predicted ratings.
R_predicted = user_knn.predict()

# 4. Examine the recommendations for a specific user (e.g., user 0).
target_user_ratings = R[0, :]
predicted_ratings_for_user = R_predicted[0, :]

# Create a ranked list of recommendations for unrated items.
unrated_items = np.where(target_user_ratings == 0)[0]
recommendations = sorted(
    zip(unrated_items, predicted_ratings_for_user[unrated_items]),
    key=lambda x: x[1],
    reverse=True
)

print(f"Original ratings for User 0: {target_user_ratings}")
print(f"Full predicted ratings for User 0: {np.round(predicted_ratings_for_user, 2)}")
print("\nTop recommendations for User 0:")
for item_id, score in recommendations:
    print(f"  Item {item_id}: Predicted Score = {score:.4f}")
```

The final output displays the predicted scores for the items the target user had not previously rated. This demonstrates the complete, end-to-end workflow of the UserKNN model: training the user similarity model and then using it to generate personalized, ranked recommendations by inferring tastes from like-minded users.

2.3.4 Comparing User-Based and Item-Based Approaches

While algorithmically similar, user-based and item-based k-NN have different practical trade-offs:

- **Accuracy and Stability.** Item-based methods are often more accurate and stable. Item similarities (e.g., two sci-fi movies are similar) are generally more static than user similarities, which can change quickly. As new users and ratings are added, the item-item similarity matrix needs less frequent recalculation than the user-user matrix.

- **Diversity and Serendipity.** User-based methods often produce more diverse and serendipitous recommendations. By tapping into the tastes of a "neighbor," a user can be exposed to items outside their immediate sphere of interest. Item-based methods, by recommending items similar to what a user already likes, can sometimes be too obvious and less novel.

- **Explainability.** Item-based methods typically offer more intuitive explanations. "Because you watched *Movie A*, you might like *Movie B*" is a direct and compelling justification that is easy to generate from the item neighborhood. User-based explanations rely on anonymous peer groups, which are less transparent.

- **Scalability.** The primary computational cost is building the similarity matrix. For user-based methods, this is O(m^2), and for item-based, it's O(n^2), where m is the number of users and n is the number of items. In most systems, the number of users is far greater than the number of items (m » n), making the initial computation for item-based methods much more tractable.

2.3.5 SlopeOne

SlopeOne is a simple, non-iterative algorithm that predicts ratings by computing average deviations (or "slopes") between item pairs, assuming linear relationships like f(x) = x + b, where b is the pre-computed average rating deviation. Introduced in a 2005 paper by Daniel Lemire and Anna Maclachlan called Slope One Predictors for Online Rating-Based Collaborative Filtering.

Key concept — It models consistent offsets in ratings (e.g., if Item B is rated 0.5 higher than Item A on average, predict accordingly for a new user); new ratings can update averages incrementally. Consider two users, U_1 and U_2, and two items, I_1 and I_2. User U_1 gave item I_1 a rating of 1 star and item I_2 a rating of 1.5 stars. If User U_2 rated item I_1 with 2 stars, we can assume the difference in ratings between the two items is the same as for User U_1. Therefore, User U_2's rating for item I_2 would be: 2 + (1.5 - 1) = 2.5 stars.

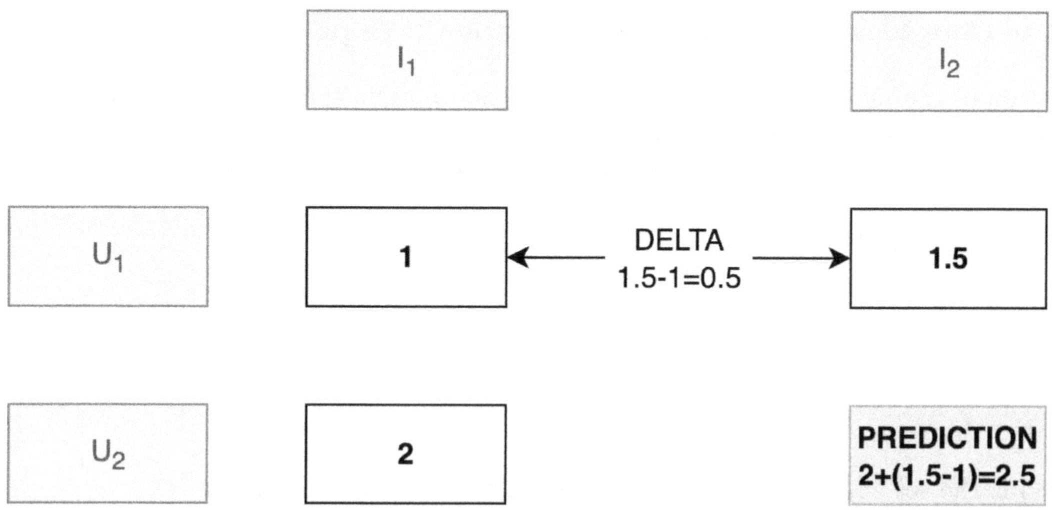

Differentiator — Extremely lightweight with no training phase ($O(n^2)$ preprocessing for n items), handles cold-start better than KNN, and supports dynamic updates with fast queries.

Use cases — Quick prototyping, mobile apps, or online systems with limited resources where numerical ratings exist and simplicity/speed trump top accuracy. Consider it when preferences have consistent offsets, you need an incremental model, or engineering overhead must be minimal.

Seminal Papers:

- Daniel Lemire, Anna Maclachlan. Slope One Predictors for Online Rating-Based Collaborative Filtering. https://arxiv.org/abs/cs/0702144.

Production Ready?

- The primary advantages of Slope One are its ease of implementation, low storage requirements, and extremely fast prediction time. These characteristics make it an excellent choice for systems with limited computational resources, as a strong and simple-to-debug baseline, or in online settings where the model needs to be updated frequently and dynamically as new ratings arrive.

Mathematical Foundations

Slope One's elegance lies in its simplicity. It consists of two straightforward steps: pre-computing the average rating differences between all item pairs and then using those differences to predict ratings for a user.

Part A: The Core Idea - Average Rating Deviation ("Slope")

The foundation of the model is a pre-computed deviation matrix that stores the average difference in ratings for every pair of items. The deviation $dev(i, j)$ represents how much higher (or lower) item i is rated than item j on average, by users who have rated both.

This deviation is calculated as:

$$dev(i, j) = \frac{\sum_{u \in S_{i,j}(U)} (r_{ui} - r_{uj})}{|S_{i,j}(U)|}$$

Where:

- $S_{i,j}(U)$ is the set of all users who have rated **both** item i and item j.
- r_{ui} and r_{uj} are user u's ratings for items i and j, respectively.
- $||S_{i,j}(U)|$ is the number of users in that set, also called the co-rating count, c_{ij}.

This calculation is performed once for all item pairs. Note that the deviation is anti-symmetric: $dev(i, j) = -dev(j, i)$.

Part B: The Prediction Model (Weighted Slope One)

To predict a rating $\hat{r}_{ui}$ for a user u on a target item i, we look at all the other items j that user u has already rated. For each such item j, we can form a simple prediction for item i by taking the user's rating for j and adding the pre-computed average deviation between i and j:

$$r_{uj} + dev(i, j)$$

The final prediction is not a simple average of these individual predictions, but a **weighted average**. Predictions derived from item pairs with more co-ratings are more reliable and are therefore given more weight.

The final prediction formula is:

$$\hat{r}_{ui} = \frac{\sum_{j \in R_u} (r_{uj} + dev(i, j)) \cdot c_{ij}}{\sum_{j \in R_u} c_{ij}}$$

Where:

- R_u is the set of all items that user u has rated (excluding item i itself).
- r_{uj} is the user's known rating for an item j in that set.

- $dev(i, j)$ is the pre-computed average deviation between items i and j.
- c_{ij} is the co-rating count for items i and j, which acts as the weight.

This weighted approach ensures that the final prediction is more heavily influenced by stable, reliable deviations calculated from a large number of users.

2.3.6 Attribute-Aware k-Nearest Neighbors

Attribute-Aware k-NN is a specialized extension of the classic k-NN algorithm that enhances the similarity metric by incorporating both collaborative (user interaction) and content-based (item attribute) signals. In this approach, item similarity is computed by combining collaborative signals (e.g., cosine similarity of user ratings) with content-based signals (e.g., similarity of item features like genre, director, or tags), often using a weighted hybrid similarity metric. This creates a more robust and nuanced measure of item similarity, which is particularly effective at alleviating the item cold-start problem, where new items lack interaction data, by leveraging metadata. However, user cold-start issues may require complementary strategies.

Hybridizing k-NN: Combining User-Based and Item-Based Models

Before diving into the details, let's define a few key terms. **Data sparsity** occurs when most users have rated only a few items, making predictions challenging. A **heuristic** is a simple rule or shortcut used to make decisions, like calculating similarity scores. An **objective function** is a mathematical formula that the model optimizes to improve predictions, such as minimizing prediction errors.

While User-Based and Item-Based k-NN are powerful on their own, they possess complementary strengths and weaknesses.

- **Item-Based k-NN** often provides higher **accuracy and stability**. Since item-to-item relationships (e.g., two sci-fi movies being similar) are more static than user tastes, the underlying similarity model requires less frequent updates. This approach also leads to more intuitive explanations, such as "Because you watched *Star Wars*, you might like *The Empire Strikes Back*".
- **User-Based k-NN** tends to generate more **diverse and serendipitous** recommendations. By tapping into the tastes of similar users, it can introduce a person to items outside their immediate sphere of interest, fostering discovery.

A hybrid model seeks to combine these advantages, creating a more robust and accurate recommender system. A formal way to achieve this is to reframe both neighborhood methods through the lens of regression modeling.

At the core, both User-Based and Item-Based neighborhood methods can be seen as simple linear models. A rating is predicted as a weighted average of other known ratings. In the classic k-NN approach, these weights are set **heuristically** using similarity scores like Pearson correlation or cosine similarity.

However, a more powerful approach is to **learn** these weights through an optimization process. By defining an objective function—typically by minimizing the squared error between predicted and actual known ratings—we can find the optimal weights that best explain the data. This regression-based perspective provides a principled mathematical framework for unifying the two methods.

A unified model predicts a rating by considering influences from both similar users and similar items simultaneously. The final prediction for user u's rating on item j, denoted as $\hat{r}_{uj}$, is constructed by combining several components:

$$\hat{r}_{uj} = b_u^{\text{user}} + b_j^{\text{item}} + \frac{\sum_{v \in P_u(j)} w_{vu}^{\text{user}} \cdot (r_{vj} - (\mu + b_v + b_j))}{\sqrt{|P_u(j)|}} + \frac{\sum_{t \in Q_j(u)} w_{tj}^{\text{item}} \cdot (r_{ut} - (\mu + b_t + b_u))}{\sqrt{|Q_j(u)|}}$$

Let's break down this formula piece by piece:

- **Baseline Predictors:** b_u^{user} and b_j^{item} are **bias** terms. They capture the average rating tendency of user u (e.g., some users are generally harsher critics) and the average rating of item j (e.g., some items are universally acclaimed). The term $\mu + b_v + b_j$ is the baseline estimate for the rating of user v on item j, where μ is the global mean rating.
- **User-Based Component:** The first summation represents the influence of the user's "neighborhood."
  - $P_u(j)$ is the set of users similar to user u who have also rated item j.
  - w_{vu}^{user} is a **learned weight** representing how much user v's opinion should influence the prediction for user u.
  - $(r_{vj} - (\mu + b_v + b_j))$ is the neighbor's rating for item j, adjusted for their baseline biases. This term captures how much more or less than average user v liked item j.
- **Item-Based Component:** The second summation represents the influence of the user's own past ratings on similar items.
  - $Q_j(u)$ is the set of items similar to item j that user u has rated.
  - w_{tj}^{item} is a **learned weight** representing how much item t's rating should influence the prediction for item j.

  - $(r_{ut} - (\mu + b_t + b_u))$ is the user's own rating for a similar item t, adjusted for baselines. This captures the user's personal preference for items related to j.

- **Normalization:** The factors $\sqrt{|P_u(j)|}$ and $\sqrt{|Q_j(u)|}$ are a common heuristic to handle **data sparsity**, reducing the impact of predictions based on few neighbor ratings. Other normalization strategies, such as linear scaling by $|P_u(j)|$, may also be used.

The weights w_{vu}^{user} and w_{tj}^{item} are learned by minimizing a loss function, such as the mean squared error between predicted and actual ratings, often with regularization to prevent overfitting. This can be achieved using techniques like gradient descent or alternating least squares.

The entire model, including all bias terms (b) and weights (w), is trained jointly by minimizing the prediction error on all known ratings in the training set. This allows the model to learn the optimal balance between user-based and item-based signals, creating a hybrid that is often more powerful than either method in isolation.

The performance of hybrid k-NN models is typically evaluated using metrics like **Root Mean Squared Error (RMSE)** for rating prediction accuracy or **precision@K** for ranking quality, ensuring the model meets the desired recommendation goals.

Python Frameworks

- **Surprise** `https://surpriselib.com/`: Provides robust implementations for explicit data, including KNNBasic, KNNWithMeans, and KNNWithZScore, allowing for various baseline and normalization strategies. It also supports attribute-aware k-NN through custom similarity measures.
- **MyMediaLite** `http://www.mymedialite.net/`: A lightweight library offering implementations of attribute-aware UserKNN and ItemKNN, combining interaction and content-based features.
- **LightFM** `https://github.com/lyst/lightfm`: A modern library that supports hybrid recommender systems combining collaborative and content-based features.

2.4 Latent Factor Models (Matrix Factorization)

These "model-based" methods address data sparsity by decomposing the user-item interaction matrix into lower-dimensional latent factor matrices for users and items. The core idea is to represent users and items in a shared latent space where their proximity reflects preference. This condenses complex interaction patterns into a small number of hidden features, moving beyond direct neighbor comparisons to uncover the underlying reasons for preferences.

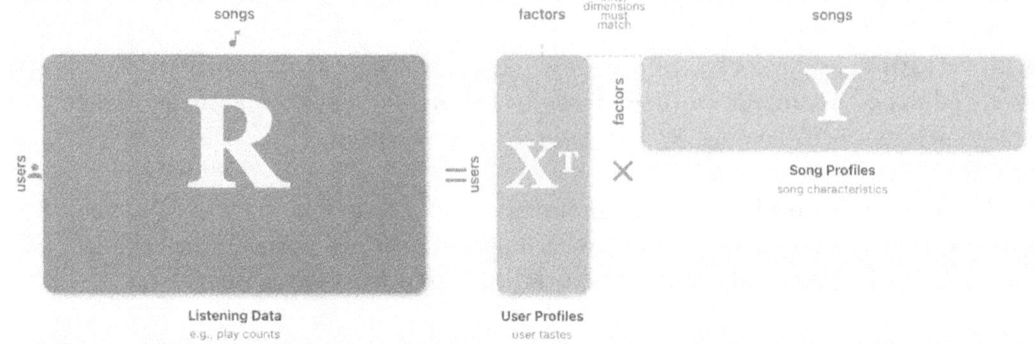

It's like creating a "taste profile" for both users and items using the same set of hidden characteristics.

Imagine you're recommending movies. Instead of just knowing which movies a person likes, the model tries to figure out why. It creates a handful of underlying characteristics, like "amount of sci-fi," "level of comedy," or "degree of romance."

Each movie gets a score for each of these characteristics. For example, a rom-com would score high on "comedy" and "romance" but low on "sci-fi." Each user gets a matching profile based on the movies they've enjoyed. Someone who loves rom-coms would get high scores for "comedy" and "romance" preferences. To make a recommendation, the system just finds movies whose characteristic scores are a great match for the user's preference scores. This way, it can recommend a new movie the user has never seen, as long as its "taste profile" fits theirs.

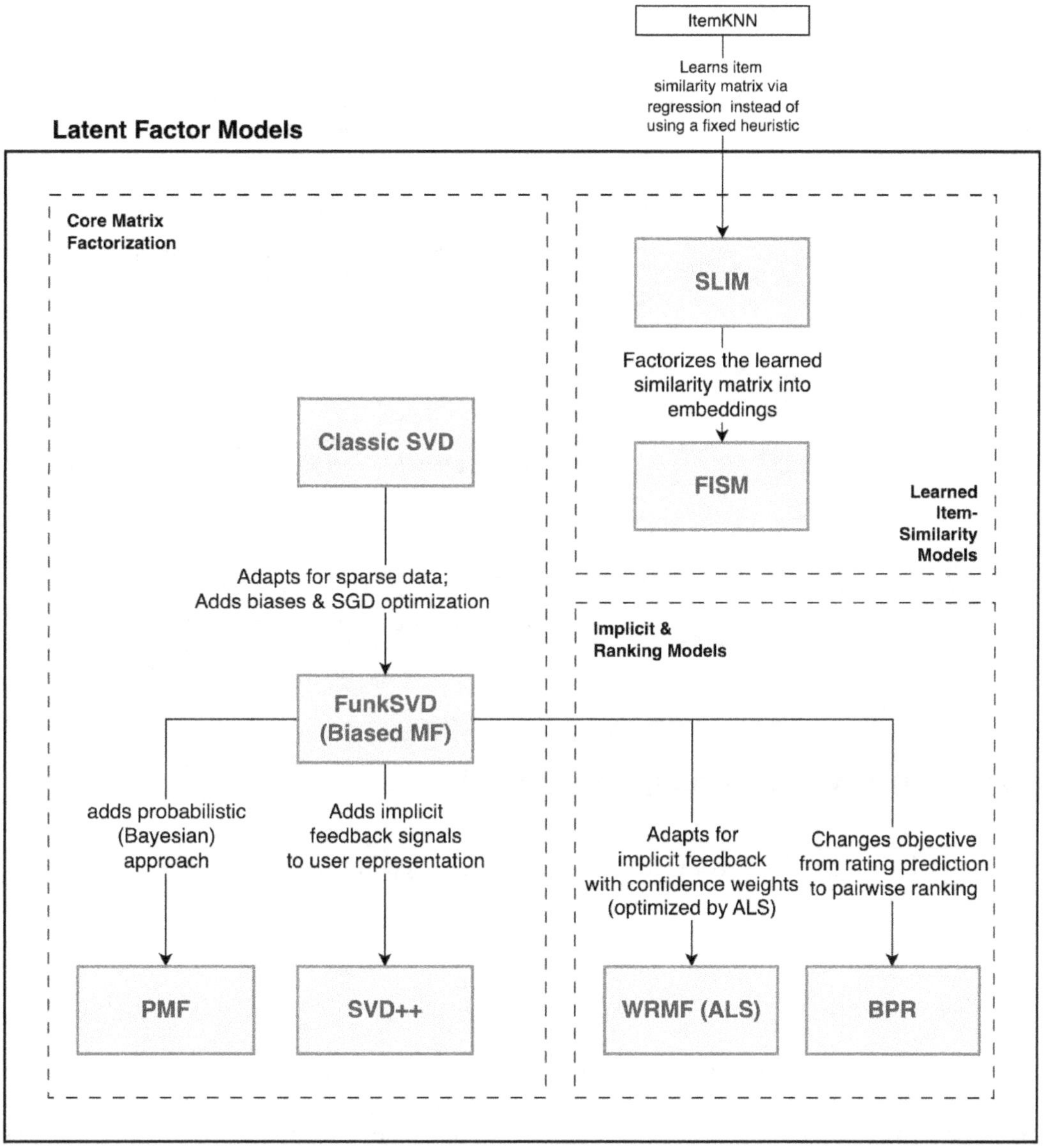
ItemKNN
Learns item similarity matrix via regression instead of using a fixed heuristic
Latent Factor Models
Core Matrix Factorization
Classic SVD
Adapts for sparse data; Adds biases & SGD optimization
FunkSVD (Biased MF)
adds probabilistic (Bayesian) approach
Adds implicit feedback signals to user representation
PMF
SVD++
SLIM
Factorizes the learned similarity matrix into embeddings
FISM
Learned Item-Similarity Models
Implicit & Ranking Models
Adapts for implicit feedback with confidence weights (optimized by ALS)
Changes objective from rating prediction to pairwise ranking
WRMF (ALS)
BPR

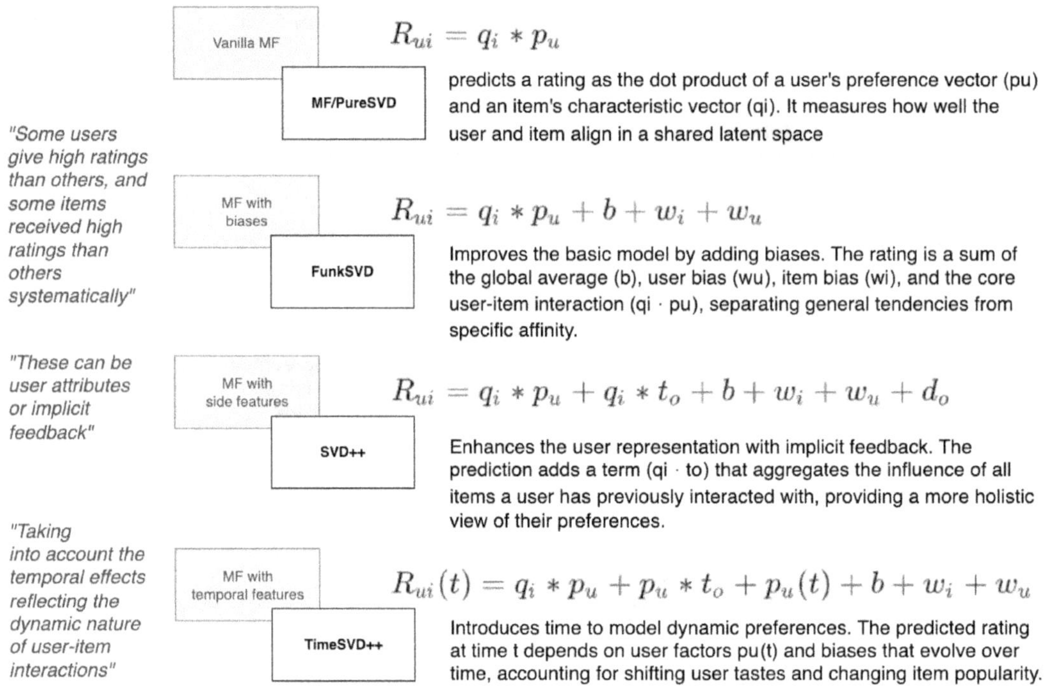

2.4.1 Classic Singular Value Decomposition (SVD)

In its pure form, SVD is a method from linear algebra that decomposes any matrix `R` into three distinct matrices: U, Σ, and V^T.

$$R = U\Sigma V^T$$

- U: A matrix of left singular vectors (representing user "features").
- Σ: A diagonal matrix of singular values (representing the importance of each "feature").
- V^T: The transpose of a matrix of right singular vectors (representing item "features").

To get recommendations, one can reduce the dimensionality (by keeping only the `k` most important features) and then multiply the matrices back together: $\hat{R} = U_k \Sigma_k V_k^T$. The resulting matrix, $\hat{R}$, would contain predicted ratings in every cell, including those that were previously empty.

Why It's Not Used in Practice for Recommendations: The Big Problem

The primary and virtually insurmountable issue with classic SVD is that **it does not work with missing values.**

(1) **Requires a Complete Matrix:** Mathematical SVD requires that every cell in the matrix `R` be filled. However, in real-world recommender systems, the user-item matrix is extremely sparse (often 99.9% empty), as users have only rated a tiny fraction of the available items.

(2) **The Imputation Problem:** To use SVD, you would first have to fill in all the missing cells with some value (a process called imputation), such as zero or the average rating for that item. This has disastrous consequences:

- **Data Distortion:** Filling millions of empty cells with zeros creates a strong but false signal that a user *dislikes* an item, when in reality, they have likely never seen it. This severely pollutes the data and leads to poor recommendations.
- **Computational Cost:** A sparse matrix is stored very efficiently in memory (only the known ratings are stored). Converting it into a dense matrix would make it astronomically large and computationally infeasible to store and process.

Five WHYs

Why does classic SVD require that every cell in the matrix `R` be filled?

Classic SVD is a mathematical technique that works only on complete matrices, meaning every cell in the user-item matrix R must have a value. This is because SVD decomposes the matrix into three matrices (U, Σ, V^T) using linear algebra, which assumes no missing data to perform the calculations correctly.

Why can't we just fill missing values with zeros to use SVD?

Filling missing values with zeros distorts the data by falsely suggesting that users dislike items they haven't rated or seen. This creates misleading patterns, leading to poor recommendation quality since SVD would treat these zeros as actual ratings.

Why is the user-item matrix in recommender systems usually sparse?

In real-world recommender systems, users only rate or interact with a small fraction of available items (e.g., movies, products). This results in a sparse matrix where most cells are empty, often 99.9% empty, because users haven't rated or seen most items.

Why does imputing missing values with averages cause problems for SVD?

Imputing missing values with averages (e.g., the average rating for an item) still distorts the data because it assumes users would rate items similarly to others, which may not be true. This can obscure true user preferences and lead to inaccurate recommendations.

Why is classic SVD computationally infeasible for large sparse matrices?

Converting a sparse matrix into a dense one by filling in missing values creates a massive matrix that requires enormous memory and computational power to process. Sparse matrices are stored efficiently by only keeping known ratings, but a dense matrix with millions of imputed values becomes too large to handle practically.

FunkSVD is a clever adaptation of the core idea of matrix decomposition, specifically engineered to solve the real-world problem of learning from sparse data, making it the true practical starting point.

2.4.2 FunkSVD (Biased Matrix Factorization)

Key concept — FunkSVD, more formally known as Biased Matrix Factorization, was a breakthrough model popularized during the Netflix Prize competition. It predicts a user's rating for an item by modeling it as the sum of four components: a global average rating, a user-specific bias, an item-specific bias, and the dot product of user and item latent factor vectors. This approach captures not just the core user-item interaction but also baseline rating tendencies.

Key differentiator — Its primary differentiator is its elegant simplicity and surprising effectiveness. Unlike a true mathematical SVD, it is an optimization-based model typically trained with Stochastic Gradient Descent (SGD). By incorporating user and item biases, it separates the general popularity of an item or the rating tendency of a user from the specific interaction component, which often leads to significantly more accurate predictions than basic matrix factorization.

Use cases — It is the quintessential model for **rating prediction** tasks where explicit feedback (e.g., 1-5 star ratings) is available. It is widely used in domains like movie recommendation (Netflix), e-commerce (product ratings), and book reviews.

When to Consider — An engineer should always consider FunkSVD as a first-pass model and a powerful baseline for any explicit-feedback recommendation task. Its straightforward implementation and strong performance make it the ideal starting point for understanding and applying latent factor models. It provides the foundation upon which more complex models like are built.

Seminal Paper/Resource:

While not a formal academic paper, the method was famously detailed by Simon Funk in a blog post during the Netflix Prize. A more formal description of the same model can be found in the papers by Yehuda Koren.

- Koren, Y., Bell, R., & Volinsky, C. (2009). *Matrix Factorization Techniques for Recommender Systems*. https://datajobs.com/data-science-repo/Recommender-Systems-[Netflix].pdf.
- Funk, S. (2006). *Netflix Update: Try This at Home*. https://sifter.org/~simon/journal/20061211.html.

Mathematical Foundations

The model is built on a simple, intuitive formula for predicting ratings and is trained by minimizing the error between its predictions and the actual known ratings.

Part A: The Prediction Model

The predicted rating $\hat{r}_{ui}$ for a user u and an item i is modeled as the sum of baseline estimates and the latent factor interaction:

$$\hat{r}_{ui} = \mu + b_u + b_i + p_u^\top q_i$$

Let's break down the components:

- μ: The **global average rating** across all known ratings in the dataset. This serves as the most basic starting point.
- b_u: The **user bias**. This term captures the tendency of user u to rate items higher or lower than the average. For example, a user who is a harsh critic will have a negative b_u.
- b_i: The **item bias**. This term captures the tendency of item i to receive higher or lower ratings than average. For example, a critically acclaimed movie will have a positive b_i.
- $p_u \in \mathbb{R}^k$: The **user latent factor vector**. This is a dense vector of size k that represents the user's preferences along a set of hidden dimensions (e.g., affinity for comedy, preference for action).
- $q_i \in \mathbb{R}^k$: The **item latent factor vector**. This is a dense vector of the same size k that represents the item's characteristics along those same hidden dimensions.

- $p_u^\top q_i$: The **dot product** of the user and item vectors. This term captures the specific interaction between user u's tastes and item i's attributes.

Part B: The Learning Process - Minimizing an Objective Function

The model learns all its parameters—the biases b_u, b_i and the factor vectors p_u, q_i—by minimizing an objective function. This function consists of two parts: the prediction error on the training data and a regularization term to prevent overfitting. The objective is to minimize the regularized sum of squared errors:

$$\min_{p*,q*,b*} \sum_{(u,i)\in\mathcal{K}} (r_{ui} - \hat{r}_{ui})^2 + \lambda \left(\sum_u ||p_u||^2 + \sum_i ||q_i||^2 + \sum_u b_u^2 + \sum_i b_i^2 \right)$$

- The first term, $\sum_{(u,i)\in\mathcal{K}}(r_{ui} - \hat{r}_{ui})^2$, is the **sum of squared errors** over all known user-item ratings in the training set $\mathcal{K}$. This pushes the model to make predictions that are as close as possible to the real ratings.

- The second term is the **L2 regularization** penalty. It penalizes large values for the biases and latent factors, which helps the model to generalize better to unseen data by preventing it from "memorizing" the training set. λ is a hyperparameter that controls the strength of this penalty.

How L2 Regularization Works

L2 regularization (also called Ridge regularization or Tikhonov regularization) is a technique that adds a "penalty" to the objective function for parameters that are too large. The main idea is to prevent overfitting, where the model fits the training data too closely, capturing noise or random patterns instead of general trends. This happens when parameters (like the vectors p_u and q_i or biases b_u, b_i) become very large, making the model overly complex.

L2 regularization addresses this by adding a term to the objective function that is proportional to the square of the magnitude of the parameters. This forces the optimizer (like Stochastic Gradient Descent, SGD) to find a balance: minimize prediction errors while keeping the parameters "small" and simple. The result is a smoother model that generalizes better to new, unseen data.

In practice:

- If λ is small (close to 0), the regularization is weak, and the model might overfit.

- If λ is large, the regularization is strong, pushing parameters toward zero, which can lead to underfitting (missing important patterns).

The value of λ is typically tuned using cross-validation.

Part C: Optimization with Stochastic Gradient Descent (SGD)

The most common method for minimizing this objective function is **Stochastic Gradient Descent (SGD)**. It works by iterating through the known ratings one by one and making small adjustments to the model parameters to reduce the error for that specific rating.

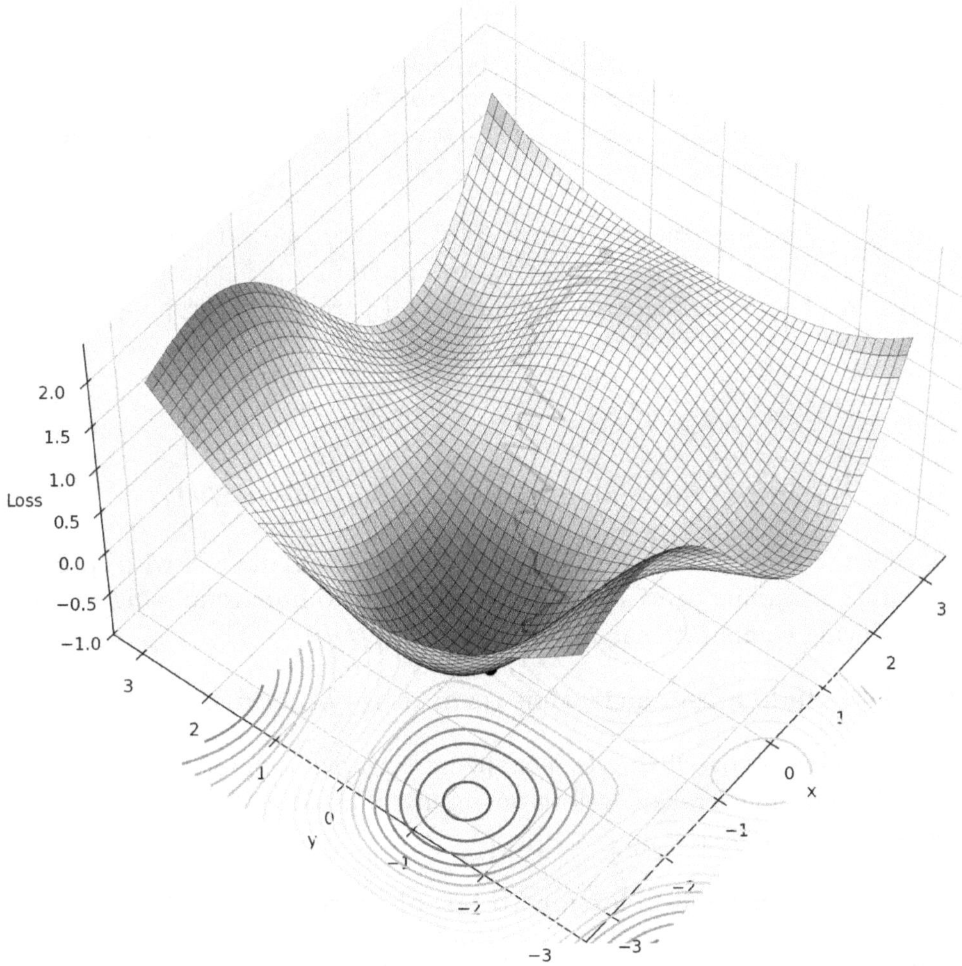

The process for a single rating r_{ui} is:

(1) Calculating the current prediction $\hat{r}_{ui}$ using the formula from Part A.

(2) Calculating the prediction error: $e_{ui} = r_{ui} - \hat{r}_{ui}$.

(3) Updating each parameter by taking a small step in the direction that reduces the error. The update rules are derived from the gradient of the squared error term:

- $b_u \leftarrow b_u + \gamma \cdot (e_{ui} - \lambda b_u)$
- $b_i \leftarrow b_i + \gamma \cdot (e_{ui} - \lambda b_i)$
- $p_u \leftarrow p_u + \gamma \cdot (e_{ui} \cdot q_i - \lambda p_u)$
- $q_i \leftarrow q_i + \gamma \cdot (e_{ui} \cdot p_u - \lambda q_i)$

Here, γ is the **learning rate**, a hyperparameter that controls the size of the update step. This process is repeated for many iterations over the entire training dataset until the parameters converge to a good solution.

You can see effect of the L2 regularization in these SGD update rules. For example, in the update $b_u \leftarrow b_u + \gamma \cdot (e_{ui} - \lambda b_u)$, the term $-\lambda b_u$ "shrinks" b_u toward zero. If b_u is positive, it gets reduced; if negative, it gets increased. This shrinking effect applies to all parameters, keeping them in check.

Five WHYs

Why is FunkSVD better suited for sparse matrices than classic SVD?

Unlike classic SVD, which requires a complete matrix, FunkSVD works directly with sparse data by only using known ratings in the training process. It avoids the need to impute missing values, preventing data distortion and reducing computational costs.

Why does FunkSVD include a regularization term in its objective function?

The regularization term prevents overfitting by penalizing large values in the biases and latent factor vectors. This ensures the model generalizes well to unseen data, avoiding "memorizing" the training set and improving recommendation quality.

Why does FunkSVD use biases in addition to latent factor vectors?

FunkSVD includes user biases (b_u) and item biases (b_i) to capture general tendencies, like a user rating items higher or lower than average or an item being generally popular or unpopular. This separates baseline rating patterns from specific user-item interactions, making predictions more accurate.

Why is FunkSVD trained with Stochastic Gradient Descent (SGD)?

SGD is used because it efficiently minimizes the error between predicted and actual ratings by iteratively updating model parameters for each known rating. This approach is computationally feasible for large, sparse datasets and helps FunkSVD learn optimal biases and latent factors.

2.4.3 Probabilistic Matrix Factorization (PMF)

Key concept — Probabilistic Matrix Factorization (PMF) reimagines matrix factorization from a probabilistic perspective. Instead of just finding two latent matrices that multiply together to approximate the original ratings, PMF treats latent factors as probability distributions. It assumes that a user's rating for an item is drawn from a bell curve (a Gaussian distribution), where the center of the curve is the dot product of the user's and item's latent vectors.

Key differentiator — Its main innovation is its fully **probabilistic and Bayesian approach**. PMF doesn't just learn a single, deterministic set of latent factors. By placing Gaussian "priors" (or initial beliefs) on the user and item vectors, it incorporates uncertainty into the model. These priors act as a principled form of regularization, gently guiding the latent factors to be small and simple. This makes the model more robust and far less prone to overfitting, especially on sparse datasets where most ratings are unknown.

Use cases — PMF is designed for **rating prediction** tasks where explicit feedback is available. It is particularly effective for large and sparse datasets, where its probabilistic nature helps it generalize well. It laid the groundwork for many subsequent Bayesian and probabilistic recommendation models.

When to Consider — Consider PMF when working with a sparse, explicit feedback dataset and you want a model with a strong theoretical, probabilistic foundation. It is an excellent starting point for understanding how Bayesian inference can be applied to collaborative filtering and serves as a powerful baseline that often demonstrates very strong performance.

Production-Ready? — Probabilistic Matrix Factorization (PMF) is not inherently outdated but is less suited for modern, large-scale production environments compared to newer models like neural collaborative filtering or graph-based recommenders. It remains production-ready for specific use cases involving sparse, explicit feedback datasets (e.g., movie ratings), offering a robust, interpretable baseline with a strong probabilistic foundation. However, its limitations—such as struggles with cold start, implicit feedback, and dynamic updates—require significant engineering (e.g., distributed computing, hybrid approaches) to scale effectively. For medium-scale systems with explicit ratings, PMF can be deployed with proper optimization and monitoring, but for cutting-edge applications, more advanced models often outperform it due to their flexibility and ability to handle diverse data types.

Seminal Paper:

- Mnih, A., & Salakhutov, R. (2008). *Probabilistic Matrix Factorization.* https://papers.nips.cc/paper_files/paper/2007/hash/d7322ed717dedf1eb4e6e52a37ea7bcd-Abstract.html).

Mathematical Foundations

PMF provides a fully probabilistic view of matrix factorization, modeling the ratings as outputs of a generative process that incorporates uncertainty.

Part A: The Probabilistic View

The core of PMF is a model that defines the probabilistic relationships between observed ratings and the unobserved (latent) factors.

(1) **The Likelihood: A Bell Curve of Ratings.** The model assumes that the rating r_{ui} a user u gives to an item i isn't a fixed number. Instead, it's drawn from a Gaussian (normal) distribution. The mean of this distribution—the center of the bell curve—is the dot product of the user's latent vector $p_u \in \mathbb{R}^k$ and the item's latent vector $q_i \in \mathbb{R}^k$.

$$p(r_{ui}|p_u, q_i, \sigma^2) = \mathcal{N}(r_{ui}|p_u^\top q_i, \sigma^2)$$

Here, $\mathcal{N}(x|\mu, \sigma^2)$ is the probability density of a Gaussian distribution with mean μ and variance σ^2. This means we don't expect the dot product to be exactly equal to the rating, but rather to be the most likely outcome in a range of possibilities.

The initial distribution:

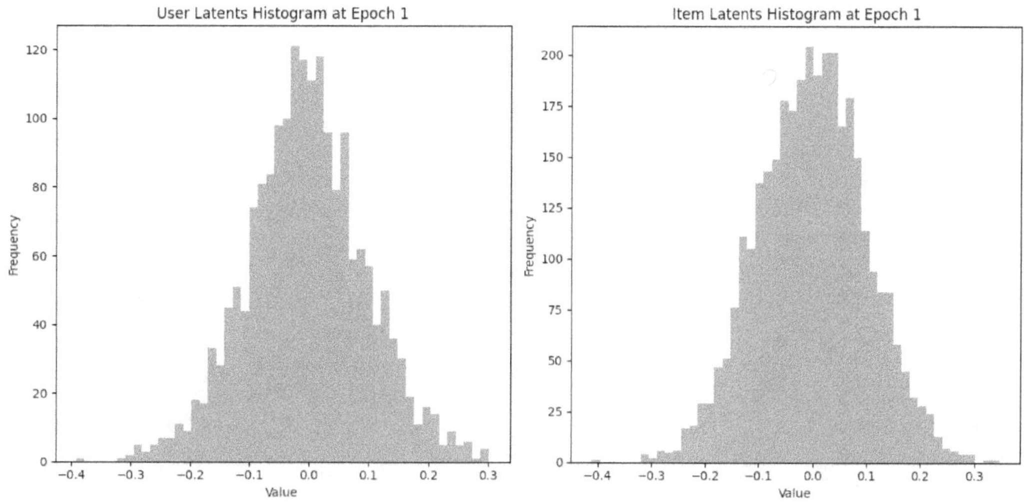

Learned after first 50 epochs:

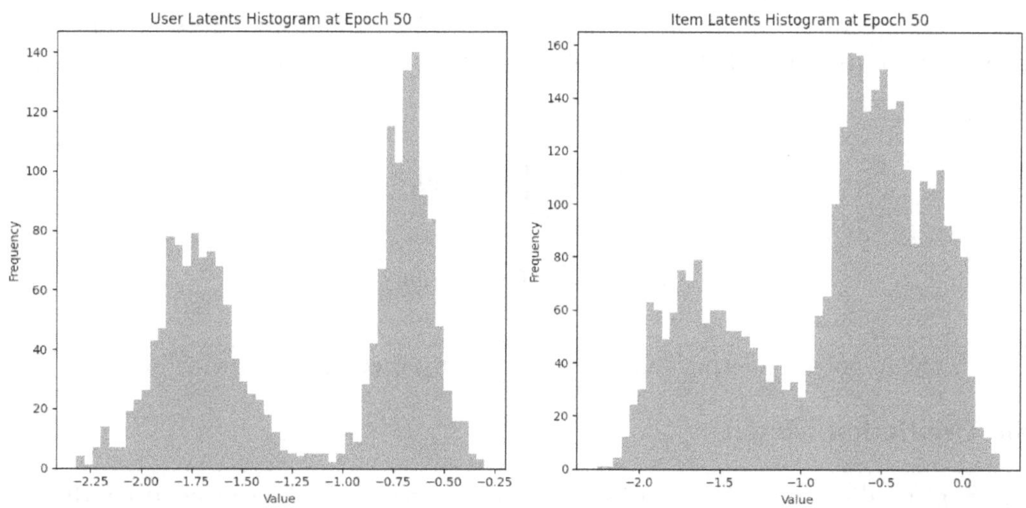

After 100 epochs:

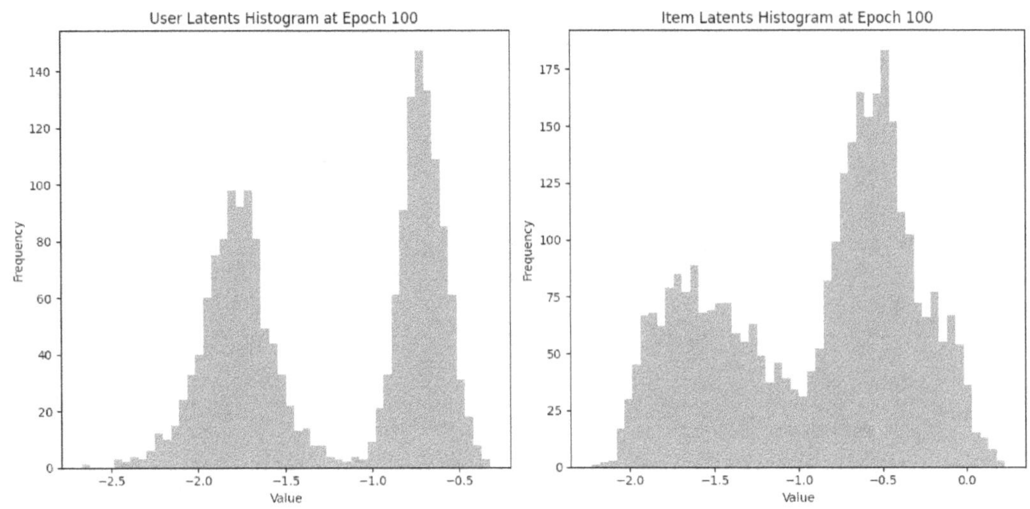

(2) **The Priors: A Gentle Nudge Against Complexity.** To make the model Bayesian and prevent overfitting, PMF places zero-mean Gaussian priors on the user and item latent factors. Think of this as a "prior belief" that the values in the latent vectors should be small and close to zero unless the data strongly suggests otherwise. This helps the model generalize better from sparse data.

$$p(P|\sigma_P^2) = \prod_{u=1}^{M} \mathcal{N}(p_u|0, \sigma_P^2 I)$$

$$p(Q|\sigma_Q^2) = \prod_{i=1}^{N} \mathcal{N}(q_i|0, \sigma_Q^2 I)$$

Here, σ_P^2 and σ_Q^2 are hyperparameters that control the variance of these prior beliefs.

Part B: The Prediction Model

For PMF, the final prediction $\hat{r}_{ui}$ is the most likely value, which is the **expected value** of the rating distribution. For a Gaussian, this is simply its mean:

$$\hat{r}_{ui} = p_u^\top q_i$$

While the prediction formula looks identical to basic matrix factorization, the way the parameters are learned is fundamentally different and more robust.

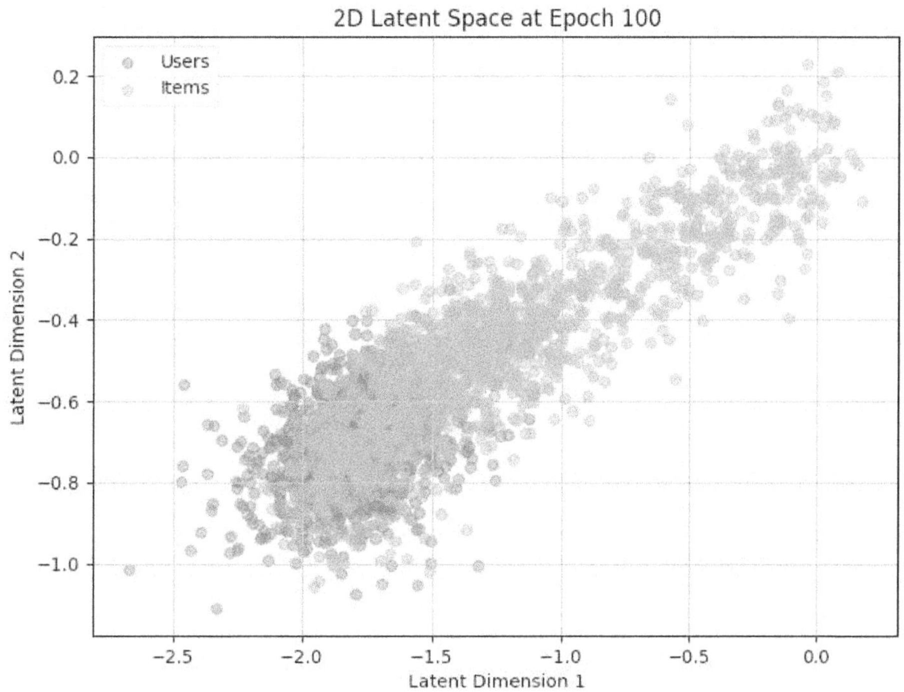

Part C: How the Model Learns

The goal is to find the user and item factors that are most probable given the observed ratings. This is achieved by maximizing the log-posterior probability of the factors which, thanks to Bayes' theorem, is proportional to the log-likelihood plus the log-priors.

$$\arg\max_{P,Q} \log p(P,Q|R) \propto \arg\max_{P,Q}[\log p(R|P,Q) + \log p(P) + \log p(Q)]$$

When we substitute the Gaussian distributions into this equation, maximizing this log-posterior turns out to be mathematically equivalent to minimizing a familiar objective function: the sum-of-squared-errors with L2 regularization.

$$\min_{P,Q} \frac{1}{2} \sum_{(u,i)\in\mathcal{K}} (r_{ui} - p_u^\top q_i)^2 + \frac{\lambda_P}{2} \sum_u ||p_u||_F^2 + \frac{\lambda_Q}{2} \sum_i ||q_i||_F^2$$

- The first term is the sum of squared errors over all known ratings, derived from the log-likelihood.

- The second and third terms are L2 regularization penalties, which are a direct result of the Gaussian log-priors. The regularization strengths, λ_P and λ_Q, are determined by the variances of the likelihood and prior distributions.

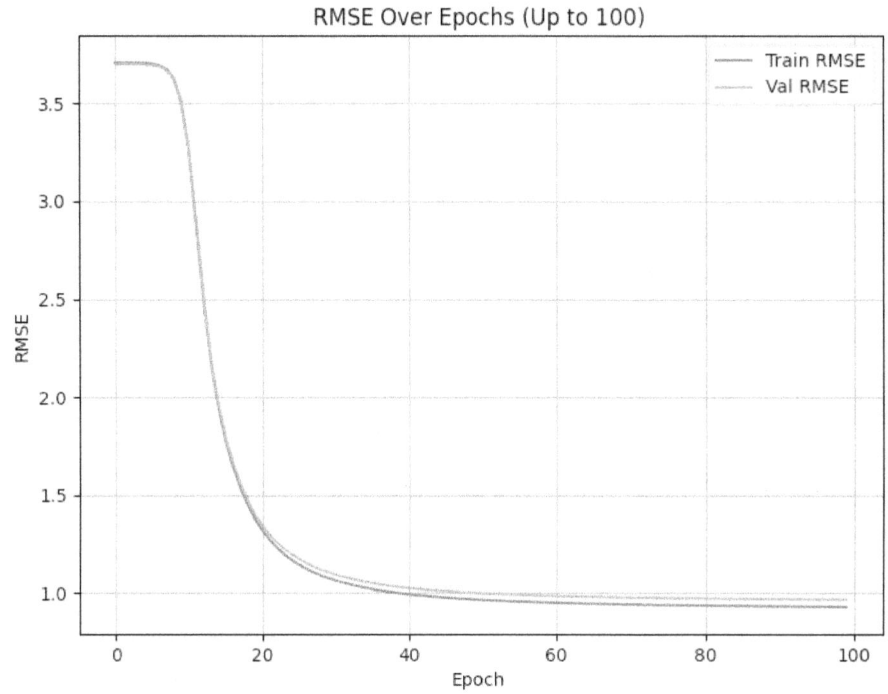

This elegant connection shows that the probabilistic formulation of PMF provides a solid theoretical justification for why L2 regularization is so effective in other matrix factorization models. This objective function can be minimized using methods like Stochastic Gradient Descent (SGD).

2.4.4 Weighted Regularized Matrix Factorization (WRMF)

WRMF is a model for implicit feedback, where non-interactions (no click) aren't treated as negatives but given less weight. Models like WRMF are key for modern systems with sparse data (lots of empty cells in the matrix). Its principles are similar to matrix factorization like SVD, just with weights and regularization.

Key concept — Weighted Regularized Matrix Factorization (WRMF) is designed for implicit feedback datasets, treating all non-interacted items as negative examples with lower confidence. It optimizes a weighted loss function, where interactions are weighted higher, and uses regularization to prevent overfitting.

Imagine the same table (matrix) of interactions as in SVD++:

- Rows are users (you, me, your friends).
- Columns are items (movies, products).
- But now, it's not ratings (1-5 stars) but binary implicit data: 1 if the user interacted (watched, clicked, bought), 0 if they didn't (or it's unknown).

The problem: A 0 doesn't mean "dislike" — maybe the user just hasn't seen the item. So, we can't treat all 0s as equally bad. WRMF solves this with weights:

- For 1s (positive interactions): High weight (confidence), like "this is a strong signal."
- For 0s: Low weight, like "maybe they don't like it, but we're not sure."

Like SVD, WRMF "breaks down" the matrix into latent factors: vectors for users and items (user_factors and item_factors). The predicted "score" is the dot product of these vectors (sometimes with biases, but pure WRMF often skips them). It also uses regularization to keep the factors from getting too big (avoid overfitting) and weighting to focus on reliable data.

For example, the matrix for movies:

- You (user 1): Watched "Star Wars" (1), "Interstellar" (1), rest are 0.
- Friend (user 2): Watched "Interstellar" (1), "The Matrix" (1).

WRMF figures out you both like sci-fi (a hidden factor) and recommends "The Matrix" to you with a high score.

Key differentiator — WRMF's focus on implicit feedback and its confidence-weighted loss make it highly effective for datasets with binary or frequency-based interactions, such as clicks or purchase histories. While WRMF defines the objective function, it is commonly optimized using an **Alternating Least Squares (ALS)** algorithm. This means ALS is the method used to find the latent factors that best fit the WRMF model.

Use cases — Top-N recommendation in domains like e-commerce or streaming, where implicit feedback (e.g., clicks, plays) is abundant but explicit ratings are scarce.

When to Consider — Use WRMF when working with implicit feedback datasets and aiming for high-quality Top-N recommendations. It is particularly effective in large-scale systems with sparse interaction data.

It is great for implicit data (clicks, views), handles sparse matrices well. Simple and scalable (ALS is fast for large matrices).

The downside is it doesn't capture sequence (like sequential models) or context. Also you needs tuning of alpha and regularization hyperparameters.

Hyperparameters

- **k (Latent Factors)**: The number of latent dimensions used to represent users and items.
- **Iterations**: Since WRMF is trained with an iterative solver (ALS), this parameter defines the number of times the algorithm will alternate between solving for user and item factors.
- **Regularization (lambda_reg)**: The regularization parameter used to penalize the magnitude of the latent factors, helping to prevent overfitting.
- **Alpha**: A confidence parameter that scales the importance of positive interactions. A higher alpha value indicates a higher confidence that a user's interaction with an item is a positive preference.

Production Ready?

- **Absolutely Production-Ready.** WRMF, especially when optimized with the Alternating Least Squares (ALS) algorithm, is a cornerstone of industrial recommender systems designed for implicit feedback. Its ability to efficiently handle massive, sparse datasets and its strong, often hard-to-beat performance make it a go-to model for many large-scale platforms, such as e-commerce sites and streaming services. It is frequently used both as a powerful standalone recommender and as a key component in larger hybrid systems.

Seminal Paper:

- Hu, Y., Koren, Y., & Volinsky, C. (2008). *Collaborative Filtering for Implicit Feedback Datasets.* https://dl.acm.org/doi/10.1109/ICDM.2008.22.

Mathematical Foundations

Weighted Regularized Matrix Factorization (WRMF) is a matrix factorization model specifically designed to handle the challenges of implicit feedback datasets (e.g., clicks, views, purchases). Its core innovation is to treat all user-item interactions, both observed and unobserved, but to assign a different level of confidence to each.

Part A: The Core Idea - Preference and Confidence

WRMF introduces two key concepts to model implicit data:

(1) **Preference (p_{ui}):** This is a binary variable indicating a user's preference. If a user u has interacted with an item i (e.g., clicked or purchased it), we assume a positive preference, so $p_{ui} = 1$. If there is no interaction, $p_{ui} = 0$.

(2) **Confidence (c_{ui}):** This variable captures our confidence in the preference observation. The model has low confidence that a user dislikes an unobserved item (they may simply be unaware of it), but high confidence that they like an item they have interacted with. The confidence is defined as:

$$c_{ui} = 1 + \alpha r_{ui}$$

Where:

- r_{ui} is the raw interaction frequency (e.g., number of clicks or views). In the simple binary case, r_{ui} is 1 for an interaction and 0 otherwise.
- α is a hyperparameter that controls the level of confidence. A higher α means we are much more confident in positive interactions. For example, with $\alpha = 40$, an interaction has a confidence of 41, while a non-interaction has a confidence of just 1.

Part B: The Objective Function

The goal is to find latent factor vectors for users ($p_u \in \mathbb{R}^k$) and items ($q_i \in \mathbb{R}^k$) that best explain the preferences, weighted by our confidence. The model minimizes a loss function consisting of the sum of squared errors, weighted by confidence, plus L2 regularization terms to prevent overfitting:

$$\min_{P,Q} \sum_{u,i} c_{ui}(p_{ui} - p_u^\top q_i)^2 + \lambda \left(\sum_u |p_u|^2 + \sum_i |q_i|^2 \right)$$

Let's break down this function:

$$\sum_{u,i} c_{ui}(p_{ui} - p_u^\top q_i)^2$$

This is the core of the loss. It measures the squared error between the observed preference (p_{ui}) and the predicted preference ($p_u^\top q_i$). Crucially, each error is weighted by the confidence score c_{ui}. This forces the model to focus heavily on fitting the observed interactions.

$$\lambda \left(\sum_u |p_u|^2 + \sum_i |q_i|^2 \right)$$

This is the standard L2 regularization term that penalizes large values in the user and item factor vectors, helping the model generalize better to unseen data.

Part C: Optimization with Alternating Least Squares (ALS)

Solving for all user factors (P) and item factors (Q) simultaneously is computationally difficult. Instead, WRMF is optimized using an efficient iterative method called **Alternating Least Squares (ALS)**. The process alternates between fixing one set of factors and solving for the other.

(1) **Fix Item Factors, Solve for User Factors:** If we keep the item factors (Q) constant, the objective function becomes a quadratic function of the user factors (P). This allows us to find the optimal value for each user's factor vector p_u by solving a linear system of equations. The solution for a single user u is:

$$p_u = (Q^\top C^u Q + \lambda I)^{-1} Q^\top C^u p(u)$$

Where:

- $p(u)$ is the vector of preferences for user u (a row from the binary interaction matrix).
- C^u is a diagonal matrix where $C^u_{ii} = c_{ui}$. It contains the confidence scores for user u across all items.

(2) **Fix User Factors, Solve for Item Factors:** Next, we keep the newly updated user factors (P) constant and solve for the item factors (Q). The logic is perfectly symmetrical. The solution for a single item i is:

$$q_i = (P^\top C^i P + \lambda I)^{-1} P^\top C^i p(i)$$

Where:

- $p(i)$ is the vector of preferences for item i (a column from the binary interaction matrix).
- C^i is a diagonal matrix containing the confidence scores for item i across all users.

These two steps are repeated for a fixed number of iterations. With each iteration, the model's approximation of the user and item factors improves, converging towards a solution that minimizes the overall objective function.

Tutorial: WRMF from Scratch

> The tutorial sections in this guide are entirely optional, though they can be extremely valuable for building intuition and a deeper understanding of the algorithms in practice. They assume, however, a basic familiarity with the libraries and frameworks being used. If you are interested in exploring why a particular method, function, or framework class is invoked at a specific point in the code, we encourage you to consult the Appendix, where we provide detailed, line-by-line commentary for selected algorithms from the Tutorial sections.

This tutorial provides a practical, step-by-step implementation of the Weighted Regularized Matrix Factorization (WRMF) algorithm, optimized via Alternating Least Squares (ALS). We will build a recommender specifically designed for implicit feedback data, where the goal is to learn user and item latent factors by treating all unobserved items as negative examples with lower confidence.

Step 1. Prepare Implicit Data

First, we need a user-item interaction matrix suitable for an implicit feedback model. We'll use a NumPy array where a `1` represents a positive interaction (e.g., a click, view, or purchase) and a `0` represents no observed interaction.

```
import numpy as np

# Create a sample user-item interaction matrix (implicit feedback)
# 1 = interacted, 0 = no interaction
R_implicit = np.array([
    [1, 1, 0, 1, 0, 0],
    [1, 0, 0, 1, 1, 1],
    [0, 1, 1, 1, 0, 1],
    [0, 1, 1, 0, 0, 0],
    [1, 0, 1, 0, 1, 1],
])
```

This binary matrix `R_implicit` is the input for our model. WRMF will learn to distinguish between the items users have interacted with and those they haven't.

Step 2. Define the WRMFRecommender Class

Next, we'll create a Python class to hold the algorithm's logic. This class will store hyperparameters like the number of latent factors (`k`), regularization (`lambda_reg`), and the confidence weight (`alpha`). The core logic will be in the `fit()` method, which trains the model using ALS.

```
class WRMFRecommender:
    def __init__(self, k, iterations=10, lambda_reg=0.1, alpha=40):
        self.k = k
        self.iterations = iterations
        self.lambda_reg = lambda_reg
        self.alpha = alpha
        self.P = None # User latent factors
        self.Q = None # Item latent factors

    def fit(self, R):
      # To be implemented in the next step
      pass

    def predict(self):
      # A simple matrix multiplication
      return self.P @ self.Q.T
```

This class structure provides a clear blueprint. The `__init__` method sets the key hyperparameters that control the learning process.

Step 3. Train the Model with Alternating Least Squares (The `fit` method)

This is the core of the WRMF algorithm. The `fit` method implements the Alternating Least Squares (ALS) optimization procedure. The process involves:

(1) Creating a **confidence matrix `C`** where observed interactions are given a much higher weight (`1 + alpha`) than unobserved ones (`1`).

(2) Iterating multiple times, alternating between two steps: a. Keeping the item factors (`Q`) fixed and solving for the optimal user factors (`P`). b. Keeping the newly updated user factors (`P`) fixed and solving for the optimal item factors (`Q`).

This iterative process finds the factor matrices `P` and `Q` that best explain the observed interactions, heavily weighted by our confidence.

```
# Continuing the WRMFRecommender class...

    def fit(self, R):
        num_users, num_items = R.shape
        # Initialize factor matrices with small random values
        self.P = np.random.normal(scale=1./self.k, size=(num_users, self.k))
        self.Q = np.random.normal(scale=1./self.k, size=(num_items, self.k))
```

```
    # Create the confidence matrix C
    C = 1 + self.alpha * R

    # Start the ALS iterations
    for i in range(self.iterations):
        # Update user factors (P)

        for u in range(num_users):
            # Create a diagonal confidence matrix for the current user
            Cu = np.diag(C[u, :])
            # Form the linear system Ax = b
            A = self.Q.T @ Cu @ self.Q + self.lambda_reg * np.eye(self.k)
            b = self.Q.T @ Cu @ (R[u, :] > 0).astype(int)
            # Solve for the user's latent factor vector
            self.P[u, :] = np.linalg.solve(A, b)

        # Update item factors (Q)

        for item_idx in range(num_items):
            # Create a diagonal confidence matrix for the current item
            Ci = np.diag(C[:, item_idx])
            # Form the linear system Ax = b
            A = self.P.T @ Ci @ self.P + self.lambda_reg * np.eye(self.k)
            b = self.P.T @ Ci @ (R[:, item_idx] > 0).astype(int)
            # Solve for the item's latent factor vector
            self.Q[item_idx, :] = np.linalg.solve(A, b)

    return self
```

After the `fit` method is run, `self.P` and `self.Q` contain the learned latent factors that represent user preferences and item characteristics, respectively.

Step 4. Generate Ranking Scores (The `predict` method)

Once the user and item factors are learned, predicting scores for all user-item pairs is a simple matrix multiplication. The predicted score for a user `u` and item `i` is the dot product of their respective latent factor vectors, `p_u` and `q_i`.

```
# The predict method is already defined in our class blueprint.
# It simply performs the matrix multiplication:
return self.P @ self.Q.T
```

The resulting matrix contains scores that can be used to rank items for each user. A higher score indicates a stronger predicted preference.

Step 5. Putting It All Together

Finally, let's instantiate our `WRMFRecommender`, train it on our implicit feedback data, and generate a ranked list of recommendations for a target user.

```
# 1. Instantiate the recommender with hyperparameters
wrmf = WRMFRecommender(k=5, iterations=15, lambda_reg=0.1, alpha=20)

# 2. Train the model on the implicit interaction data
wrmf.fit(R_implicit)

# 3. Generate the full matrix of ranking scores
R_scores = wrmf.predict()

# 4. Get recommendations for a specific user (e.g., user 0)
target_user_interactions = R_implicit[0, :]
scores_for_user = R_scores[0, :]

# 5. Generate a ranked list of items the user has not seen
unseen_items = np.where(target_user_interactions == 0)[0]
recommendations = sorted(
    zip(unseen_items, scores_for_user[unseen_items]),
    key=lambda x: x[1],
    reverse=True
)

print(f"User 0 interacted with items: {np.where(target_user_interactions > 0)[0]}")
print(f"Ranking scores for all items for User 0: {np.round(scores_for_user, 2)}")
print("\nTop recommendations for User 0:")
for item_id, score in recommendations:
```

```
    print(f"  Item {item_id}: Ranking Score = {score:.4f}")
```

The output shows the ranking scores for all items. The ranked list highlights which new items the model predicts the user is most likely to interact with, demonstrating the end-to-end workflow of the WRMF model for implicit feedback.

2.4.5 Pairwise Ranking Objective: BPR (Bayesian Personalized Ranking)

Key concept — BPR reframes the recommendation problem as a ranking task, focusing on predicting preference orders rather than specific rating scores. It assumes that for a given user, an item they have interacted with (positive item) should rank higher than an item they have not interacted with (negative item). The model maximizes the probability of correctly ordering these item pairs using a pairwise ranking loss.

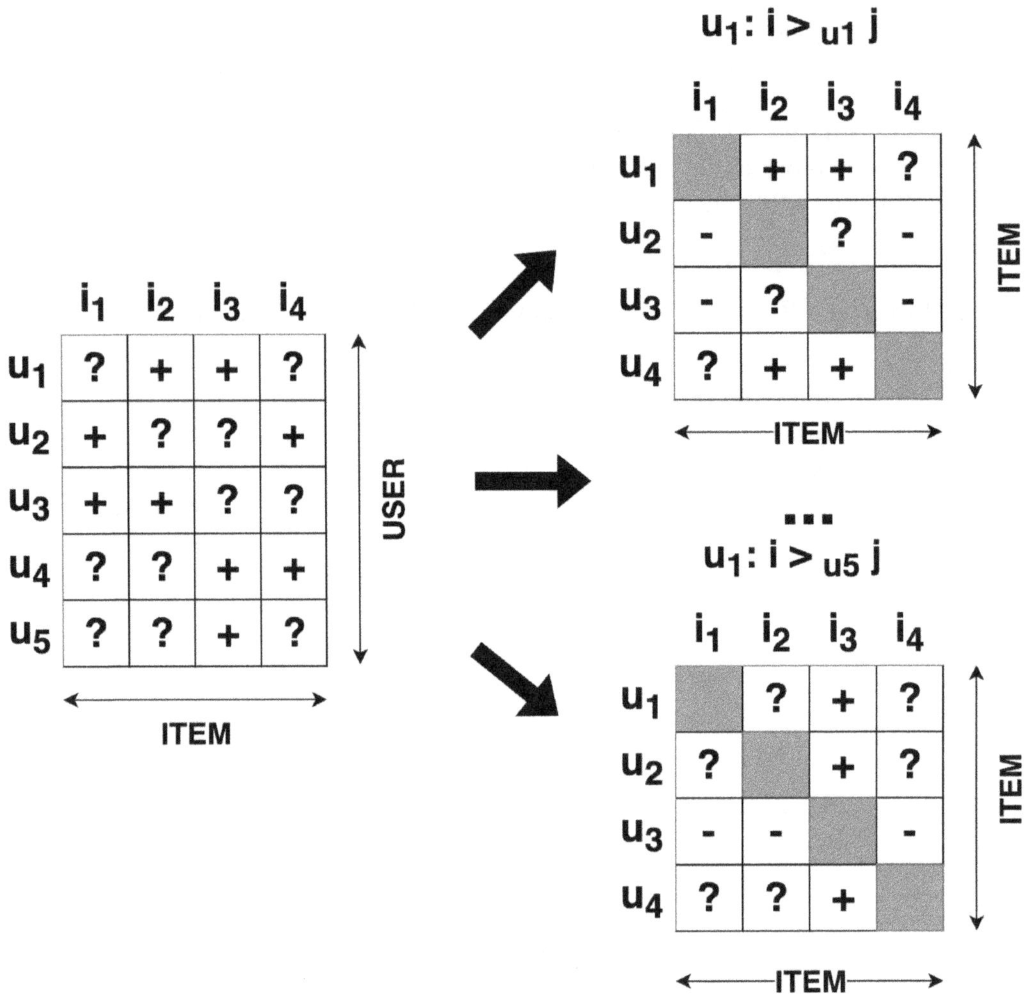

Key differentiator — BPR marked a significant shift in recommender systems by prioritizing ranking optimization over traditional rating prediction metrics like RMSE. Unlike earlier models that focused on predicting exact ratings, BPR aligns directly with the practical goal of delivering high-quality ranked lists, making it particularly effective for implicit feedback data (e.g., clicks, purchases) where explicit negative feedback is absent, and only unobserved items are available as negative samples.

Key findings from replicability study — A 2024 study by Deldjoo et al. revisited BPR's performance to assess its robustness and replicability across modern datasets and settings (Deldjoo, Y., et al., 2024, *Revisiting BPR: A Replicability Study of a Common Recommender System Baseline*). The study confirms BPR's effectiveness as a strong baseline for Top-N recommendation tasks, particularly for implicit feedback. However, it highlights that BPR's performance can vary significantly depending on dataset characteristics, such as sparsity and item popularity skew. The study also notes that while BPR remains competitive, modern neural models may outperform it in dense datasets or when incorporating side information (e.g., item features). Additionally, hyperparameter tuning, particularly the learning rate and regularization, is critical for achieving optimal performance, and the study emphasizes the importance of standardized evaluation protocols to ensure fair comparisons.

Use cases — BPR is a standard approach for modeling implicit feedback in scenarios requiring ranked recommendation lists, such as e-commerce (product recommendations), media streaming (movie or music suggestions), and online advertising. It excels in environments where explicit ratings are sparse or unavailable but user interactions are abundant.

When to Consider — Choose BPR for Top-N recommendation tasks where the goal is to produce a ranked list of items based on implicit feedback. It is particularly effective in sparse data settings and remains a robust baseline, though engineers should consider dataset characteristics and explore modern alternatives for dense datasets or feature-rich environments.

Hyperparameters

- **k (Latent Factors)**: This defines the dimensionality of the user and item vectors. It controls the complexity of the model, with a higher `k` allowing for more nuanced representations at the risk of overfitting.

- **Iterations**: The number of passes the algorithm makes through the training data. For BPR, this means iterating over the user-item pairs to update the latent factor vectors.

- **Learning Rate**: This parameter controls the step size of the updates made to the latent factors during training. A well-tuned learning rate is critical for the model to converge to an optimal solution without overshooting it.

- **Regularization (lambda_reg)**: This term is added to the loss function to penalize large values in the user and item factor vectors. It helps prevent the model from overfitting to the training data, ensuring it generalizes better to unseen items.

Production Ready?

- **Absolutely Production-Ready.** BPR is more than just an algorithm; it's a foundational optimization framework that has become a standard for training recommender systems on implicit feedback. Its pairwise ranking objective is highly effective because it directly optimizes for the quality of the ranked list, which is precisely what users see. BPR is widely implemented in production systems and serves as one of the most important and powerful baselines for any Top-N recommendation task.

Seminal Paper:

- Rendle, S., Freudenthaler, C., Gantner, Z., & Schmidt-Thieme, L. (2009). *BPR: Bayesian personalized ranking from implicit feedback.* https://arxiv.org/abs/1205.2618.

Replicability Study:

- Deldjoo, Y., et al. (2024). *Revisiting BPR: A Replicability Study of a Common Recommender System Baseline.* https://arxiv.org/abs/2409.14217

Useful links:

- Recommender System using Bayesian Personalized Ranking
- "BPR and Recommendation System" from Abby Yeh

2.4.6 SVD++

Key concept — SVD++ extends the **Biased Matrix Factorization** model by incorporating implicit feedback (e.g., clicks, views) into the matrix factorization process. It was proposed in 2008 by Yehuda Koren during the Netflix Prize, a competition to improve movie recommendations. The algorithm models user preferences using both explicit ratings and implicit interactions, adding a set of latent factors for implicit feedback to enhance prediction accuracy.

Key differentiator — By integrating implicit feedback, SVD++ captures richer user behavior patterns, making it more robust for sparse datasets with both explicit and implicit signals.

If you watched 10 sci-fi movies (even without ratings), your vector "shifts" toward sci-fi, and the algorithm better understands what to recommend.

Use cases — Recommending items in systems with mixed feedback, such as movie platforms where users provide ratings and watch histories. It excels in improving prediction accuracy for sparse datasets.

When to Consider — Use SVD++ when you have both explicit and implicit feedback data and want to leverage both to improve recommendation quality. It is a strong choice for enhancing traditional SVD in hybrid scenarios.

Hyperparameters

- **k (Latent Factors)**: The dimensionality of the user and item latent factor vectors.
- **Iterations**: The number of times the algorithm will iterate over the training data to optimize the latent factors.
- **Learning Rate**: The step size used in the stochastic gradient descent (SGD) optimization process to update the model's parameters.

- **Regularization (lambda_reg)**: A penalty term applied to the latent factors and biases to prevent overfitting by discouraging overly complex models.

Advantages:

- Improves accuracy over basic SVD, especially when explicit ratings are scarce (common in real-world systems).
- Incorporates context: implicit interactions add "depth" to the user's profile.
- Works well in collaborative filtering, where recommendations are based on user/item similarity.

In the Netflix Prize, SVD++ achieved state-of-the-art results.

Disadvantages:

- High computational complexity: the sum over $N(u)$ for each prediction can be costly if $N(u)$ is large (mitigated with approximations).
- Requires tuning hyperparameters (k, λ).
- Doesn't account for the sequence of interactions (more advanced models like Recurrent Neural Networks or Transformer-based recsys handle this).
- Sensitive to data quality: noise in implicit signals can degrade performance.

Production Ready?

- SVD++ is used in recommendation systems on platforms like Netflix, Amazon, and YouTube. Overall, SVD++ is a classic in recommendation systems, but it's often combined with deep learning approaches (e.g., Neural Collaborative Filtering) for better results today.

Seminal Paper:

- Koren, Y. (2008). *Factorization Meets the Neighborhood: A Multifaceted Collaborative Filtering Model.* https://dl.acm.org/doi/10.1145/1401890.1401944.

Mathematical Foundations

SVD++ is a direct and powerful extension of the Biased Matrix Factorization model. It enhances the prediction accuracy by enriching the user's latent representation with a signal derived from their implicit interactions.

Part A: The Foundation - Biased Matrix Factorization

First, let's recall the standard Biased Matrix Factorization (or "FunkSVD") model, which SVD++ builds upon. The predicted rating $\hat{r}_{ui}$ for a user u and item i is modeled as the sum of global, user, and item biases, plus the interaction between user and item latent factors:

$$\hat{r}_{ui} = \mu + b_u + b_i + p_u^\top q_i$$

Where:

- μ is the global average rating.
- b_u and b_i are the learned biases for user u and item i.
- $p_u \in \mathbb{R}^k$ is the latent factor vector for user u.
- $q_i \in \mathbb{R}^k$ is the latent factor vector for item i.

In this model, the user is represented solely by the vector p_u.

Part B: The Innovation - Incorporating Implicit Feedback

The key insight of SVD++ is that knowing *which* items a user has rated (or clicked, viewed, etc.), regardless of the specific rating, provides a valuable signal about their preferences. SVD++ models this implicit feedback by augmenting the user's latent representation.

To achieve this, the model introduces a **second set of item latent factors**, denoted by $y_j \in \mathbb{R}^k$. While the q_i vectors represent items as things to be rated, the y_j vectors represent items as things that a user has interacted with, thus contributing to the user's overall profile.

The user's preference is no longer captured by p_u alone. Instead, it's represented by the sum of their explicit factor p_u and an aggregated factor derived from the set of items they have implicitly provided feedback on.

Part C: The SVD++ Prediction Model

The final SVD++ prediction formula integrates this new implicit user profile directly into the biased MF equation. The dot product term $p_u^\top q_i$ is replaced with a more comprehensive interaction term:

$$\hat{r}_{ui} = \mu + b_u + b_i + \left(p_u + \frac{1}{|N(u)|^{1/2}} \sum_{j \in N(u)} y_j \right)^\top q_i$$

Where:

- $N(u)$ is the set of items that user u has provided implicit feedback for (in the original paper, this is the set of all items the user rated).
- y_j is the latent factor vector for an item j that the user has interacted with.
- The term $\sum_{j \in N(u)} y_j$ represents the user's implicit profile, aggregated from their interaction history.
- $\frac{1}{|N(u)|^{1/2}}$ is a normalization factor to dampen the effect for users with a large number of interactions, ensuring they don't dominate the signal.

In essence, the prediction now depends not just on the user's explicit latent profile (p_u), but also on a summary of the latent profiles of all the items they have interacted with in the past. This provides a much richer and more nuanced representation of the user, leading to more accurate predictions.

Tutorial: SVD++ (Biased Matrix Factorization) From Scratch

> The tutorial sections in this guide are entirely optional, though they can be extremely valuable for building intuition and a deeper understanding of the algorithms in practice. They assume, however, a basic familiarity with the libraries and frameworks being used. If you are interested in exploring why a particular method, function, or framework class is invoked at a specific point in the code, we encourage you to consult the Appendix, where we provide detailed, line-by-line commentary for selected algorithms from the Tutorial sections.

This tutorial provides a step-by-step implementation of the Biased Matrix Factorization model, which is the core of the SVD++ algorithm. We will build a recommender from scratch that learns latent factors and biases for users and items using Stochastic Gradient Descent (SGD), mirroring the mathematical principles described previously.

Step 1. Prepare Data

First, we need a user-item interaction matrix. As in our previous examples, we'll use a small NumPy array where rows are users, columns are items, and values are ratings. A zero indicates an unrated item.

```
import numpy as np

# Create a sample user-item rating matrix
# Rows: Users, Columns: Items
# 0 indicates no rating
R = np.array([
    [5, 3, 0, 1, 4, 0],
    [4, 0, 0, 1, 3, 5],
```

```
    [1, 1, 5, 5, 0, 4],
    [0, 1, 4, 4, 0, 0],
    [2, 0, 3, 0, 5, 4],
])
```

This matrix R contains the known ratings that our model will learn from.

Step 2. Define the SVDppRecommender Class

Next, we'll create a Python class to encapsulate the logic. This class will store hyperparameters (learning rate, regularization), the learned matrices (P, Q), and the bias terms. The main methods will be `fit()` for training and `predict()` for generating the full matrix of scores.

```
class SVDppRecommender:
    def __init__(self, k=2, iterations=20, learning_rate=0.005, lambda_reg=0.02):
        self.k = k
        self.iterations = iterations
        self.learning_rate = learning_rate
        self.lambda_reg = lambda_reg
        self.P = None  # User factors
        self.Q = None  # Item factors
        self.user_bias = None
        self.item_bias = None
        self.global_mean = None
        self.R_predicted = None

    def fit(self, R):
      # To be implemented in the next step
      pass

    def predict(self):
      # To be implemented later
      pass
```

This class structure provides a clean blueprint. The `__init__` method sets the key hyperparameters that control the training process.

Step 3. Train the Model (The `fit` method)

This is the core training step where the model learns the latent factors and biases using **Stochastic Gradient Descent (SGD)**. For each known rating in the matrix, the model makes a prediction, calculates the error, and updates the corresponding user factor, item factor, user bias, and item bias to reduce that error.

```
# Continuing the SVDppRecommender class...

def fit(self, R):
 num_users, num_items = R.shape

 # Initialize factor matrices and biases
 self.P = np.random.normal(scale=1./self.k, size=(num_users, self.k))
 self.Q = np.random.normal(scale=1./self.k, size=(num_items, self.k))
 self.user_bias = np.zeros(num_users)
 self.item_bias = np.zeros(num_items)
 self.global_mean = R[R > 0].mean()

 # Stochastic Gradient Descent loop
 for i in range(self.iterations):
     # Iterate over all known ratings
     for u, item_idx in np.argwhere(R > 0):
       # Make a prediction
       pred = (self.global_mean + self.user_bias[u] +
               self.item_bias[item_idx] +
               self.P[u, :] @ self.Q[item_idx, :].T)

       # Calculate the error
       error = R[u, item_idx] - pred

       # Update biases and factors with learning rate and regularization
       bu = self.user_bias[u]
       bi = self.item_bias[item_idx]
       pu = self.P[u, :]
       qi = self.Q[item_idx, :]

       self.user_bias[u] += (
               self.learning_rate * (error - self.lambda_reg * bu)
       )
       self.item_bias[item_idx] += (
               self.learning_rate * (error - self.lambda_reg * bi)
       )
       self.P[u, :] += (
               self.learning_rate * (error * qi - self.lambda_reg * pu)
       )
       self.Q[item_idx, :] += (
                 self.learning_rate * (error * pu - self.lambda_reg * qi)
       )
```

```
        return self
```

When `fit` method completes, the matrices `P` and `Q` and the bias vectors will contain the optimized values that best approximate the original rating matrix.

Step 4. Make Predictions (The `predict` method)

Once the model is trained, generating the full matrix of predicted ratings is a straightforward process. We simply reconstruct the matrix using the learned components: the global mean, the user and item biases, and the dot product of the user and item factor matrices.

```
# Continuing the SVDppRecommender class...

    def predict(self):
        # Reconstruct the full ratings matrix from the learned components
        user_bias_matrix = np.repeat(self.user_bias[:, np.newaxis],
                                     self.Q.shape[0], axis=1)
        item_bias_matrix = np.repeat(self.item_bias[np.newaxis, :],
                                     self.P.shape[0], axis=0)

        self.R_predicted = (self.global_mean + user_bias_matrix +
                            item_bias_matrix + (self.P @ self.Q.T))
        return self.R_predicted
```

This method efficiently calculates the predicted score for every user-item pair, allowing us to rank items for any user.

Step 5. Putting It All Together

Finally, let's instantiate our recommender, train it on our sample data, and generate the complete matrix of predicted ratings. We will then examine the top recommendations for a specific user.

```
# 1. Instantiate the recommender
svdpp = SVDppRecommender(k=2, iterations=30, learning_rate=0.01, lambda_reg=0.1)

# 2. Train the model on the rating data
svdpp.fit(R)

# 3. Generate the full matrix of predicted ratings
R_predicted = svdpp.predict()

# 4. Examine recommendations for a specific user (e.g., user 0)
target_user_ratings = R[0, :]
```

```
predicted_ratings_for_user = R_predicted[0, :]

# Create a ranked list of recommendations for unrated items
unrated_items = np.where(target_user_ratings == 0)[0]
recommendations = sorted(
    zip(unrated_items, predicted_ratings_for_user[unrated_items]),
    key=lambda x: x[1],
    reverse=True
)

print(f"Original ratings for User 0: {target_user_ratings}")
print(f"Predicted ratings for User 0: {np.round(predicted_ratings_for_user, 2)}")
print("\nTop recommendations for User 0:")
for item_id, score in recommendations:
    print(f"  Item {item_id}: Predicted Score = {score:.4f}")
```

The output shows the predicted ratings for all items, including those the user has not yet seen. The ranked list highlights which new items the model believes the user will like the most. This demonstrates the end-to-end workflow of the Biased Matrix Factorization model.

2.4.7 TimeSVD++ (Time-aware SVD++)

Key concept — TimeSVD++ is a temporal extension of the SVD++ model, designed to capture the dynamic and time-drifting nature of user preferences and item properties. It models a rating not as a static event, but as an interaction occurring at a specific point in time, acknowledging that a user's tastes can evolve and an item's perceived value can change.

Key differentiator — Its primary innovation is the incorporation of multiple temporal dynamics directly into the matrix factorization model. The biases and user factors are no longer static parameters but are modeled as functions of time. This allows the model to capture complex temporal effects, such as users becoming stricter or more lenient raters over time, items losing popularity after their initial release, and seasonal preference shifts.

Use cases — Rating prediction in domains where timestamps are available and temporal context is critical. It is highly effective for datasets where preferences are not static, such as movie recommendations (a film's popularity peaks and then wanes), e-commerce (seasonal trends in products), or news recommendations (where content relevance is highly time-sensitive).

When to Consider — TimeSVD++ is a powerful choice when the dataset contains timestamps and there is a strong hypothesis that user behavior or item relevance changes over time. It serves as a crucial bridge between static latent factor models and modern, fully sequential recommender systems, demonstrating how temporal signals can be integrated into a collaborative filtering framework for a significant accuracy boost.

Seminal Paper:

- Koren, Y. (2009). *Collaborative filtering with temporal dynamics.* https://dl.acm.org/doi/10.1145/1557019.1557044.

Mathematical Foundations

The TimeSVD++ model builds directly upon the SVD++ framework by making its core components time-dependent. The goal is to predict a rating r_{ui} made at a specific time t.

Part A: The Foundation - SVD++ Model

As a starting point, recall the prediction formula for SVD++, which combines user and item biases with a user representation enriched by implicit feedback:

$$\hat{r}_{ui} = \mu + b_u + b_i + q_i^\top \left(p_u + |N(u)|^{-1/2} \sum_{j \in N(u)} y_j \right)$$

TimeSVD++ extends this by transforming the static parameters b_u, b_i, and p_u into functions of time t.

Part B: Modeling Time-Varying Biases

The first temporal extension is to model the user and item biases as dynamic.

(1) **Item Biases ($b_i(t)$):** An item's popularity is often not constant. For example, a movie's perceived value is highest shortly after its release and then fades. This is modeled by splitting time into discrete bins (e.g., days or weeks) and learning a separate bias for each bin.

$$b_i(t) = b_i + b_{i,Bin(t)}$$

Here, b_i is the static bias for item i, and $b_{i,Bin(t)}$ is a time-specific bias corresponding to the time bin in which the rating was made.

(2) **User Biases ($b_u(t)$):** A user's rating tendency can also drift. For instance, a new user might give generous ratings initially and become more critical over time. This is modeled with a continuous function:

$$b_u(t) = b_u + \alpha_u \cdot dev_u(t)$$

- b_u is the static user bias.
- $dev_u(t) = sign(t - t_u) \cdot |t - t_u|^\beta$ represents the deviation of the rating time t from the user's mean rating time t_u. This term captures a steady drift in the user's rating behavior. The parameter β (typically around 0.4) dampens the effect of very long-term deviations.
- α_u is a learnable parameter that controls the magnitude of this drift for user u.

Part C: Modeling Dynamic User Factors

Just as a user's rating bias can change, so can their fundamental preferences. The user's latent factor vector p_u is also modeled as a function of time to capture this evolving taste:

$$p_u(t)$$

The model allows each component k of the user's factor vector to drift over time, similar to the user bias:

$$p_{uk}(t) = p_{uk} + \alpha_{uk} \cdot dev_u(t)$$

This allows the model to learn, for example, that a user's affinity for the "comedy" factor has been gradually increasing over the years.

Part D: The Final TimeSVD++ Prediction Model

By substituting these time-aware components back into the original SVD++ formula, we arrive at the final prediction equation for TimeSVD++:

$$\hat{r}_{ui}(t) = \mu + b_u(t) + b_i(t) + q_i^\top \left(p_u(t) + |N(u)|^{-1/2} \sum_{j \in N(u)} y_j \right)$$

This complete model captures a rich set of temporal dynamics, including long-term preference drifts and short-term, item-specific effects. All parameters, including the static and dynamic components, are learned jointly by minimizing a regularized squared error function over the training data using methods like Stochastic Gradient Descent.

2.4.8 Item-based Latent Models: SLIM & FISM

Key concept — These models blend the straightforwardness of item-based recommendation methods with the advanced capabilities of latent factor models. Rather than just counting how often items appear together in user data, they use machine learning to directly learn a matrix that shows similarities between items, based on user interactions like clicks or purchases.

Key differentiator:

- **SLIM (Sparse Linear Methods)** learns an item-to-item similarity matrix, called `W`, by treating the problem as a set of separate prediction tasks (like regressions). The main goal is to recreate the original user-item interaction matrix, `A`, by multiplying it with this learned similarity matrix: $A \approx AW$. To do this, SLIM solves an optimization problem that mixes L1 and L2 regularization (similar to a technique called Elastic Net) and requires the weights in `W` to be non-negative (zero or positive). The L1 penalty is especially important because it encourages sparsity—this means most entries in `W` become zero, so each item's recommendation is based on just a handful of truly similar items. This sparsity keeps the model fast to run and easy to understand, as you can see exactly which items are influencing others.
- **FISM (Factored Item Similarity Models)** uses a mixed approach. Instead of learning the entire item-item similarity matrix all at once, it breaks it down (factorizes it) into two smaller matrices of item embeddings. This factorization helps the model capture indirect connections between items—for example, if item A is similar to B, and B is similar to C, then A and C could be seen as related, even if no user has interacted with both A and C directly. This makes FISM stronger in datasets where interactions are very rare and spread out.

1. Why does SLIM use L1 and L2 regularization in its optimization problem?

SLIM uses L1 and L2 regularization to balance accuracy and simplicity when learning the item-to-item similarity matrix `W`. The **L1 regularization** encourages sparsity, meaning it pushes many weights in `W` to zero. This is important because it ensures each item's recommendation relies on only a few highly similar items, making the model faster (fewer calculations) and easier to interpret (you can see exactly which items matter). For example, if you're recommending books, sparsity ensures a sci-fi novel's recommendation depends on just a handful of other sci-fi books, not everything in the store. The **L2 regularization** prevents any single weight from becoming too large, which helps the model generalize better to new users or items, avoiding overfitting where it just memorizes the training data. Together, they make SLIM's predictions both accurate and practical.

2. Why does SLIM require the weights in the similarity matrix `W` to be non-negative?

SLIM enforces non-negative weights (zero or positive) in `W` because it deals with implicit feedback, like clicks or purchases, where negative similarities don't make intuitive sense. Implicit data reflects positive actions (e.g., a user clicked a movie), so a negative weight suggesting "dislike" wouldn't align with the data's meaning. Non-negativity also makes recommendations easier to understand—for instance, if a user liked a sci-fi movie, SLIM uses positive weights to suggest other similar movies, not to push away unrelated ones. This constraint keeps the model's outputs clear and aligned with how people think about recommendations.

3. Why does SLIM treat the problem as a set of separate prediction tasks (like regressions)?

SLIM breaks the problem into separate prediction tasks—one for each item—to make learning the similarity matrix `W` more manageable and scalable. Each task focuses on predicting how users interact with one item based on their interactions with all other items, like solving a regression problem. For example, to recommend a specific book, SLIM learns how other books' interactions predict that book's popularity. By treating each item independently, SLIM can solve these tasks in parallel (like splitting work across multiple computers), which speeds up training, especially for huge datasets like those on e-commerce sites with millions of products. This approach keeps SLIM efficient while still capturing item similarities accurately.

4. Why is sparsity in SLIM's similarity matrix `W` considered a benefit?

Sparsity in `W` means most weights are zero, so each item's recommendation depends on just a few other items. This is a benefit because it makes SLIM faster—fewer non-zero weights mean fewer calculations when predicting scores, which is critical for real-time systems like streaming services. It also makes the model easier to understand, as you can see exactly which items influence a recommendation. For instance, if SLIM suggests a mystery novel, sparsity ensures it's based on a small set of similar novels, not a confusing mix of unrelated ones. This clarity and efficiency make SLIM practical for real-world use.

5. Why does FISM factorize the item-item similarity matrix into two smaller matrices instead of learning it directly like SLIM?

FISM factorizes the similarity matrix into two smaller matrices of item embeddings to capture indirect connections between items, which is especially useful when data is very sparse (i.e., users interact with few items). By breaking the matrix down, FISM can find patterns like: if item A is similar to B, and B to C, then A and C might be related, even if no user has interacted with both A and C. For example, if one user likes a sci-fi movie and another likes a sci-fi book, FISM's embeddings can link the movie and book through shared traits, even without direct overlap. This makes FISM stronger than SLIM in datasets where interactions are rare, as it generalizes better to uncover hidden similarities.

6. Why is FISM better suited for datasets with very rare and spread-out interactions?

FISM excels in sparse datasets because its factorization approach allows it to discover indirect relationships between items that don't directly co-occur in user interactions. In very sparse data, where most users interact with only a tiny fraction of items, direct methods like SLIM might struggle to find enough shared interactions to link items. FISM's use of embeddings means it can infer similarities through latent patterns—for example, connecting two products because they share similar features, even if no user bought both. This ability to generalize makes FISM more effective when data is limited, like in niche markets or new platforms with few user actions.

> **A Note on FISM Performance:** The training process for FISM can be significantly slower than for other models like SLIM or ALS. This is due to its implementation, which often relies on multiple nested loops (iterating through epochs, users, and items). In particular, for each user-item pair, the model must then iterate again through all other items the user has interacted with to perform the weight updates. This leads to high computational complexity. While highly effective, be prepared for longer training times, especially on larger datasets.

Use cases — Both models are designed for Top-N recommendation from implicit feedback. SLIM is highly effective and efficient, making it a strong baseline and suitable for production systems where speed and interpretability are critical. Because each item's similarity vector (a column in `W`) is learned independently, the training process is highly parallelizable. FISM is particularly advantageous in scenarios with very high data sparsity, where learning latent relationships is crucial.

When to Consider — Choose **SLIM** when you need a fast, scalable, and interpretable item-based model. It's an excellent choice when you want a "learned" item-item similarity model and is often cited as a powerful baseline that can outperform more complex deep learning models in rigorous evaluations. Consider **FISM** when facing extreme data sparsity. Its ability to generalize and find similarities between items that do not co-occur in the training data gives it a distinct advantage in such challenging scenarios.

Accelerating Training with fsSLIM (Feature Selection SLIM)

To address the computational cost of training, especially on large datasets, a practical variant called **fsSLIM** was introduced. The core idea is to significantly reduce the complexity of the learning problem by applying **feature selection** before solving the regression task for each item. Instead of using all other items as potential predictors, fsSLIM first identifies a smaller subset of the most promising candidates—typically the k most similar items, determined using a simple metric like cosine similarity (similar to ItemKNN). The optimization is then performed using only this reduced set of features. This dramatically speeds up the training process with minimal impact on recommendation quality, making the SLIM framework more scalable and efficient for production environments.

Hyperparameters (SLIM)

- **l1_reg (L1 Regularization)**: This parameter controls the penalty applied to the absolute values of the coefficients in the similarity matrix. A higher `l1_reg` value promotes sparsity, meaning more coefficients will be pushed to exactly zero. This makes the model more efficient and interpretable.
- **l2_reg (L2 Regularization)**: This parameter controls the penalty applied to the squared values of the coefficients. It helps to prevent the model from assigning excessively large weights to any single item, which can improve generalization and prevent overfitting.

Production Ready?

- **SLIM: Production-Ready as a strong baseline.** Due to its simplicity, efficiency, and interpretability, SLIM is a very practical choice for production environments. Its training is parallelizable, and the resulting sparse similarity matrix allows for fast predictions. It often serves as a powerful benchmark that more complex models struggle to beat.
- **FISM: More of a powerful baseline than a plug-and-play production model.** While the concept is strong, especially for sparse data, its typical implementation involves computationally intensive training loops that make it slow. For production use, FISM would require significant optimization (e.g., implementing the core loops in a lower-level language like C++ or Cython) to meet the latency requirements of a real-time system.

Seminal Papers:

- **SLIM:** Ning, X., & Karypis, G. (2011). *SLIM: sparse linear methods for top-n recommender systems.* https://www.researchgate.net/publication/220765374_SLIM_Sparse_Linear_Methods_for_Top-N_Recommender_Systems.
- **FISM:** Kabbur, S., Badrul, S., & Karypis, G. (2013). *FISM: factored item similarity models for top-n recommender systems.* http://chbrown.github.io/kdd-2013-usb/kdd/p659.pdf.

Useful links:

- "SLIM: A Fast and Interpretable Baseline for Recommender Algorithms" from Michael Roizner
- The implementation of SLIM was written by George Karypis with contributions by Xia Ning, Athanasios N. Nikolakopoulos, Zeren Shui and Mohit Sharma.

Mathematical Foundations of SLIM

SLIM (Sparse Linear Methods) is a recommendation system designed to suggest items (like movies, books, or products) to users based on their past interactions, such as clicks or purchases, rather than explicit ratings (like 5 stars). This section explains how SLIM works in four parts: how it predicts what users might like, how it learns to make those predictions, and why it's efficient for large datasets, and how authors proposed to make it even more efficient. We'll keep it simple, using examples and clear formulas.

Part A: How SLIM Makes Predictions

SLIM predicts how much a user will like an item by looking at what other items they've interacted with. Imagine you're shopping online, and you've bought a sci-fi book and a mystery novel. SLIM might suggest a new sci-fi novel by checking how similar it is to the books you already liked.

The predicted score for user u liking item i, denoted $\hat{r}_{ui}$, is calculated as:

$$\hat{r}_{ui} = \sum_{j \neq i} r_{uj} \cdot w_{ji}$$

Here's what this means:

- r_{uj}: This is 1 if user u interacted with item j (e.g., clicked or bought it) and 0 otherwise.
- w_{ji}: A weight that shows how similar item j is to item i. SLIM learns these weights to capture patterns, like "if you liked this sci-fi book, you'll probably like that one."
- The sum skips $j = i$ to avoid an item predicting itself (e.g., "you liked this book, so you'll like this book" is not helpful).

In matrix form, SLIM applies this idea to all users and items at once. The predicted scores for all user-item pairs form a matrix $\hat{R}$, which is calculated as:

$$\hat{R} = RW$$

Where:

- R: A matrix of size $m \times n$, where m is the number of users and n is the number of items. Each entry r_{uj} shows whether user u interacted with item j.
- W: A square matrix of size $n \times n$, where w_{ji} represents how much item j influences the prediction for item i.

- $\hat{R}$: The predicted interaction matrix, with scores for how much each user might like each item.

Think of this as a compact way to make recommendations for everyone at once, based on learned similarities between items.

Part B: How SLIM Learns the Weights

To make accurate predictions, SLIM needs to find the best weights for the matrix W. It does this by solving an optimization problem, like tweaking a recipe to match the taste of a dish as closely as possible. The goal is to make the predicted matrix RW match the actual interaction matrix R, while keeping the model simple to avoid overfitting (i.e., memorizing the data instead of finding general patterns).

SLIM uses an *Elastic Net* approach, which balances accuracy and simplicity. The optimization problem is:

$$\min_{W} \frac{1}{2}|R - RW|_F^2 + \lambda_1|W|_1 + \frac{\lambda_2}{2}|W|_F^2$$

Let's break it down:

- **Prediction accuracy** ($\frac{1}{2}|R - RW|_F^2$): The Frobenius norm $|R - RW|_F^2$ measures the total difference between the actual interactions R and the predicted ones RW. The Frobenius norm is like the sum of squared differences across all entries in the matrices, ensuring predictions are close to reality. Mathematically:

$$|R - RW|_F^2 = \sum_{u=1}^{m}\sum_{i=1}^{n}(r_{ui} - \hat{r}_{ui})^2$$

- **Sparsity** : The L1 norm

$$|W|_1 = \sum_{i,j}|w_{ji}|$$

encourages most weights in W to be zero. This means only a few items influence the prediction for any given item, making the model simpler and easier to interpret (e.g., only a few books are truly similar to a sci-fi novel).

- **Smoothness** : The L2 norm

$$|W|_F^2 = \sum_{i,j} w_{ji}^2$$

prevents weights from becoming too large, helping the model generalize to new users or items.

- λ_1 and λ_2: These are tuning parameters that control how much emphasis is placed on sparsity and smoothness.

SLIM also enforces two constraints:

(1) **Non-negativity** ($W \geq 0$): All weights in W must be zero or positive, since negative similarities don't make sense for implicit feedback (like clicks or purchases). This also makes the model's recommendations easier to understand.

(2) **Zero diagonal** ($w_{ii} = 0$): The diagonal of W is set to zero, so an item doesn't influence its own prediction. This avoids unhelpful recommendations like "you liked this movie, so you'll like this movie."

Part C: Why SLIM is Efficient

Training SLIM means finding the best W to solve the optimization problem. A key advantage is that the problem can be split into smaller, independent tasks, making it fast even for huge datasets (like millions of products on an e-commerce site).

The optimization problem breaks down into one sub-problem for each item i. For each item, SLIM finds the column w_i of W, which shows how all other items influence predictions for item i:

$$\min_{w_i} \frac{1}{2}|r_i - Rw_i|_2^2 + \lambda_1|w_i|_1 + \frac{\lambda_2}{2}|w_i|_2^2$$

Here:

- r_i: The column of R for item i, showing how all users interacted with that item.
- Rw_i: The predicted interactions for item i, based on other items' interactions and their weights.
- The terms are similar to Part B: the L2 norm ($|r_i - Rw_i|_2^2$) measures prediction error for item i, while the L1 ($|w_i|_1$) and L2 ($|w_i|_2^2$) terms ensure sparsity and smoothness.

Each sub-problem is an Elastic Net regression, which can be solved efficiently using algorithms like *coordinate descent*. This method adjusts one weight at a time while keeping others fixed, gradually improving the solution. Since each item's weights are independent, these sub-problems can be solved in parallel, like splitting a big task across multiple computers. This makes SLIM *highly scalable*, ideal for platforms with millions of items, like streaming services or online stores.

For example, if you're recommending movies on a platform with millions of titles, SLIM can compute similarities for each movie independently, speeding up the process by spreading the work across multiple machines.

Part D: Efficient Learning with Feature Selection (fsSLIM)

The main computational bottleneck in training SLIM is solving the optimization problem for each of the n items, where each problem involves a feature matrix of size $m \times (n-1)$. fsSLIM accelerates this by reducing the number of features (the columns of R) before the optimization step.

The process for a target item i becomes:

(1) **Feature Selection:** First, a set of candidate features, $\mathcal{F}_i$, is selected from all other items. A common heuristic is to choose the top-k items most similar to item i based on cosine similarity, similar to the ItemKNN approach.

(2) **Reduced Optimization Problem:** A reduced interaction matrix, $R_{\mathcal{F}_i}$, is constructed containing only the columns corresponding to the features in $\mathcal{F}_i$. The optimization problem from Part C is then solved on this much smaller problem:

$$\min_{w_i'} \frac{1}{2}\|r_i - R_{\mathcal{F}_i} w_i'\|_2^2 + \lambda_1 \|w_i'\|_1 + \frac{\lambda_2}{2}\|w_i'\|_2^2$$

Here, w_i' is the smaller vector of coefficients corresponding only to the selected features. By dramatically reducing the number of variables in the regression, fsSLIM achieves a substantial speedup in training time.

Tutorial: SLIM for Top-N Recommendation From Scratch

> The tutorial sections in this guide are entirely optional, though they can be extremely valuable for building intuition and a deeper understanding of the algorithms in practice. They assume, however, a basic familiarity with the libraries and frameworks being used. If you are interested in exploring why a particular method, function, or framework class is invoked at a specific point in the code, we encourage you to consult the Appendix, where we provide detailed, line-by-line commentary for selected algorithms from the Tutorial sections.

This tutorial provides a step-by-step implementation of the SLIM (Sparse Linear Methods) algorithm, correctly framed for its intended task: **Top-N item ranking from implicit feedback**. Unlike neighborhood-based models that use predefined similarity metrics, SLIM learns a sparse item-item similarity matrix by treating the problem as a series of regression tasks. We will use scikit-learn's `ElasticNet` model to learn the similarity coefficients that are optimized for producing a ranked list of recommendations.

Step 1. Prepare Implicit Feedback Data

First, we'll import the necessary libraries. For this example, we will use a **binary, implicit** user-item interaction matrix. A `1` indicates a user has interacted with an item (e.g., clicked, viewed, or purchased it), and a `0` indicates no interaction. This data type is the ideal fit for SLIM.

```
import numpy as np
from sklearn.linear_model import ElasticNet
from sklearn.exceptions import ConvergenceWarning
```

```
import warnings

# Create a sample user-item interaction matrix (implicit feedback)
# Rows: Users, Columns: Items
# 1 = interacted (viewed, clicked, purchased), 0 = no interaction
R_implicit = np.array([
    [1, 1, 0, 1, 0, 0],
    [1, 0, 0, 1, 1, 1],
    [0, 1, 1, 1, 0, 1],
    [0, 1, 1, 0, 0, 0],
    [1, 0, 1, 0, 1, 1],
])
```

This matrix `R_implicit` is the core input for our model. SLIM will learn which items are similar based on co-occurrence patterns in user interaction histories.

Step 2. Define the SLIMRecommender Class

Next, we will encapsulate the algorithm's logic within a Python class. This class will store the model's hyperparameters (`l1_reg`, `l2_reg`), the learned similarity matrix, and the training data. The main methods will be `fit()` to train the model and `predict()` to generate the ranking scores.

```
class SLIMRecommender:
    def __init__(self, l1_reg=0.001, l2_reg=0.0001):
        self.l1_reg = l1_reg
        self.l2_reg = l2_reg
        self.similarity_matrix_ = None
        self.train_data_ = None

    def fit(self, R):
      # To be implemented in the next step
      pass

    def predict(self, R_input):
      # To be implemented later
      pass
```

The `__init__` method sets the L1 and L2 regularization parameters, which are crucial for learning a **sparse** and stable similarity matrix, making the model efficient and interpretable.

Step 3. Learn the Similarity Matrix (The `fit` method)

This is the core training step where we build the item similarity matrix. SLIM learns this matrix by solving a separate regression problem for each item. For a target item `j`, the model learns to predict its interaction vector (`y = R[:, j]`) using all other items as features (`X`). The learned coefficients from the regression model become the similarity scores.

```
# Continuing the SLIMRecommender class...
def fit(self, R):
    self.train_data_ = R
    num_items = R.shape[1]
    self.similarity_matrix_ = np.zeros((num_items, num_items))

    # We use ElasticNet which combines L1 and L2 penalties.
    alpha = self.l1_reg + self.l2_reg
    l1_ratio = self.l1_reg / alpha if alpha > 0 else 0

    model = ElasticNet(
        alpha=alpha,
        l1_ratio=l1_ratio,
        positive=True, # Enforce non-negative similarity coefficients
        fit_intercept=False,
        copy_X=False,
        max_iter=1000
    )

    warnings.filterwarnings("ignore", category=ConvergenceWarning)

    # Train a model for each item
    for j in range(num_items):
        y = R[:, j]
        X = np.delete(R, j, axis=1)
        model.fit(X, y)
        self.similarity_matrix_[j, :] = np.insert(model.coef_, j, 0)

    warnings.resetwarnings()
    return self
```

After the `fit` method runs, `self.similarity_matrix_` contains the learned relationships between all pairs of items. This matrix is pre-computed, allowing for very fast prediction.

Step 4. Generate Ranking Scores (The `predict` method)

With the learned similarity matrix, generating scores for ranking is a single, efficient matrix multiplication. The predicted score matrix `R_scores` is the user-item interaction matrix `R` multiplied by the item-item similarity matrix `W`. We then return these scores only for items the user has not already interacted with.

```
# Continuing the SLIMRecommender class...
def predict(self, R_input):
    # Prediction is a matrix multiplication of user interactions
    # and the learned similarity matrix.
    R_scores = R_input @ self.similarity_matrix_

    # We only care about scores for items the user has NOT seen.
    # Set scores for already-seen items to 0.
    return np.where(R_input > 0, 0, R_scores)
```

This method directly implements the SLIM prediction formula `R_scores $\approx$ R @ W`. The output scores are **not** probabilities or ratings; they are simply values used to rank items.

Step 5. Putting It All Together

Finally, let's instantiate our recommender, train it, and generate a ranked list of recommendations for a target user. We'll show which unseen items the model recommends most highly based on their ranking scores.

```
# 1. Instantiate the recommender with hyperparameters
slim_rec = SLIMRecommender(l1_reg=0.01, l2_reg=0.01)

# 2. Train the model on the implicit interaction data
slim_rec.fit(R_implicit)

# 3. Generate the full matrix of ranking scores
R_scores = slim_rec.predict(R_implicit)

# 4. Get recommendations for a specific user (e.g., user 0)
target_user_interactions = R_implicit[0, :]
scores_for_user = R_scores[0, :]

# 5. Generate the final ranked list of items the user has not seen
unseen_items = np.where(target_user_interactions == 0)[0]
recommendations = sorted(
    zip(unseen_items, scores_for_user[unseen_items]),
    key=lambda x: x[1],
```

```
    reverse=True
)
ir=np.where(target_user_interactions > 0)[0]
pr=np.round(scores_for_user[unseen_items], 4)
print(f"User 0 interacted with items: {ir}")
print(f"Ranking scores for unseen items: {pr}")
print("\nTop recommendations for User 0:")
for item_id, score in recommendations:
    # Only show recommendations with a positive score
    if score > 0:
        print(f"  Item {item_id}: Ranking Score = {score:.4f}")
```

2.4.9 Non-Negative Matrix Factorization (NonNegMF)

Key concept — Non-Negative Matrix Factorization (NonNegMF) decomposes the user-item matrix into two non-negative matrices representing user and item latent factors. It ensures all latent factors are non-negative, which can lead to more interpretable features (e.g., representing genres or preferences).

Key differentiator — The non-negativity constraint makes the latent factors more interpretable and can improve performance in domains where negative weights are less meaningful, such as implicit feedback datasets.

Use cases — Recommending items in domains like e-commerce or media streaming, where interpretable latent factors (e.g., user preference for a specific genre) are valuable. It is effective for both explicit and implicit feedback.

When to Consider — Use NonNegMF when interpretability of latent factors is important or when dealing with implicit feedback data where non-negative representations align with the domain's semantics.

Production Ready?

- **Production-Ready, often as a specialized tool.** While not as universally deployed as standard SVD or WRMF, NonNegMF is a robust and valuable algorithm in production environments where the **interpretability** of the latent factors is a key requirement. Its ability to produce additive, parts-based representations (e.g., a user's preference is a sum of positive genre affinities) makes it useful for model diagnostics, explaining recommendations, and understanding user behavior. It serves as a strong baseline, particularly for implicit feedback tasks.

Seminal Paper:

- Lee, D. D., & Seung, H. S. (1999). *Learning the Parts of Objects by Non-Negative Matrix Factorization.* https://www.nature.com/articles/44565.

Mathematical Foundations

Non-Negative Matrix Factorization (NonNegMF) is a variant of matrix factorization that adds a crucial constraint: all learned latent factors must be non-negative. This constraint often leads to more interpretable, parts-based representations, as it models user preferences and item attributes as an additive combination of concepts.

Part A: The Prediction Model

The prediction mechanism in NonNegMF is identical to that of standard matrix factorization. The predicted rating $\hat{r}_{ui}$ for a user u and an item i is the dot product of their respective latent factor vectors, p_u and q_i:

$$\hat{r}_{ui} = p_u^\top q_i = \sum_{k=1}^{K} p_{uk} \cdot q_{ik}$$

Where:

- $p_u \in \mathbb{R}^K$ is the latent factor vector for user u.
- $q_i \in \mathbb{R}^K$ is the latent factor vector for item i.
- K is the number of latent factors.

The key difference lies in the **non-negativity constraint** imposed on the factor matrices P (for users) and Q (for items):

$$p_{uk} \geq 0 \quad \text{and} \quad q_{ik} \geq 0 \quad \forall u, i, k$$

This means that the model can only represent preferences and attributes in an additive manner. For example, a user's preference for a movie is built by adding up their positive affinities for different latent features (e.g., genres, directors). A user cannot have a "negative" affinity for sci-fi; they can only have zero or some positive level of interest.

Part B: The Objective Function

The goal of NonNegMF is to find the non-negative matrices P and Q whose product, $PQ^\top$, best approximates the original user-item interaction matrix R. This is typically formulated as minimizing the sum of squared errors between the actual ratings and the predicted ratings, plus L2 regularization to prevent overfitting.

The objective function to minimize is:

$$\min_{P,Q\geq 0} \sum_{(u,i)\in\mathcal{K}} (r_{ui} - p_u^\top q_i)^2 + \lambda \left(\sum_u ||p_u||_F^2 + \sum_i ||q_i||_F^2 \right)$$

Let's break down this function:

- **Reconstruction Error:** The first term,

$$\sum_{(u,i)\in\mathcal{K}} (r_{ui} - p_u^\top q_i)^2$$

measures the sum of squared differences between the known ratings r_{ui} and the predicted ratings $p_u^\top q_i$. The model tries to make this error as small as possible. The summation is only over the set of known ratings, $\mathcal{K}$.

- **Regularization:** The second term,

$$\lambda \left(\sum_u ||p_u||_F^2 + \sum_i ||q_i||_F^2 \right)$$

is the L2 regularization penalty. It penalizes large values in the latent factor vectors, which helps to prevent the model from overfitting to the training data and improves its ability to generalize.

- **Non-Negativity Constraint:** The term $P, Q \geq 0$ under the `min` operator explicitly states that the optimization must be performed while ensuring all elements in the factor matrices remain non-negative.

Part C: Optimization with Multiplicative Update Rules

The non-negativity constraint makes standard optimization algorithms like Stochastic Gradient Descent (SGD) less straightforward to apply. The most common method for solving NMF is through **Multiplicative Update Rules**. These are iterative rules that update the values in P and Q in a way that guarantees they remain non-negative, while gradually minimizing the objective function.

The update rules for the user factors (P) and item factors (Q) are:

(1) **Update Rule for User Factors (P):**

$$P \leftarrow P \odot \frac{RQ}{PQ^\top Q}$$

(2) **Update Rule for Item Factors (Q):**

$$Q \leftarrow Q \odot \frac{R^\top P}{QP^\top P}$$

How these updates work:

- The notation $\odot$ represents element-wise multiplication, and the division is also element-wise.
- Think of the fraction in each rule as a **correction factor**.
- The numerator (e.g., RQ for the user update) is related to the actual data R.
- The denominator (e.g., $PQ^\top Q$) is related to the current reconstruction of the data.
- If the reconstruction is underestimating the actual data, the fraction will be greater than 1, and the corresponding factor will be increased. If it is overestimating, the fraction will be less than 1, and the factor will be decreased.
- Because the current factor values are always non-negative and are multiplied by a non-negative correction factor, the updated values are guaranteed to remain non-negative.

The algorithm alternates between updating P while keeping Q fixed, and then updating Q while keeping the new P fixed, repeating this process for a set number of iterations or until the values converge.

2.4.10 Collaborative Metric Learning (CML)

Key concept — Collaborative Metric Learning (CML) reframes collaborative filtering as a metric learning problem, learning a shared embedding space where the distance between user and item embeddings reflects their compatibility. It uses a pairwise loss to minimize distances for positive interactions and maximize them for negative ones.

Key differentiator — Unlike traditional matrix factorization, CML focuses on distances in the embedding space, which can capture more nuanced relationships and is robust to cold-start scenarios when combined with content features.

Use cases — Top-N recommendation in systems with implicit feedback, such as social media or e-commerce, where capturing fine-grained user-item compatibility is crucial.

When to Consider — Use CML when you need a flexible approach that can incorporate side information (e.g., item metadata) and handle cold-start problems. It is a strong alternative to BPR for ranking tasks.

Hyperparameters

- **k (Latent Factors)**: The dimensionality of the embedding space where user and item vectors are represented.
- **Iterations**: The number of training epochs, where the model iterates over the user-item interaction pairs.
- **Learning Rate**: The step size for the gradient descent updates that adjust the positions of the user and item embeddings.
- **Regularization (lambda_reg)**: A penalty applied to the embeddings to prevent them from growing too large, which helps in generalizing the model.
- **Margin**: A threshold used in the pairwise loss function. It defines how much closer a positive user-item pair should be in the embedding space compared to a negative pair.

Production Ready?

- **Production-Ready, but more common as an advanced baseline or in specialized applications.** CML is a powerful and flexible framework that has influenced modern recommendation research. While not as commonly deployed as WRMF or BPR, its metric learning approach is highly valuable in production systems where **handling cold-start scenarios** or **integrating side information** (content features) is critical. For real-time inference on large catalogs, a production deployment requires an efficient Approximate Nearest Neighbor (ANN) search index to quickly find the closest items to a user's embedding.

Seminal Paper:

- Hsieh, C. K., Yang, L., Cui, Y., Lin, T. Y., Belongie, S., & Estrin, D. (2017). *Collaborative Metric Learning.* https://arxiv.org/abs/1701.02398.
- Shilong Bao, Qianqian Xu, Zhiyong Yang, Yuan He, Xiaochun Cao, Qingming Huang. The Minority Matters: A Diversity-Promoting Collaborative Metric Learning Algorithm https://arxiv.org/abs/2209.15292

Python Frameworks

- **Surprise** https://surpriselib.com/: Offers popular and well-documented implementations of SVD, SVD++, Probabilistic Matrix Factorization (PMF), and NonNegMF, with support for custom loss functions.
- **implicit** https://github.com/benfred/implicit: Provides high-performance implementations of ALS, BPR, and WRMF, optimized for implicit feedback datasets.
- **Cornac** https://github.com/preferredAI/cornac: Includes implementations of PMF, NonNegMF, and other MF variants as part of its comparative framework.
- **RecTools** https://github.com/MobileTeleSystems/RecTools: Provides wrappers and implementations of matrix factorization models, including PureSVD and FunkSVD.
- **RecBole** https://github.com/RUCAIBox/RecBole: Offers implementations of SLIM (as SLIMElastic), WRMF, and CML, with support for various regularization techniques.
- **LightFM** https://github.com/lyst/lightfm: Supports WRMF and hybrid models that can incorporate side information, useful for CML.

Production Ready?

- Matrix factorization is one of the most influential and widely deployed techniques in the history of recommender systems. Its ability to generalize from sparse data by learning latent representations made it a breakthrough technology, famously popularized by its success in the Netflix Prize competition. It remains a core component of many large-scale production systems and serves as the conceptual foundation for many advanced deep learning architectures, such as Neural Collaborative Filtering. SLIM and its variants have demonstrated very strong performance in academic studies for the top-N recommendation task, often outperforming more complex methods. However, they are less commonly seen as standalone models in production systems compared to matrix factorization or k-NN. Their principles have influenced subsequent research, and they serve as powerful baselines for evaluating new item-based recommendation algorithms.

Mathematical Foundations

Collaborative Metric Learning (CML) shifts the perspective from predicting a score (like matrix factorization's dot product) to learning a geometric space where distances represent user-item compatibility. The core idea is that the distance between a user's and an item's vector should be small if the user likes the item and large otherwise.

Part A: The Core Idea - A Shared Metric Space

CML maps both users and items into the same low-dimensional latent space, typically a Euclidean space $\mathbb{R}^k$.

- Each user u is represented by a vector $p_u \in \mathbb{R}^k$.
- Each item i is represented by a vector $q_i \in \mathbb{R}^k$.

Unlike matrix factorization, which uses the dot product $p_u^\top q_i$ to measure similarity, CML uses the **squared Euclidean distance** to measure dissimilarity or "incompatibility." The distance between user u and item i is defined as:

$$d(u,i)^2 = |p_u - q_i|_2^2 = \sum_{k=1}^{K} (p_{uk} - q_{ik})^2$$

A smaller distance implies a stronger preference of user u for item i. The goal of the model is to learn the embedding vectors p_u and q_i such that this geometric relationship holds true for all user-item interactions.

Part B: The Pairwise Learning Objective

CML is optimized for ranking, making it ideal for implicit feedback. It learns from triplets of (u, i, j), where:

- u is the target user.
- i is a **positive item** that user u has interacted with (e.g., clicked, purchased).
- j is a **negative item** that user u has not interacted with (sampled from the unobserved items).

The fundamental goal is to ensure that for any user u, the distance to a positive item i is smaller than the distance to a negative item j. To make this relationship robust, the model enforces a **margin** m, requiring that the negative item be farther away by at least this amount. This leads to the desired geometric arrangement:

$$d(u,i)^2 + m < d(u,j)^2$$

Part C: The Loss Function (Triplet Hinge Loss)

To achieve the objective described above, CML is trained by minimizing a **triplet hinge loss** function. This loss penalizes the model whenever the geometric arrangement of a triplet is incorrect. The objective function is:

$$\mathcal{L} = \sum_{(u,i,j)\in\mathcal{T}} \max(0, m + d(u,i)^2 - d(u,j)^2) + \lambda \left(\sum_u |p_u|_2^2 + \sum_i |q_i|_2^2 \right)$$

Let's break down this function:

- **Triplet Hinge Loss:** The first term, $\sum_{(u,i,j)\in\mathcal{T}} \max(0, m + d(u,i)^2 - d(u,j)^2)$, is the core of the learning process.
  - The summation is over all training triplets $\mathcal{T}$.
  - The term $m + d(u,i)^2 - d(u,j)^2$ will be positive if the negative item j is not sufficiently far away from the user u compared to the positive item i (i.e., if the condition $d(u,i)^2 + m < d(u,j)^2$ is violated).
  - The $\max(0, \ldots)$ function means that if the condition is satisfied (the term is negative), the loss for that triplet is 0. Otherwise, the model incurs a positive penalty, and the gradients will push p_u and q_i closer while pushing p_u and q_j farther apart.
- **Regularization:** The second term, $\lambda \left(\sum_u |p_u|_2^2 + \sum_i |q_i|_2^2 \right)$, is the standard L2 regularization. It penalizes large values in the embedding vectors, which helps to prevent overfitting and improves the model's ability to generalize to unseen data.

2.5 Deep Learning Hybrids & Representation Learning

In the previous section, we explored how matrix factorization can be used to generate embeddings. However, this approach has some notable drawbacks:

- Limited use of additional features. Matrix factorization primarily relies on user and item IDs, making it difficult to incorporate other contextual or descriptive information. Consequently, the model is restricted to recommending only users or items it has already encountered during training.
- Recommendations are too generic. When similarity is measured with a dot product, the system often favors popular items, leading to less personalized suggestions. This makes it harder to reflect an individual user's unique preferences.

Deep learning overcome these challenges by offering a more flexible design. Since the input layer of a deep neural network can handle a wide range of user and item attributes, the model can integrate richer information. This capability enables it to better capture users' specific interests and deliver more relevant recommendations.

Thus, this category marks the transition from linear latent factor models to more expressive, non-linear models powered by neural networks. By replacing the simple dot product with deep learning architectures, these models can capture more complex and subtle user-item interaction patterns that traditional methods might miss.

What are non-linear relationships?

Think of it like this: a linear model assumes that if you like action movies twice as much, you'll get twice the enjoyment from an action scene. A **non-linear model** understands that the relationship is more complex. Maybe you love action movies, but after two hours, your enjoyment plateaus or even drops. Neural networks are excellent at learning these kinds of nuanced, "it depends" relationships from the data automatically.

2.5.1 Neural Collaborative Filtering (NCF) Framework and NeuMF

Key concept — NCF is a framework that generalizes Matrix Factorization (MF) by replacing its simple dot product with a more powerful and flexible neural network. Instead of being limited to a linear multiplication of user and item latent vectors, NCF learns an arbitrary, complex interaction function from the data itself. This allows it to capture **complex, non-linear patterns** that traditional MF misses. For example, it can learn that a user's preference for the "sci-fi" genre and the "Christopher Nolan" director *together* creates a much stronger signal than the sum of the individual preferences.

The NCF paper proposes a flagship model called **Neural Matrix Factorization (NeuMF)**, which fuses two pathways to achieve state-of-the-art performance.

Neural Matrix Factorization (NeuMF): The Fused Model

The relationship between Neural Collaborative Filtering (NCF) and Neural Matrix Factorization (NeuMF) is that of a conceptual framework to a specific implementation. NCF is the overarching framework that proposes generalizing traditional Matrix Factorization by replacing its simple dot product with a more powerful neural network to capture complex, non-linear user-item interaction patterns. NeuMF is the flagship model proposed within the original NCF paper that puts this idea into practice. It combines the strengths of linearity (for simple, predictable patterns) and non-linearity (for complex, nuanced patterns) in a single architecture.

Key differentiator — NeuMF's hybrid architecture leverages both linear and non-linear modeling by fusing two specialized neural layers, offering superior performance over simpler models. It balances the representational power of matrix factorization with the expressiveness of deep learning. It consists of two parallel components that are fused at the final layer. The two pathways are:

1. **GMF (Generalized Matrix Factorization) Path:** This "linear" path performs an element-wise product on a set of user and item embeddings. It acts as a learned, generalized version of the classic matrix factorization dot product, capturing the linear relationships in the data.

2. **MLP (Multi-Layer Perceptron) Path:** This "non-linear" path first concatenates a *separate* set of user and item embeddings and then processes them through a standard stack of deep neural network layers (an MLP). This allows the model to learn highly complex and arbitrary interaction patterns.

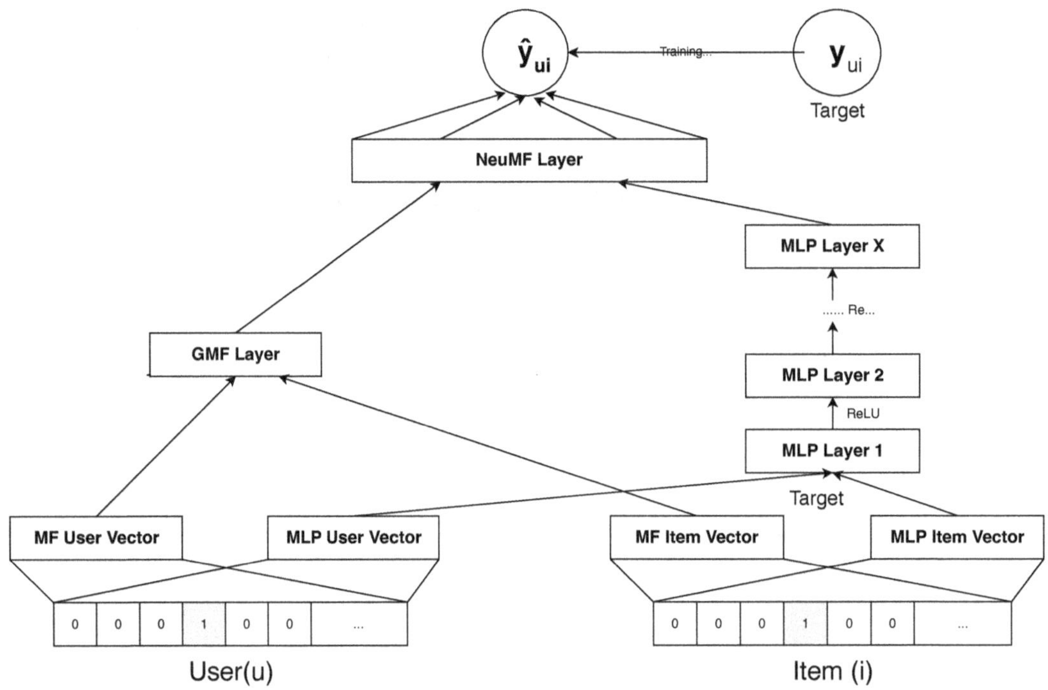

The output vectors from both the GMF and MLP paths are then concatenated and fed into a final prediction layer, which outputs the probability of interaction. By training all components jointly, NeuMF learns the optimal way to combine simple and complex signals for the most accurate recommendations.

Use cases — NeuMF is a high-performance model for Top-N recommendation from implicit feedback. It is ideal for scenarios with abundant data where user-item interactions might have complex patterns that simpler models cannot capture.

When to Consider — Use NeuMF when you need a high-performance model and have sufficient data to train a hybrid neural architecture without overfitting. It is a logical and powerful step up from standard matrix factorization or simpler NCF variants.

Seminal Paper:

- He, X., Liao, L., Zhang, H., Nie, L., Hu, X., & Chua, T. S. (2017). *Neural Collaborative Filtering.* https://arxiv.org/abs/1708.05031.

Five WHYs

1. Why is the simple dot product used in Matrix Factorization not good enough?

The dot product is a powerful tool, but it's fundamentally a linear operation. This means it assumes the relationship between a user's preference and an item's characteristics is simple and additive. For example, it might learn a user's general preference for "sci-fi" and an item's "sci-fi" score, but it struggles to capture more complex interactions. The NCF framework was created because the simple dot product can't effectively model the nuanced, non-linear patterns in user behavior, such as when the combination of two features (like "sci-fi" genre and "Christopher Nolan" director) creates a much stronger preference than just the sum of their individual parts.

2. Why use a neural network to replace the dot product?

Neural networks, particularly Multi-Layer Perceptrons (MLPs), are excellent at learning complex and non-linear relationships directly from data. By replacing the rigid dot product with a flexible neural network, the NCF framework allows the model to learn its own specialized interaction function. The MLP path in the NeuMF model, for instance, concatenates user and item vectors and processes them through several layers, giving it the capacity to discover intricate and subtle patterns in user preferences that a linear model like matrix factorization would completely miss.

3. Why does the NeuMF model have two separate paths (GMF and MLP)? Why not just use the more powerful MLP?

While the MLP path is powerful for learning complex patterns, it may not be the most efficient way to learn simpler ones. The NeuMF model uses two paths to get the best of both worlds. The **GMF path** acts like a generalized, learnable version of the classic dot product, making it very good at capturing the simple, linear relationships that matrix factorization excels at. The **MLP path** is dedicated to finding the complex, non-linear interactions. By fusing them, the model doesn't have to force one architecture to do everything; it allows each component to specialize, leading to a more powerful and accurate model overall.

4. Why does NeuMF learn *separate* embedding vectors for the GMF and MLP paths? Wouldn't it be more efficient to share them?

Using separate embeddings for each pathway gives the model more flexibility and has been shown to improve its final performance. You can think of the embeddings for the GMF path (p_u^{GMF}, q_i^{GMF}) as learning to represent users and items in a way that is best for capturing broad, multiplicative similarities. In contrast, the embeddings for the MLP path (p_u^{MLP}, q_i^{MLP}) might learn to encode features that are more useful for the complex, non-linear logic of the deep neural network. Forcing a single set of embeddings to be good at both tasks could create a compromise that is optimal for neither. By keeping them separate, each pathway can learn the most effective representations for its specific job.

5. Why are the outputs of the GMF and MLP paths concatenated and fed into a final layer? Why not just average their predictions?

Simply averaging the outputs would assume that the linear (GMF) and non-linear (MLP) signals are always equally important for every prediction. By concatenating the output vectors from both paths and feeding them into a final prediction layer, NeuMF allows the model to *learn* the optimal way to combine these signals. This final layer can assign different weights to the outputs from the GMF and MLP paths, essentially deciding how much to trust the "simple" versus the "complex" patterns for a specific user-item pair. This learned fusion is more powerful and adaptive than a fixed rule like averaging and is a key reason for the model's high performance.

Mathematical Foundations of NeuMF

The NeuMF model fuses a linear and a non-linear pathway, each with its own set of embeddings, to create a final prediction.

(1) Input and Embedding Layers

The model begins by creating two separate sets of embeddings for a given user u and item i:

- For the GMF path: User embedding p_u^{GMF} and item embedding q_i^{GMF}.
- For the MLP path: User embedding p_u^{MLP} and item embedding q_i^{MLP}.

Allowing the pathways to learn separate embeddings provides the model with more flexibility and has been shown to improve performance.

(2) Parallel Modeling Pathways

- **GMF Path:** This pathway models linear interactions via an element-wise product of the GMF embeddings:

$$\phi^{GMF} = p_u^{GMF} \odot q_i^{GMF}$$

This captures multiplicative interactions similar to standard Matrix Factorization.

- **MLP Path:** This pathway models non-linear interactions by first concatenating the MLP embeddings and then feeding them through a standard MLP tower with ReLU activations:

$$z_1 = \begin{bmatrix} p_u^{MLP} \\ q_i^{MLP} \end{bmatrix} \phi^{MLP} = a_L(W_L^\top(...a_2(W_2^\top z_1 + b_2)...) + b_L)$$

This structure allows the model to learn arbitrarily complex functions between the user and item embeddings.

(3) Fusion and Objective Function

The output vectors from both pathways are concatenated and projected by a final dense layer with a sigmoid activation function to produce the predicted interaction probability $\hat{y}_{ui}$:

$$\hat{y}_{ui} = \sigma\left(h^\top \begin{bmatrix} \phi^{GMF} \\ \phi^{MLP} \end{bmatrix}\right)$$

The entire model is trained end-to-end by minimizing the **Binary Cross-Entropy (Log Loss)**, which is ideal for the implicit feedback task of predicting the probability of an interaction.

$$\mathcal{L} = -\sum_{(u,i)\in\mathcal{Y}\cup\mathcal{Y}^-} y_{ui}\log\hat{y}_{ui} + (1 - y_{ui})\log(1 - \hat{y}_{ui})$$

where $\mathcal{Y}$ is the set of observed positive interactions (label $y_{ui} = 1$) and $\mathcal{Y}^-$ is a set of sampled negative interactions (label $y_{ui} = 0$).

Python Frameworks

- **Tensorflow** https://github.com/tensorflow/tensorflow: The TensorFlow Model Garden includes an official implementation and tutorial for building NCF and NeuMF models.
- **Microsoft Recommenders** https://github.com/recommenders-team/recommenders: Provides a detailed Jupyter notebook implementation of NCF and NeuMF, explaining both theory and practical application. Also includes an example notebook for xDeepFM.
- **Cornac** https://github.com/PreferredAI/cornac: Features an implementation of BiVAECF (Bilateral Variational Autoencoder for Collaborative Filtering).
- **RecBole** https://recbole.io/docs/user_guide/model/context/deepfm.html: Provides implementations of DeepFM, xDeepFM, and NeuMF.

- **LibRecommender** https://github.com/massquantity/LibRecommender: Offers a TensorFlow-based implementation of DeepFM and NeuMF with extensive configuration options.

Production Ready?

- NCF is a seminal deep learning model for recommendation that has had a significant impact on the field. It is widely used in industry, both as a powerful standalone model and as a strong baseline for evaluating more advanced architectures. Its core architectural principles have influenced the design of many subsequent models.

2.5.2 Factorization Machine-based: DeepFM & xDeepFM

Key concept — These models are advanced hybrid architectures designed primarily for Click-Through Rate (CTR) prediction. They combine a "wide" component for learning simple, memorable feature interactions and a "deep" component for learning complex, generalizable patterns. Both components share the same input embeddings, making training highly efficient.

What is Click-Through Rate (CTR) Prediction?

CTR prediction is the task of estimating the probability that a user will click on an item (like an ad, a product, or a news article) if it is shown to them. It's a critical task in online advertising and recommendation, as it directly relates to engagement and revenue. Models that are good at CTR prediction excel at understanding what makes a user click in a specific context.

Key differentiator:

- **DeepFM** combines a **Factorization Machine (FM)** for the "wide" part and a standard MLP for the "deep" part. The FM component is highly effective at learning 2nd-order feature interactions (e.g., how the combination of "user is a teenager" and "item is a video game" affects clicks) without manual effort.

- **xDeepFM (eXtreme DeepFM)** improves upon this by replacing the standard MLP with a **Compressed Interaction Network (CIN)**. The CIN is specifically designed to explicitly learn high-order feature interactions in a more controlled, vector-wise manner, which can be more powerful and interpretable than the implicit interactions learned by an MLP.

Use cases — Both models are state-of-the-art for CTR prediction in large-scale industrial recommender systems, such as those used in online advertising, e-commerce, and news feeds. They are designed to handle high-dimensional, sparse, and multi-field categorical features (e.g., user demographics, item category, time of day).

When to Consider — You may consider these models for any feature-rich recommendation task, especially CTR prediction. **DeepFM** is a powerful and widely used baseline. However, if you believe that explicit, high-order feature combinations are particularly important in your domain (e.g., "young user" + "sports category" + "weekend"), **xDeepFM**'s CIN component offers a more targeted mechanism for learning them.

Seminal Papers:

- **DeepFM:** Guo, H., Tang, R., Ye, Y., Li, Z., & He, X. (2017). *DeepFM: A Factorization-Machine based Neural Network for CTR Prediction.* https://arxiv.org/abs/1703.04247.
- **xDeepFM:** Lian, J., Zhou, X., Zhang, F., Chen, Z., Xie, X., & Sun, G. (2018). *xDeepFM: Combining Explicit and Implicit Feature Interactions for Recommender Systems.* https://arxiv.org/abs/1803.05170.

Mathematical Foundations

These models are designed to handle high-dimensional and sparse categorical features common in CTR prediction tasks. Their core idea is to process these features through different pathways to capture both low-order and high-order interactions efficiently.

Part A: The Shared Foundation - Feature Embeddings

Both DeepFM and xDeepFM begin with the same input structure. The input data consists of multiple fields (e.g., User ID, Item ID, Item Category, Time of Day). Each value within these fields (e.g., User 'A', Item '123') is a sparse, high-dimensional feature.

The first layer of the model is an **embedding layer**. Each sparse feature is mapped to its own low-dimensional, dense vector called an embedding. If we have m feature fields, the input to the main model architecture is a set of m embedding vectors $\{e_1, e_2, \ldots, e_m\}$, where each $e_i \in \mathbb{R}^k$ and k is the embedding dimension. These embeddings are shared across the different components of the model.

Part B: The DeepFM Architecture

DeepFM processes the input embeddings through two parallel components—a Factorization Machine and a Deep Neural Network—whose outputs are then summed for the final prediction.

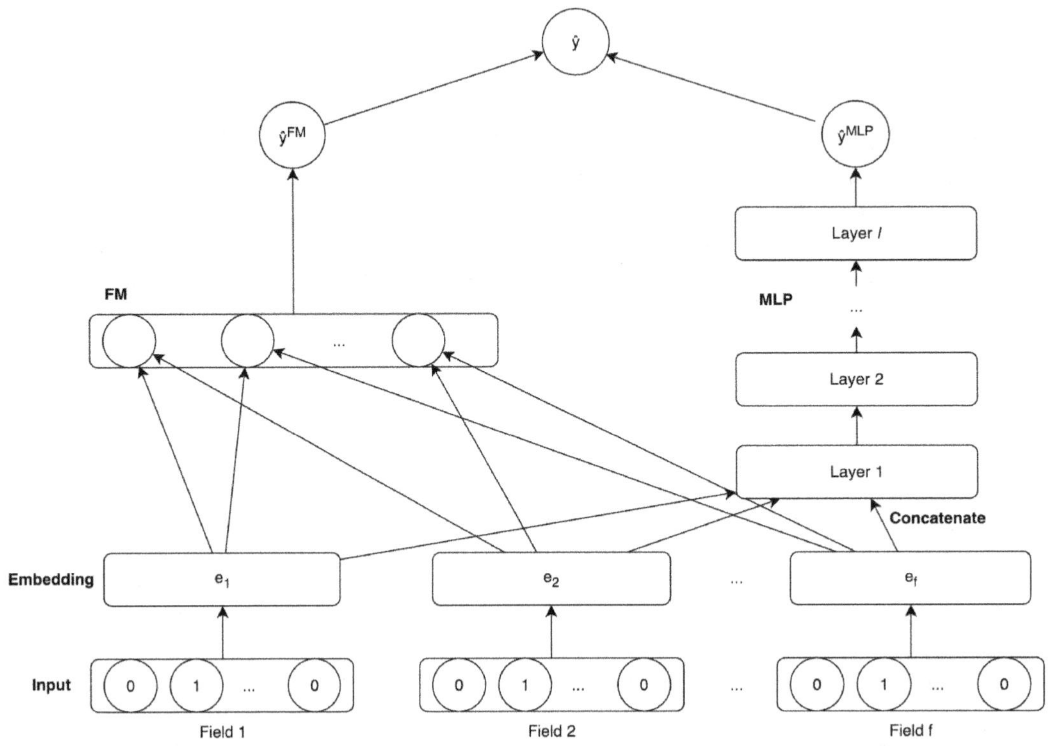

(1) **FM Component:** This part is responsible for modeling low-order (1st and 2nd) feature interactions. Its output, y_{FM}, is the sum of a linear part and a second-order interaction part:

$$y_{FM} = \langle w, x \rangle + \sum_{i=1}^{m} \sum_{j=i+1}^{m} \langle e_i, e_j \rangle$$

- $\langle w, x \rangle$: This is the 1st-order part, representing the linear sum of feature effects (addition unit).
- $\sum\sum\langle e_i, e_j \rangle$: This is the 2nd-order part. It computes the dot product for every pair of feature embeddings, efficiently capturing their pairwise interactions.

(2) **Deep Component (MLP):** This part uses a standard Multi-Layer Perceptron to automatically learn high-order, implicit feature interactions.

- The embedding vectors for all fields are first concatenated into a single large vector:

$$a^{(0)} = [e_1, e_2, \ldots, e_m]$$

- This vector is then fed through a series of dense layers (the MLP):

$$a^{(l+1)} = \sigma(W^{(l)} a^{(l)} + b^{(l)})$$

- The output of the final layer, $y_{MLP} = \sigma(W_{out} a^{(L)} + b_{out})$, captures the complex, high-order interactions.

(3) **Final Prediction:** The outputs of both components are combined to produce the final prediction:

$$\hat{y} = \text{sigmoid}(y_{FM} + y_{MLP})$$

Part C: The xDeepFM Architecture (CIN)

xDeepFM improves on DeepFM by replacing the implicit MLP component with a **Compressed Interaction Network (CIN)**, which is designed to learn high-order feature interactions explicitly and in a vector-wise manner.

(1) **Linear Component:** Same as the 1st-order part of the FM: $y_{Linear} = \langle w, x \rangle$.

(2) **Compressed Interaction Network (CIN):** This is the core of xDeepFM. It operates on the matrix of input embeddings, $X^0 \in \mathbb{R}^{m \times k}$. The CIN builds explicit high-order interactions layer by layer.

- Let $X^k \in \mathbb{R}^{H_k \times k}$ be the output of the k-th layer, where H_k is the number of feature vectors in that layer.

- Each vector in layer k is computed based on the interactions between the vectors in the previous layer, X^{k-1}, and the original embedding matrix, X^0. Conceptually, for each layer k:

(1) A **vector-wise outer product** is computed between X^{k-1} and X^0, resulting in a tensor that captures all pairwise interactions between the two sets of vectors.

(2) This tensor is then treated as an "image," and a set of "filters" (convolutions) are applied to sum up these interactions and generate the new set of vectors, X^k.

- After each layer k, a **sum pooling** is performed on the output matrix X^k along the embedding dimension, resulting in a vector $p^k \in \mathbb{R}^{H_k}$.

- The final output of the CIN is the concatenation of the pooled vectors from all layers: $p^+ = [p^1, p^2, \ldots, p^D]$.

(3) **Final Prediction:** The output of the CIN is passed through a dense layer to get a single score, y_{CIN}. This is combined with the linear component for the final prediction.

$$\hat{y} = \text{sigmoid}(y_{Linear} + y_{CIN})$$

2.5.3 Autoencoder-based: DAE & VAE

Key concept — This approach treats collaborative filtering as a reconstruction task. It takes a user's complete interaction history—represented as a sparse vector where each entry indicates whether the user has engaged with a particular item—and feeds it into a neural network called an autoencoder. The network compresses this information into a compact, low-dimensional representation and then attempts to reconstruct the original interaction vector as accurately as possible. By learning to rebuild the input from this compressed form, the model uncovers hidden patterns in user behavior, which can then be used to predict new recommendations.

What is an Autoencoder?

An autoencoder is a neural network designed to learn an efficient representation of data by copying its input to its output. It consists of two main parts: an **encoder** that reduces the input to a lower-dimensional form (often called the latent space or bottleneck), and a **decoder** that expands this compressed representation back to the original dimensions. The challenge of passing data through this bottleneck compels the network to prioritize the most essential features, making it a powerful tool for discovering structure in high-dimensional data like user-item interactions.

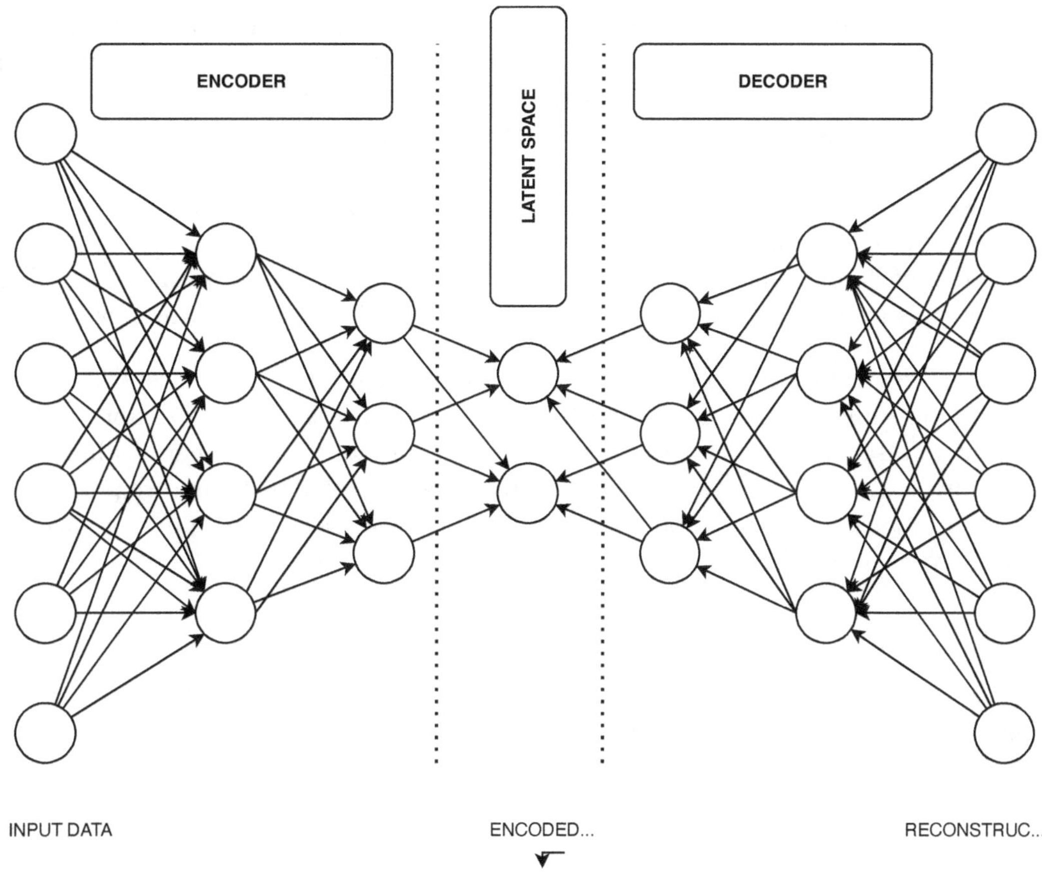

Key differentiator — Autoencoders stand out by focusing on self-supervised learning: the model trains on the data itself without needing explicit labels, using reconstruction as the guiding objective. Specific variants build on this foundation in distinct ways:

- **Collaborative Denoising Autoencoder (CDAE):** This model enhances robustness by introducing noise during training—it corrupts the input by randomly masking some interactions and then requires the network to reconstruct the full, original vector. This process helps the model generalize better to incomplete or noisy real-world data.
- **Multi-VAE (Multinomial Variational Autoencoder):** This extends the basic autoencoder into a probabilistic framework known as a variational autoencoder (VAE). Instead of producing a fixed latent representation, it outputs a probability distribution over possible representations, allowing it to capture uncertainty in user preferences. The "multinomial" aspect refers to its use of a distribution suited for count-based data, making it particularly effective for implicit feedback like clicks or views.

- **EASE (Embarrassingly Shallow Autoencoders):** A surprisingly simple linear version of the autoencoder that skips the neural network layers altogether. It solves the reconstruction problem analytically in a closed form, without iterative training, yet often rivals or surpasses more complex models—demonstrating that depth is not always necessary for strong performance.

Use cases — These models excel in top-N recommendation scenarios based on implicit feedback, such as suggesting products on e-commerce sites or videos on streaming platforms. Multi-VAE, for instance, has become a benchmark for collaborative filtering tasks, delivering high accuracy in ranking unseen items. EASE serves as a reliable, computationally efficient baseline for validating new algorithms.

When to Consider — Turn to autoencoder-based methods when traditional latent factor models fall short in capturing non-linear patterns or handling sparse data. Start with a denoising autoencoder like CDAE if your dataset includes noisy interactions. Opt for Multi-VAE when dealing with implicit feedback and seeking state-of-the-art ranking performance, as its probabilistic nature provides a nuanced understanding of user variability. If simplicity and speed are priorities, EASE offers an accessible entry point that still delivers competitive results.

Seminal Papers:

- **DAE (for RecSys):** Wu, Y., DuBois, C., Zheng, A. X., & Ester, M. (2016). *Collaborative Denoising Auto-Encoders for Top-N Recommender Systems.* https://dl.acm.org/doi/10.1145/2835776.2835837.

- **VAE (for RecSys):** Liang, D., Krishnan, R. G., Hoffman, M. D., & Jebara, T. (2018). *Variational Autoencoders for Collaborative Filtering.* https://arxiv.org/abs/1802.05814.

Mathematical Foundations

Autoencoder-based models transform collaborative filtering into a process of data compression and reconstruction. We begin with the basic framework and progressively introduce more advanced variants, explaining each step to build understanding.

Part A: The General Autoencoder Framework

Consider a user's interaction history as a vector $x_u \in \mathbb{R}^N$, where N is the total number of items in the catalog. Typically, this vector is sparse: $x_{ui} = 1$ if user u has interacted with item i (e.g., clicked or purchased), and 0 otherwise.

The autoencoder processes this vector through two functions:

(1) **Encoder (g):** This maps the high-dimensional input x_u to a lower-dimensional latent vector $z_u \in \mathbb{R}^k$, where $k \ll N$ (e.g., $k = 50$):

$$z_u = g(x_u)$$

In practice, the encoder is often a neural network with layers that progressively reduce the dimensionality.

(2) **Decoder (f):** This takes the latent vector z_u and reconstructs an approximation of the original input, $\hat{x}_u$:

$$\hat{x}_u = f(z_u)$$

The entries in $\hat{x}_u$ serve as predicted scores for ranking items—the higher the score for an unseen item, the stronger the recommendation.

Training minimizes a reconstruction loss, such as the mean squared error between x_u and $\hat{x}_u$ across all users:

$$\mathcal{L} = \sum_u \|x_u - \hat{x}_u\|^2$$

This objective encourages the model to retain only the most informative patterns in the latent space.

Part B: Collaborative Denoising Autoencoder (CDAE)

To make the model more resilient to incomplete data—a common issue in recommendations—CDAE introduces a denoising step. Before encoding, the input x_u is corrupted to create $\tilde{x}_u$, for example by randomly setting some 1's to 0 (simulating missing interactions).

The forward pass then becomes:

$$\hat{x}_u = f(g(\tilde{x}_u))$$

The loss remains the reconstruction of the original x_u:

$$\mathcal{L} = \sum_u \|x_u - f(g(\tilde{x}_u))\|^2$$

This corruption acts as a regularizer, compelling the model to infer hidden connections between items rather than memorizing the input exactly. For instance, if a user's interaction with a sci-fi movie is masked, the model must rely on patterns from similar items to reconstruct it.

Part C: Multi-VAE (Variational Autoencoder with Multinomial Likelihood)

To make the math approachable, we'll start with a simplified view of the objective and then build up to the full formulation.

Step 1: The Encoder's Probabilistic Output

In a standard autoencoder, the encoder outputs a single latent vector z_u for user u. In Multi-VAE, the encoder instead produces parameters of a probability distribution—typically a Gaussian. Think of this as defining a "cloud" of possible latent representations for the user. For simplicity, let's say the encoder outputs:

- μ_u: The center of this cloud (the mean of the Gaussian).
- σ_u^2: The spread of the cloud (the variance, indicating uncertainty).

The actual latent vector z_u is sampled from this distribution:

$$z_u \sim \mathcal{N}(\mu_u, \sigma_u^2)$$

This sampling introduces randomness, allowing the model to explore different possible representations of the user's preferences during training.

Step 2: The Decoder and Multinomial Likelihood

The decoder takes a sampled z_u and produces a probability vector π_u over all N items, where π_{ui} is the predicted probability that user u will interact with item i. To ensure these probabilities sum to 1, the decoder applies a softmax function:

$$\pi_u = \text{softmax}(f(z_u))$$

Here, $f(z_u)$ is the decoder's output (e.g., a neural network layer), and the softmax converts raw scores into probabilities:

$$\pi_{ui} = \frac{\exp(f(z_u)_i)}{\sum_{j=1}^{N} \exp(f(z_u)_j)}$$

For implicit feedback, Multi-VAE assumes the user's interaction vector x_u follows a multinomial distribution based on π_u. The likelihood of observing x_u given z_u is proportional to:

$$p(x_u | z_u) \propto \prod_{i=1}^{N} \pi_{ui}^{x_{ui}}$$

Taking the logarithm for numerical stability, the log-likelihood becomes:

$$\log p(x_u | z_u) \propto \sum_{i=1}^{N} x_{ui} \log \pi_{ui}$$

This term measures how well the model predicts the user's actual interactions: higher π_{ui} for items where $x_{ui} = 1$ increases the likelihood, aligning predictions with observed behavior.

Step 3: The Training Objective (Simplified)

Training aims to maximize the likelihood of the data while keeping the latent distribution reasonable. A simplified version of the objective for a single user is to maximize:

$$\text{Reconstruction Quality} - \text{Latent Distribution Penalty}$$

- **Reconstruction Quality**: This measures how well the model reconstructs x_u using the log-likelihood above.
- **Latent Distribution Penalty**: This ensures the encoder's output distribution $\mathcal{N}(\mu_u, \sigma_u^2)$ doesn't stray too far from a standard Gaussian $\mathcal{N}(0, I)$, preventing overfitting to noisy patterns.

Step 4: The Full Objective (Evidence Lower Bound)

The full training objective is called the Evidence Lower Bound (ELBO), which balances these goals. For a single user, it can be written as:

$$\mathcal{L}_u = \mathbb{E}_{q(z_u|x_u)}[\log p(x_u|z_u)] - \beta \cdot \mathrm{KL}(q(z_u|x_u)\|p(z))$$

Let's unpack this:

- **Reconstruction Term**: $\mathbb{E}_{q(z_u|x_u)}[\log p(x_u|z_u)]$ is the expected log-likelihood over samples z_u drawn from the encoder's distribution $q(z_u|x_u) = \mathcal{N}(\mu_u, \sigma_u^2)$. Since sampling is random, we approximate this expectation using one or a few samples during training. This term encourages accurate reconstruction of x_u.
- **KL Divergence Term**: $\mathrm{KL}(q(z_u|x_u)\|p(z))$ measures how much the encoder's distribution deviates from a standard Gaussian prior $p(z) = \mathcal{N}(0, I)$. The KL divergence acts as a regularizer, ensuring the latent space is structured and generalizable. The parameter β (often gradually increased from 0 to 1 during training) controls the strength of this regularization.

The total loss is the negative ELBO summed over all users:

$$\mathcal{L} = \sum_u \left(-\mathbb{E}_{q(z_u|x_u)}[\log p(x_u|z_u)] + \beta \cdot \mathrm{KL}(q(z_u|x_u)\|p(z))\right)$$

Minimizing this loss trains the model to balance accurate predictions with a well-behaved latent space.

Why It Works

The probabilistic nature of Multi-VAE allows it to handle uncertainty in sparse data, where most items have no interactions. The multinomial likelihood aligns with the nature of implicit feedback, treating interactions as counts. The KL divergence ensures the model doesn't overfit to specific users, making it robust for top-N recommendations. In practice, Multi-VAE often outperforms simpler models by capturing complex patterns while remaining computationally feasible for large datasets.

2.5.4 A Modern Baseline for CF: SimpleX

SimpleX stands as a powerful testament to the principle of "less is more" in modern recommender systems. It is a simple yet remarkably strong baseline for collaborative filtering that often achieves or surpasses the performance of much more complex architectures like GNNs or sequential models. It uses a standard bi-encoder (two-tower) architecture, but derives its power from a well-formulated **contrastive learning** objective and a focus on effective training techniques.

Key concept — SimpleX learns user and item embeddings by optimizing them directly for similarity. For each positive user-item interaction in a training batch, the model is trained to maximize the similarity score between that pair's embeddings. Simultaneously, it is trained to minimize the similarity scores between that same user's embedding and the embeddings of all *other* items in the same batch (so-called "in-batch negatives"). This process effectively teaches the model to pull positive pairs together in the embedding space while pushing them far apart from negative pairs.

Key differentiator — Its primary differentiator is achieving state-of-the-art performance through radical simplicity. Unlike models that require complex graph convolutions or recurrent layers, SimpleX relies on a basic bi-encoder. Its strength comes from three key aspects of its training:

(1) **A powerful loss function (InfoNCE)**, which is highly effective for learning from implicit feedback.

(2) **Effective hard negative mining**, as the in-batch negatives strategy naturally provides a diverse and challenging set of negative examples for each positive interaction.

(3) **Consistency regularization**, which improves the model's robustness by ensuring that embeddings for the same user or item remain stable even under minor perturbations like neural network dropout.

Use cases — SimpleX is a high-performance model for Top-N recommendation from implicit feedback. Its main role in the field is as a formidable baseline. Any new, more complex collaborative filtering model should be benchmarked against it to justify its added complexity.

When to Consider — An engineer should use SimpleX as a primary baseline for any new collaborative filtering project. Given its ease of implementation and top-tier performance, it is an excellent starting point. If a more sophisticated model fails to significantly outperform SimpleX, it is a strong signal that the simpler approach is likely sufficient and more practical.

Seminal Paper:

- Mao, K., Zhu, J., Zhang, Y., Wang, J., He, X., & Li, D. (2021). *SimpleX: A Simple and Strong Baseline for Collaborative Filtering.* https://arxiv.org/abs/2109.12613.

Mathematical Foundations

The effectiveness of SimpleX comes from its carefully designed training objective, rather than a complex model architecture.

(1) The Bi-Encoder Architecture

The model consists of two simple embedding lookups:

- **User Encoder:** Maps a user ID u to a user embedding $p_u \in \mathbb{R}^d$.
- **Item Encoder:** Maps an item ID i to an item embedding $q_i \in \mathbb{R}^d$.

The predicted relevance score between a user and an item is simply the dot product of their embeddings: $s(u,i) = p_u^\top q_i$.

(2) The Contrastive Learning Objective (InfoNCE)

The model is trained using a contrastive loss that operates over a mini-batch of user-item interactions. For a single positive pair (u,i) within a batch $\mathcal{B}$, the item i is the positive sample for user u. All other items j within the same batch ($j \in \mathcal{B}, j \neq i$) are treated as **in-batch negatives**.

The InfoNCE loss for this positive pair is defined as:

$$\mathcal{L}_{infoNCE}^{(u,i)} = -\log \frac{\exp(p_u^\top q_i/\tau)}{\sum_{j\in\mathcal{B}} \exp(p_u^\top q_j/\tau)}$$

Let's break this down:

- The term $p_u^\top q_j$ calculates the similarity score between user u and an item j.
- The numerator promotes a high similarity score for the positive pair (u,i).
- The denominator is the sum of similarity scores for the user u against *all* items in the batch (one positive, many negatives).

- This structure is effectively a softmax function over the item similarities. The loss is minimized when the probability of the positive item is maximized.
- τ is the **temperature** hyperparameter, which adjusts the penalty on hard-to-classify negative examples.

The total loss for the batch is the average of this loss calculated for all positive pairs in $\mathcal{B}$.

(3) Consistency Regularization

To improve robustness, SimpleX adds a simple but effective consistency loss. The idea is to pass the same user and item IDs through the encoders twice, with dropout enabled differently each time. This produces two slightly different embeddings for the same user (p_u and p'_u) and item (q_i and q'_i). The consistency loss then encourages these two embeddings to be close to each other, typically using a Mean Squared Error (MSE):

$$\mathcal{L}_{consist} = \frac{1}{|\mathcal{B}|} \sum_{(u,i)\in\mathcal{B}} \left(|p_u - p'_u|_2^2 + |q_i - q'_i|_2^2 \right)$$

This acts as a regularizer, forcing the model to learn representations that are stable and less sensitive to random noise from dropout.

(4) The Final Objective

The final loss function combines the contrastive loss and the consistency loss:

$$\mathcal{L} = \mathcal{L}_{infoNCE} + \gamma \mathcal{L}_{consist}$$

where γ is a hyperparameter that controls the strength of the consistency regularization.

Production Ready?

- **Highly.** The bi-encoder architecture is an industry standard for large-scale retrieval systems because user and item embeddings can be pre-computed and served efficiently. SimpleX provides a state-of-the-art recipe for training such an architecture, making it a very practical and powerful choice for production environments.

Python Frameworks:

- SimpleX is straightforward to implement using standard deep learning libraries like **PyTorch** or **TensorFlow**.
- **RecBole**: Includes a high-quality implementation of SimpleX.

2.5.5 EASE (Embarrassingly Shallow Autoencoders)

Key concept — EASE is a non-neural, linear autoencoder for top-N recommendation from implicit feedback. It learns an item-item similarity matrix by solving a simple, closed-form regression problem. The goal is to find a similarity matrix B that can reconstruct the original user-item interaction matrix X as closely as possible, such that $X \approx XB$. Despite its simplicity, it is an extremely powerful baseline that often outperforms complex deep learning models.

Key differentiator — Its most significant feature is the existence of a **closed-form (analytical) solution**. Unlike deep learning models that require iterative optimization via stochastic gradient descent (SGD), EASE computes its item similarity matrix directly by solving a single matrix equation. This completely eliminates the need to tune hyperparameters like learning rates, the number of epochs, or network architecture, making the model incredibly simple, fast to "train," and perfectly reproducible.

Use cases — Top-N recommendation from implicit feedback. Its primary role in research and industry is to serve as a very strong and difficult-to-beat baseline against which new, more complex collaborative filtering algorithms should be compared.

When to Consider — EASE should be considered one of the very first and most important baselines for any collaborative filtering task. It is ideal when you need to quickly establish a high-performance benchmark. However, be aware that computing the closed-form solution requires inverting an $N \times N$ matrix (where N is the number of items), which can be computationally expensive for catalogs with millions of items.

Mathematical Foundations

The objective of EASE is to learn an item-to-item similarity matrix B of size $N \times N$ that minimizes the reconstruction error of the user-item interaction matrix X (size $M \times N$).

Objective Function — The model minimizes the sum of squared reconstruction errors with L2 regularization to prevent overfitting:

$$\min_B ||X - XB||_F^2 + \lambda ||B||_F^2$$

A key constraint is that the diagonal elements of B must be zero ($\text{diag}(B) = 0$). This prevents the trivial solution where the model simply learns to recommend an item to itself ($B = I$).

Analytical Solution — This optimization problem has a direct, closed-form solution. First, we compute the Gram matrix (the item-item co-occurrence matrix) $G = X^T X$. The solution for B is then derived from G:

(1) First, calculate an intermediate matrix P by inverting the regularized Gram matrix:

$$P = (G + \lambda I)^{-1}$$

(2) The final similarity matrix B is then derived from P by normalizing its elements and setting the diagonal to zero:

$$B_{ij} = \begin{cases} -\frac{P_{ij}}{P_{jj}} & \text{if } i \neq j \\ 0 & \text{if } i = j \end{cases}$$

Once the matrix B is computed, the prediction scores for all users are generated by the matrix multiplication $\hat{X} = XB$. The items with the highest scores for each user are then selected as the top-N recommendations.

2.6 Sequential & Session-Based Models

This paradigm marks a fundamental shift from treating user interactions as an unordered set to modeling them as an ordered sequence. The goal is to predict the user's *next* action based on the temporal dynamics of their recent behavior. While earlier models like **TimeSVD++** integrated time-drifting effects into the matrix factorization framework, this new paradigm represents a more comprehensive approach. It reflects a powerful conceptual convergence with the field of Natural Language Processing (NLP), where a sequence of user interactions is treated analogously to a sequence of words in a sentence.

Why does order matter?

Imagine a shopping session. A user who clicks on "iPhone → iPhone Case → Screen Protector" has a very clear and different intent from a user who clicks on "iPhone, then Laptop, then Headphones." The first user is accessorizing a specific product, while the second is browsing different categories. Sequential models are designed to understand these ordered patterns to make much more contextually relevant "what's next" predictions.

2.6.1 RNN-based: GRU4Rec

Key concept — GRU4Rec was a pioneering model that applied Recurrent Neural Networks (RNNs) to session-based recommendation. It processes a sequence of user interactions one by one, maintaining a "memory" or hidden state that evolves with each new item. This state captures the user's current intent, which is then used to predict the very next item they are likely to interact with.

What is an RNN?

A **Recurrent Neural Network (RNN)** is a type of neural network designed for sequential data. Think of it as having a short-term memory. As it reads a sequence (like words in a sentence or items in a session), it passes information from one step to the next. This allows it to understand context and order, making it perfect for predicting what comes next based on what happened before. The **GRU (Gated Recurrent Unit)** is an advanced and efficient type of RNN.

Key differentiator — Its core innovation was using RNNs to handle variable-length, anonymous user sessions. Unlike static models, GRU4Rec captures the evolving nature of user intent within a single session. It also introduced ranking-aware loss functions to directly optimize for the quality of the recommended list, not just prediction accuracy.

Use cases — GRU4Rec is designed for session-based recommendation, where user identity may be unknown or irrelevant (e.g., guest shoppers). It is common in e-commerce for predicting the next product click, in media streaming for the next song or video, and in news for the next article.

When to Consider — GRU4Rec is a strong baseline for any sequential or session-based task where short-term context and the order of interactions are critical. It's particularly useful when a user's intent evolves throughout a session and you need to make real-time, next-step predictions.

Seminal Paper:

- Hidasi, B., Karatzoglou, A., Baltrunas, L., & Tikk, D. (2016). *Session-based Recommendations with Recurrent Neural Networks.* https://arxiv.org/abs/1511.06939.

Mathematical Foundations

GRU4Rec models user sessions by processing the sequence of item interactions one at a time. At each step, it updates an internal "memory" (the hidden state) that summarizes the user's intent so far and uses this memory to predict the next item.

Part A: The Sequential Input and Embedding

The input to the model is a user session, which is an ordered sequence of item interactions, $S = (i_1, i_2, \ldots, i_n)$. The model is trained to predict the next item in the sequence given the items seen so far.

At each time step t in the session, the model takes the current item, i_t, as input. This item ID is first converted into a dense, low-dimensional vector representation called an **embedding**, e_t. This is done via a lookup in an item embedding matrix E that is learned during training.

Part B: The Core - Gated Recurrent Unit (GRU)

The heart of GRU4Rec is the GRU cell, which is responsible for maintaining the session's memory. The GRU takes the current item embedding e_t and the previous hidden state h_{t-1} to compute the new hidden state h_t. This state h_t is a vector that represents a compressed summary of the session up to step t.

The GRU uses two "gates" to control the flow of information, which prevents issues like vanishing gradients and allows it to capture dependencies over longer sequences.

(1) **Reset Gate (r_t):** This gate determines how much of the past information (from h_{t-1}) should be forgotten.

$$r_t = \sigma(W_r e_t + U_r h_{t-1})$$

(2) **Update Gate (z_t):** This gate determines how much of the new information should be combined with the old hidden state. A value close to 1 means the old state is mostly ignored, while a value close to 0 means the new information is mostly ignored.

$$z_t = \sigma(W_z e_t + U_z h_{t-1})$$

(3) **Candidate Hidden State:** This computes a "candidate" new state by combining the current input e_t with a selectively forgotten version of the previous state h_{t-1} (controlled by the reset gate r_t):

$$\tilde{h}_t = \tanh(W_h e_t + U_h(r_t \odot h_{t-1}))$$

(4) **New Hidden State (h_t):** The final hidden state is a linear interpolation between the previous state h_{t-1} and the candidate state $\tilde{h}_t$, controlled by the update gate z_t.

$$h_t = (1 - z_t) \odot h_{t-1} + z_t \odot \tilde{h}_t$$

Here, the W and U matrices are learnable weights, σ is the sigmoid function, and $\odot$ denotes the element-wise product.

Part C: Prediction and Objective Function

After updating the hidden state to h_t, the model uses it to predict the *next* item in the session, i_{t+1}.

(1) **Output Layer:** The hidden state h_t is passed through a final dense layer to compute a score, s_j, for every possible item j in the entire catalog. These scores are then typically converted into a probability distribution using the softmax function.

$$\hat{y}_t = \text{softmax}(W_o h_t + b_o)$$

The vector $\hat{y}_t$ contains the probabilities for each item being the next one in the session. Recommendations are made by ranking items by these probabilities.

(2) **Objective Function:** The model minimizes a loss function to align predicted probabilities with the actual next item in the sequence. While standard **categorical cross-entropy** can be used, the GRU4Rec paper introduced session-aware, ranking-based losses that often perform better.

- **TOP1 Loss:** A popular ranking loss that encourages the score of the correct next item ($s_{i_{t+1}}$) to be higher than the scores of negatively sampled items (s_j). It is a regularized approximation of the rank of the positive item.
- **BPR Loss (Bayesian Personalized Ranking):** A pairwise loss that also aims to maximize the difference between the score of the positive item and the scores of negative items.

2.6.2 CNN-based: NextItNet

Key concept — NextItNet applies Convolutional Neural Networks (CNNs), traditionally used for image processing, to model sequences of user interactions. It treats an embedded sequence of items as a 1D "image" and uses stacked layers of *dilated convolutions* to efficiently identify patterns and long-range dependencies.

> **How can a CNN work on a sequence?**
>
> Imagine the sequence of items is laid out like a single row of pixels. A **CNN** applies "filters" that slide across this row to recognize local patterns (e.g., "item A is often followed by item B"). By using **dilated convolutions**, which skip inputs at varying rates, the network can create a very large receptive field, allowing it to see how an item at the beginning of a long session influences an item at the end, all without the step-by-step processing of an RNN.

Key differentiator — The main advantage of NextItNet over RNNs is **efficiency and parallelism**. CNNs can process all parts of a sequence simultaneously, making training much faster. Its use of dilated convolutions and residual blocks allows it to build very deep networks that can capture dependencies across extremely long sequences (hundreds of items) where RNNs might struggle with vanishing gradients.

Use cases — NextItNet is used for session-based and sequential Top-N item recommendation. It is particularly well-suited for scenarios with very long user interaction sequences and where training efficiency on large datasets is a major concern.

When to Consider — Consider NextItNet when training speed is a priority or when dealing with very long sequences where capturing long-range dependencies is crucial. It represents a powerful and scalable architectural alternative to RNNs for modeling sequential data.

Seminal Paper:

- Yuan, F., Karatzoglou, A., Arapakis, I., Jose, J. M., & He, X. (2019). *A Simple Convolutional Generative Network for Next Item Recommendation.* https://dl.acm.org/doi/10.1145/3289600.3290975.

Mathematical Foundations

NextItNet leverages concepts from computer vision, treating a sequence of item embeddings as a 1D "image" and applying stacked convolutional layers to learn sequential patterns. Its key components are dilated and causal convolutions, which allow it to efficiently capture long-range dependencies in parallel.

Part A: The Sequential Input as an "Image"

The model's input is a user's interaction history, typically a fixed-length subsequence of the most recent L items, $S = (i_1, i_2, \dots, i_L)$.

Embedding Layer — This sequence of item IDs is first transformed into a matrix of dense embedding vectors by looking up each item's corresponding vector in a shared embedding matrix.

$$E = [e_1, e_2, \dots, e_L]^\top \in \mathbb{R}^{L \times k}$$

Here, $e_t \in \mathbb{R}^k$ is the embedding for the item at position t, and k is the embedding dimension. This matrix E serves as the input "image" for the subsequent convolutional layers.

Part B: The Core - Dilated Causal Convolutions

The main building block of NextItNet is the 1D dilated causal convolution. Let's break down each term:

(1) **Convolution:** A standard 1D convolution applies a filter (or kernel) f of size K that slides across the input sequence E. At each position t, it computes a weighted sum of the embeddings in a local neighborhood.

(2) **Causal:** To predict the *next* item, the model must only use information from the past. A causal convolution ensures this by only looking at the current position and previous positions. This is typically implemented by padding the beginning of the sequence. The formula for a causal convolution at position t is:

$$(E * f)(t) = \sum_{s=0}^{K-1} f(s) \cdot E_{t-s}$$

(3) **Dilated:** This is the key to capturing long-range dependencies efficiently. A dilated convolution skips inputs with a certain step size, known as the **dilation rate** d. This allows the filter to cover a wider range of the sequence without increasing the number of parameters. The formula for a 1D dilated convolution is:

$$(E *_d f)(t) = \sum_{s=0}^{K-1} f(s) \cdot E_{t-d \cdot s}$$

By stacking convolutional layers and exponentially increasing the dilation rate in each layer (e.g., $d = 1, 2, 4, 8, \ldots$), the network's **receptive field** (how far back in the sequence it can "see") grows exponentially. This allows the model to connect an item at the very beginning of a long session to the prediction at the very end with just a few layers.

Part C: Stacking Blocks and Prediction

The overall architecture of NextItNet consists of stacking several residual blocks of these convolutional layers.

(1) **Residual Blocks:** To enable the training of a very deep network, NextItNet uses residual connections. The input to a block is added to its output, allowing gradients to flow more easily. A typical block looks like this:

$$H_1 = \text{ReLU}(\text{Conv}_{d_1}(E)) H_2 = \text{ReLU}(\text{Conv}_{d_2}(H_1)) \text{Output} = H_2 + E \quad \text{(element-wise sum)}$$

(2)**Prediction:** After passing the input through all the stacked residual blocks, we take the output vector at the very last position in the sequence, h_L. This vector is a rich representation of the entire preceding sequence. It is then passed through a final dense layer to produce a score for every item in the catalog.

$$\hat{y} = \text{softmax}(W h_L + b)$$

The vector $\hat{y}$ contains the predicted probabilities for the next item.

(3) **Objective Function:** The model is trained to predict the actual next item in the sequence. The standard loss function for this multi-class classification task is **Categorical Cross-Entropy**.

$$\mathcal{L} = -\sum_{i=1}^{|V|} y_i \log(\hat{y}_i)$$

Where $|V|$ is the total number of items, and y is the one-hot encoded vector of the true next item.

2.6.3 Attention/Transformer-based: SASRec & BERT4Rec

Key concept — This family of models leverages the **self-attention mechanism**, the core component of the Transformer architecture that has revolutionized NLP. Self-attention allows the model to dynamically weigh the importance of *all* other items in a sequence when making a prediction for the next item, overcoming the sequential processing bottleneck of RNNs and the fixed receptive field of CNNs.

> **What is Self-Attention?**
>
> **Self-attention** is a mechanism that allows a model to look at other items in the input sequence and decide which ones are most important for understanding the current item. For recommendation, this means that to predict your next action, the model can pay more attention to the very first item you clicked on, or a specific item you lingered on, regardless of its position in the sequence. It learns to identify the most influential past actions on the fly.

Key differentiator — The key innovation is the use of self-attention, providing a global view of the sequence. The distinction between the two main models is crucial:

- **SASRec (Self-Attentive Sequential Recommendation)** is **unidirectional** (autoregressive). It only considers past items to predict the future, strictly respecting the temporal flow of user actions. It excels at identifying which of the previous items are most relevant for the *next* choice.
- **BERT4Rec (Bidirectional Encoder Representations from Transformers for Recommendation)** is **bidirectional**. Inspired by BERT in NLP, it is trained using a "cloze task" where it predicts a randomly masked item in the sequence using both its left and right context (items that came before and after). This allows it to learn a richer, more holistic representation of user interests.

Use cases — These models represent the state-of-the-art for sequential recommendation tasks. **SASRec** is a powerful general-purpose model for next-item prediction. **BERT4Rec** is particularly effective when a user's overall interest is a reflection of their entire history. Specialized variants extend this architecture for specific domains; for example, **NRMS** is designed for news recommendation, using attention to model article content, while **TiSASRec** incorporates timestamps to better model the time intervals between user interactions.

When to Consider — Transformer-based models should be the default choice for high-performance sequential recommendation. Choose **SASRec** for tasks where strict temporal order is paramount. Consider **BERT4Rec** when you have dense data and believe a user's intent is better captured by their holistic interaction history.

Seminal Papers:

- **SASRec:** Kang, W. C., & McAuley, J. (2018). *Self-Attentive Sequential Recommendation.* https://arxiv.org/abs/1808.09781.
- **BERT4Rec:** Sun, F., Liu, J., Wu, J., Pei, C., Lin, X., Ou, W., & Jiang, P. (2019). *BERT4Rec: Sequential Recommendation with Bidirectional Encoder Representations from Transformer.* https://arxiv.org/abs/1904.06690.

Mathematical Foundations

Transformer-based models capture complex dependencies within a sequence by using a self-attention mechanism, which allows every item to directly weigh its relationship with every other item. This provides a global view of the user's interaction history.

The Shared Foundation: Input and Positional Embeddings

The input is a sequence of the user's most recent L interactions, $S = (i_1, i_2, \ldots, i_L)$.

(1) **Item Embeddings:** The sequence of item IDs is converted into a matrix of dense embeddings, $E = [e_1, \ldots, e_L]^\top \in \mathbb{R}^{L \times k}$.

(2) **Positional Embeddings:** The self-attention mechanism is permutation-invariant, meaning it has no inherent sense of order. To fix this, we inject positional information by adding a **positional embedding** to each item embedding. The final input to the model is the sum of these two embeddings:

$$M = E + P$$

Where $P = [p_1, \ldots, p_L]^\top \in \mathbb{R}^{L \times k}$ is the matrix of positional embeddings, which are learned during training.

The Core Mechanism: Scaled Dot-Product Attention

The central component of the Transformer is the self-attention layer. For each item in the input matrix M, we create three vectors by multiplying it with learned weight matrices: a **Query** (Q), a **Key** (K), and a **Value** (V).

$$Q = MW^Q, \quad K = MW^K, \quad V = MW^V$$

The attention mechanism then computes the output as a weighted sum of the Value vectors, where the weights are determined by the similarity between Query and Key vectors.

$$\text{Attention}(Q, K, V) = \text{softmax}\left(\frac{QK^\top}{\sqrt{d_k}}\right)V$$

- The term $QK^\top$ computes the dot-product similarity between every query and every key.
- The scaling factor $\frac{1}{\sqrt{d_k}}$ (where d_k is the dimension of the key vectors) stabilizes the gradients.
- The **softmax** function converts these similarity scores into attention weights that sum to 1.
- The final matrix is the weighted sum of the Value vectors, allowing the model to focus on the most relevant items in the sequence.

This is typically extended to **multi-head attention**, where several attention "heads" are computed in parallel with different weight matrices, and their results are concatenated. This allows the model to learn different types of relationships simultaneously. The full Transformer block also includes a Position-wise Feed-Forward Network, residual connections, and layer normalization.

The Models: SASRec vs. BERT4Rec

The key difference between the two models lies in how they apply the self-attention mechanism and how they are trained.

SASRec (Unidirectional)

SASRec is an **autoregressive** model designed for next-item prediction. To predict the item at step $t+1$, it must only use information from items at steps $1, \ldots, t$. This is enforced by applying a **causal mask** to the attention scores before the softmax function. The mask sets the scores for all future positions to $-\infty$, effectively making their attention weights zero.

$$\text{Attention Scores}_{\text{masked}}(i, j) = \begin{cases} (QK^\top)_{ij} & \text{if } j \leq i \\ -\infty & \text{if } j > i \end{cases}$$

Prediction — The output vector from the final Transformer block at the last position, F_L, is used to predict the next item via a dense layer. The model is trained with a **categorical cross-entropy** loss on the true next item.

BERT4Rec (Bidirectional)

BERT4Rec is designed to learn a deep, bidirectional representation of the entire user sequence. It does not use a causal mask, allowing every item to attend to every other item (both past and future).

Training (Cloze Task) — Its training objective is inspired by BERT. A random fraction of items in the input sequence are replaced with a special `[mask]` token. The model is then trained to predict the original IDs of these masked items based on the surrounding unmasked items.

Prediction — For each masked position t, the output vector from the final Transformer block, F_t, is used to predict the original item i_t. The model is trained with a **categorical cross-entropy** loss over all masked items in the sequence. This forces the model to learn a rich, holistic understanding of the user's interests from their entire history.

2.6.4 With Contrastive Learning: CL4SRec

Key concept — CL4SRec is a framework that enhances sequential models by adding a **contrastive self-supervised learning** objective. In addition to the primary task of predicting the next item, the model is trained to recognize that two different *augmented* views of the same user sequence should have similar representations, while being distinct from the sequences of other users.

> **What is Contrastive Learning?**
>
> **Contrastive learning** is a technique where a model learns by comparing things. You teach it what makes two things similar and what makes them different. For sequential recommendation, you take a user's interaction history, create two slightly modified versions of it (e.g., by hiding or cropping a few items), and tell the model: "These two augmented sequences represent the same underlying preference, so their representations should be close. Push them away from the representations of all other sequences." This helps the model learn the essential, robust essence of a user's taste.

Key differentiator — Its key innovation lies in designing data augmentation strategies specifically for user interaction sequences (e.g., **Item Crop**, **Item Mask**). This self-supervised task acts as a powerful regularizer, forcing the model to learn more robust and generalizable user representations, which is especially helpful in sparse data scenarios.

Use cases — CL4SRec is used to enhance any underlying sequential recommendation model (like SASRec). It is particularly effective in scenarios with high data sparsity or noisy interactions, as the additional self-supervised signal helps the model learn meaningful user representations from limited data.

When to Consider — Consider integrating a contrastive learning framework like CL4SRec when your sequential model is underperforming due to data sparsity or overfitting. It can significantly boost performance by forcing the model to learn the core semantic properties of a user's preference sequence, often improving recall for long-tail items.

Seminal Paper:

- Xie, X., Sun, F., Liu, Z., Wu, J., Zhang, H., & Lin, X. (2020). *Contrastive Learning for Sequential Recommendation.* https://arxiv.org/abs/2010.14395.

Mathematical Foundations

CL4SRec is not a new model architecture, but rather a **multi-task training framework** that can be applied to any existing sequential recommendation model (the "backbone encoder"). It enhances the training process by adding a self-supervised contrastive learning objective alongside the primary next-item prediction task.

A Hybrid Training Framework

The framework operates on two parallel objectives:

(1) **Next-Item Prediction:** The standard supervised task where the model, given a sequence of items, tries to predict the very next item.

(2) **Contrastive Learning:** A self-supervised task where the model learns to identify different *augmented views* of the same sequence as being similar, while pushing them away from other sequences.

The final loss is a weighted sum of the losses from these two tasks.

Data Augmentation for Sequences

The foundation of the contrastive task is **data augmentation**. For each sequence S_i in a training mini-batch, two distinct but correlated views, S_i^a and S_i^b, are created using stochastic augmentation operators. Common operators for sequential data include:

- **Crop:** Randomly select a contiguous subsequence.
- **Mask:** Randomly set a fraction of the items in the sequence to a special `[mask]` token.
- **Reorder:** Randomly swap the positions of a few items within a small subsequence.

Let $f(\cdot)$ be the backbone sequential encoder (e.g., SASRec). The two augmented sequences are passed through this shared encoder to produce two vector representations:

$$h_i^a = f(S_i^a), \quad h_i^b = f(S_i^b)$$

The Contrastive Learning Objective (InfoNCE)

The goal of the contrastive loss is to pull the representations of the two augmented views from the same original sequence (h_i^a and h_i^b) closer together in the embedding space, while pushing them apart from the representations of all other sequences in the mini-batch.

Within a mini-batch of size N:

- (h_i^a, h_i^b) is considered a **positive pair**.
- (h_i^a, h_j^b) for all $j \neq i$ are considered **negative pairs**.

The loss function used is a form of **InfoNCE (Noise-Contrastive Estimation)**. For a given positive pair (h_i^a, h_i^b), the loss is formulated as:

$$\mathcal{L}_{CL}^{(i)} = -\log \frac{\exp(\text{sim}(h_i^a, h_i^b)/\tau)}{\sum_{j=1}^{N} \exp(\text{sim}(h_i^a, h_j^b)/\tau)}$$

- $\text{sim}(u, v)$ is a similarity function, typically the **cosine similarity**: $\frac{u^\top v}{|u||v|}$.
- τ is a **temperature** hyperparameter that scales the scores, controlling the sharpness of the softmax distribution. A smaller τ makes the penalty for misclassifying negative samples harsher.

The total contrastive loss for the batch is the average over all pairs.

The Combined Loss Function

The final training objective for the model is a linear combination of the standard next-item prediction loss ($\mathcal{L}_{\text{prediction}}$, e.g., categorical cross-entropy) and the contrastive loss ($\mathcal{L}_{CL}$):

$$\mathcal{L} = \mathcal{L}_{\text{prediction}} + \lambda \mathcal{L}_{CL}$$

where λ is a hyperparameter that balances the two tasks. By training on this combined objective, the model is forced to learn representations that are not only good for predicting the next item but are also robust to the perturbations introduced by the data augmentation, leading to better generalization.

Python Frameworks

- **GRU4Rec:**
  - **RecBole:** https://github.com/RUCAIBox/RecBole Provides a well-maintained implementation.
  - **Microsoft Recommenders:** https://github.com/recommenders-team/recommenders Includes a notebook demonstrating a GRU-based model for sequential recommendation.
  - The original authors maintain a **Theano** implementation https://github.com/pascanur/theano_optimize and strongly caution against using unverified third-party versions.
- **NextItNet** https://github.com/fajieyuan/WSDM2019-nextitnet:
  - **RecBole:** https://github.com/RUCAIBox/RecBole Includes a supported implementation.
  - **Microsoft Recommenders:** https://github.com/recommenders-team/recommenders Provides a notebook showcasing its application.
- **SASRec & BERT4Rec:**
  - **RecBole** https://github.com/RUCAIBox/RecBole & **SELFRec:** https://github.com/Coder-Yu/SELFRec Offer robust implementations of both models.
  - **Transformers4Rec (NVIDIA):** https://github.com/NVIDIA-Merlin/Transformers4Rec A powerful library designed to adapt HuggingFace Transformers for recommendation tasks, providing an excellent environment for experimenting with these models.
- **CL4SRec:**
  - **SELFRec:** https://github.com/Coder-Yu/SELFRec A Python framework specifically designed for self-supervised recommendation, featuring CL4SRec as one of its flagship implementations.

Production Ready?

- **GRU4Rec:** While often surpassed by Transformers on benchmarks, it remains a **powerful and relevant baseline**. Its recurrent nature can be more efficient during real-time inference for step-by-step predictions, making it a viable production choice.
- **NextItNet:** A **strong and efficient** model. Its parallelizable convolutional architecture makes it a competitive choice for production systems, especially for its ability to model long sequences effectively.
- **SASRec & BERT4Rec: State-of-the-art and Production-Ready.** These models represent the cutting edge for sequential recommendation. Their effectiveness has led to their increasing adoption in industrial production systems at major tech companies.
- **CL4SRec: Rapidly moving from Research to Production.** Contrastive learning has consistently demonstrated significant performance improvements on academic benchmarks. Its proven ability to enhance model robustness and alleviate data sparsity makes it highly attractive, and its principles are being rapidly integrated into the training pipelines of production models.

2.6.5 Generative Adversarial Networks (GANs): IRGAN

Key concept — IRGAN adapts the GAN framework to recommendation by setting up a competitive game between two neural networks:

(1) A **Generator**, which acts as the recommender. It tries to learn the true distribution of a user's preferences and generates "fake" (user, item) pairs that it predicts are relevant.

(2) A **Discriminator**, which acts as a critic. It is trained to distinguish between the "fake" items suggested by the Generator and the actual items from the user's real interaction history.

Through this adversarial training, the Generator is forced to produce increasingly realistic recommendations to "fool" the Discriminator, thereby learning a more robust model of user preferences.

Key differentiator — The **adversarial training process** itself is unique. It creates a dynamic optimization landscape where the Generator effectively performs "hard negative mining" by trying to find the most challenging examples to fool the Discriminator. This can help the model learn to recommend more diverse and novel items, overcoming biases in the training data.

Use cases — IRGAN is a general framework applicable to web search, item recommendation, and other information retrieval tasks. It's used to learn the distribution of user preferences and generate a ranked list of items, with the potential to improve coverage of long-tail items.

When to Consider — Consider exploring GANs for research-oriented projects or when traditional models seem to be underperforming due to data bias. While conceptually powerful, GAN-based recommenders are notoriously difficult and unstable to train, which has limited their widespread adoption in production.

Seminal Paper:

- Wang, J., Yu, L., Zhang, W., Gong, Y., Xu, Y., Wang, B., Zhang, P., & Zhang, D. (2017). *IRGAN: A Minimax Game for Unifying Generative and Discriminative Information Retrieval Models.* https://arxiv.org/abs/1705.10513.

Mathematical Foundations

Part A: The Core Idea - An Adversarial Game

The framework involves two players:

(1) **The Generator (G_ϕ):** This is our recommender model, parameterized by ϕ. Given a user u, its goal is to learn a policy $G_\phi(i|u)$ that generates a ranked list of items that the user is likely to find relevant. It tries to generate items that are so plausible they can "fool" the Discriminator.

(2) **The Discriminator (D_θ):** This is a binary classifier, parameterized by θ. Its job is to distinguish between real, relevant items for a user and the "fake" items proposed by the Generator. It outputs a probability $D_\theta(u, i)$ that item i is a truly relevant item for user u.

These two models are trained in opposition to one another. The Discriminator's improvement forces the Generator to produce better, more realistic recommendations, and the Generator's improvement provides more challenging "negative" examples for the Discriminator to learn from.

Part B: The Generator's Role and Objective

The Generator's goal is to learn the true underlying preference distribution of a user, $p_{\text{true}}(i|u)$. It is modeled as a stochastic policy that produces a probability distribution over all items for a given user.

- **Prediction:** The Generator's output, $G_\phi(i|u)$, can be modeled using any standard recommendation algorithm structure. For example, it can be based on the dot product of user and item embeddings (similar to **Matrix Factorization**), where the resulting scores are converted into a probability distribution using a softmax function:

$$G_\phi(i|u) = \frac{\exp(\text{score}(u, i))}{\sum_{j \in \mathcal{I}} \exp(\text{score}(u, j))}$$

Here, $\mathcal{I}$ is the entire item catalog.

- **Objective:** The Generator's objective is to maximize the probability that the Discriminator classifies its generated items as "real." In other words, it wants to maximize the reward it gets from the Discriminator. The Generator's objective function, $J_G(\phi)$, is to maximize the expected reward:

$$J_G(\phi) = \mathbb{E}_{i \sim G_\phi(\cdot|u)}[\log D_\theta(u, i)]$$

Maximizing this term is equivalent to training the Generator to produce items that the Discriminator believes have a high probability of being real.

Part C: The Discriminator's Role and Objective

The Discriminator is a binary classifier that learns to differentiate between positive (real) user-item pairs and negative (generated) pairs.

- **Prediction:** The Discriminator takes a user u and an item i as input (typically their embedding vectors) and outputs a single probability score, often using a sigmoid function:

$$D_\theta(u, i) = \sigma(f(u, i; \theta))$$

where f is a neural network (e.g., an MLP) that models the interaction.

- **Objective:** The Discriminator is trained using a standard **binary cross-entropy loss**. It aims to maximize the log-probability of correctly classifying both the real positive samples from the ground truth data and the fake negative samples from the Generator. The objective function to maximize is:

$$J_D(\theta) = \mathbb{E}_{i \sim p_{\text{true}}(\cdot|u)}[\log D_\theta(u, i)] + \mathbb{E}_{i \sim G_\phi(\cdot|u)}[\log(1 - D_\theta(u, i))]$$

The first term pushes $D_\theta(u, i)$ towards 1 for real items, and the second term pushes it towards 0 for generated items.

Part D: The Minimax Game and Unified Objective

The training process is a two-player game where the Generator and Discriminator optimize a single value function $V(G_\phi, D_\theta)$ from opposite sides. The Generator tries to minimize the value function, while the Discriminator tries to maximize it:

$$\min_\phi \max_\theta V(G_\phi, D_\theta) = \mathbb{E}_{i \sim p_{\text{true}}(\cdot|u)}[\log D_\theta(u, i)] + \mathbb{E}_{i \sim G_\phi(\cdot|u)}[\log(1 - D_\theta(u, i))]$$

Training proceeds in an alternating fashion:

(1) **Train the Discriminator:** For a fixed number of steps, we sample positive items from the real data and negative items from the current Generator. We then update the Discriminator's parameters θ by ascending the stochastic gradient of $J_D(\theta)$.

(2) **Train the Generator:** For a fixed number of steps, we keep the Discriminator fixed. We then update the Generator's parameters ϕ to produce items that are more likely to fool the Discriminator.

Part E: Practical Training with Policy Gradient (REINFORCE)

Because the process of selecting an item is a discrete action, we cannot directly backpropagate the gradient from the Discriminator's output through to the Generator's parameters. Instead, IRGAN uses a policy gradient method from reinforcement learning, specifically the **REINFORCE algorithm**.

In this view, the Generator is an "agent" that takes an "action" (selecting an item i) to receive a "reward." The reward for generating item i is simply the score given by the current Discriminator, $D_\theta(u,i)$. The gradient of the Generator's objective $J_G(\phi)$ is calculated as:

$$\nabla_\phi J_G(\phi) = \mathbb{E}_{i \sim G_\phi(\cdot|u)}[\nabla_\phi \log G_\phi(i|u) \cdot D_\theta(u,i)]$$

This formula allows us to update the Generator's parameters ϕ by:

(1) Sampling an item i from the Generator's current policy $G_\phi(i|u)$.

(2) Getting a reward for that item from the Discriminator, $D_\theta(u,i)$.

(3) Increasing the log-probability of sampling that item, scaled by the reward it received.

This process encourages the Generator to produce more of the kinds of items that the Discriminator finds convincing, driving the adversarial training loop.

2.6.6 Diffusion for CF: DiffRec

DiffRec adapts Denoising Diffusion Probabilistic Models (DDPMs), a powerful class of generative models from computer vision, to the task of collaborative filtering. The core concept is to learn the distribution of user preferences by systematically destroying a user's interaction profile with noise and then training a neural network to meticulously reverse that process. This is done in two stages: a fixed **forward (diffusion) process** and a learned **reverse (denoising) process**.

Key concept — DiffRec adapts the powerful Denoising Diffusion Probabilistic Models (DDPMs) from image generation to recommendation. The process has two stages:

(1) **Forward (Diffusion) Process:** It starts with a user's true interaction vector (e.g., a multi-hot vector of liked items) and gradually adds Gaussian noise over a series of steps, eventually corrupting it into pure noise.

(2) **Reverse (Denoising) Process:** A neural network is trained to reverse this process. It learns to take a noisy vector at any step and predict the noise that was added, thereby iteratively denoising it back to the original, clean interaction vector.

To generate recommendations, the model starts with random noise and, conditioned on a user's profile, runs this reverse process to generate a new, plausible interaction vector.

Key differentiator — The iterative **denoising process** is a fundamentally different generative paradigm from GANs or VAEs. It is often more stable to train than GANs and can model highly complex data distributions, leading to high-quality and diverse generated outputs. This makes it particularly well-suited for capturing the uncertainty and multi-modal nature of user preferences.

Use cases — DiffRec is a generative model for Top-N recommendation from implicit feedback. Its strength lies in its ability to model complex preference distributions and its robustness to noisy interactions in the training data.

When to Consider — Consider DiffRec when you need a powerful generative model that can capture complex user preferences and where recommendation **diversity and novelty** are key objectives. It represents the cutting edge of generative modeling, but be mindful that it is computationally intensive, especially during the iterative sampling process at inference time.

Seminal Paper:

- Wang, W., Feng, F., He, X., Wang, X., & Wang, Q. (2023). *Diffusion Recommender Model.* https://arxiv.org/abs/2304.04971.

Mathematical Foundations

Part A: The Forward (Diffusion) Process - Gradually Adding Noise

The forward process is a fixed procedure that does not involve any learning. It takes a user's true interaction history and progressively corrupts it by adding Gaussian noise over a series of T timesteps.

(1) **Initial State (x_0):** We start with a user's clean interaction vector, x_0. This is a multi-hot vector where the dimensions correspond to all items in the catalog. A value of 1 indicates the user has interacted with an item, and 0 otherwise.

(2) **Markov Chain:** The diffusion process is a Markov chain where the state at step t, denoted as x_t, is generated by adding a small amount of Gaussian noise to the state at the previous step, x_{t-1}. This is defined by a Gaussian transition kernel:

$$q(x_t|x_{t-1}) = \mathcal{N}(x_t; \sqrt{1-\beta_t}x_{t-1}, \beta_t I)$$

Here, β_t is a small, pre-defined constant from a variance schedule ($0 < \beta_1 < \ldots < \beta_T < 1$) that controls how much noise is added at each step. As t increases, the vector becomes progressively noisier.

(3) **Closed-Form Sampling:** A key property of this process is that we can sample the noisy vector x_t at any arbitrary timestep t directly from the original vector x_0, without having to iterate. This is done using the following formula:

$$x_t = \sqrt{\bar{\alpha}_t}x_0 + \sqrt{1-\bar{\alpha}_t}\epsilon$$

Where $\alpha_t = 1 - \beta_t$, $\bar{\alpha}_t = \prod_{s=1}^{t} \alpha_s$, and ϵ is a random noise vector sampled from a standard Gaussian distribution, $\epsilon \sim \mathcal{N}(0, I)$. As t approaches the final step T, the term $\bar{\alpha}_T$ approaches 0, and x_T becomes indistinguishable from pure Gaussian noise.

Part B: The Reverse (Denoising) Process - Learning to Remove Noise

The reverse process is where the model learns. The goal is to train a neural network that can undo the noising process, step by step, starting from pure noise and gradually denoising it back into a valid user interaction profile.

- **The Goal:** The model needs to learn the reverse transition probability, $p_\theta(x_{t-1}|x_t)$.
- **The Trick (Noise Prediction):** Directly modeling this probability is difficult. Instead, the model is reparameterized to predict the **noise** (ϵ) that was added to the data at step t. This simplifies the learning task and makes training more stable.
- **The Model (ϵ_θ):** We train a neural network, $\epsilon_\theta(x_t, t)$, which takes the noisy user vector x_t and the current timestep t as input and outputs a prediction of the noise that was added. The network architecture is typically a Multi-Layer Perceptron (MLP).

Part C: The Objective Function

The model is trained by minimizing the difference between the actual noise that was added during the forward process and the noise predicted by the neural network. The objective is a simple mean squared error between the true and predicted noise vectors.

The simplified loss function is:

$$\mathcal{L}(\theta) = \mathbb{E}_{t,x_0,\epsilon}\left[|\epsilon - \epsilon_\theta(\sqrt{\bar{\alpha}_t}x_0 + \sqrt{1-\bar{\alpha}_t}\epsilon, t)|^2\right]$$

The training process works as follows:

(1) Pick a random user's interaction vector x_0 from the training data.

(2) Pick a random timestep t from $\{1, \ldots, T\}$.

(3) Sample a random noise vector $\epsilon \sim \mathcal{N}(0, I)$.

(4) Create the noisy vector x_t using the closed-form sampling formula from Part A.

(5) Feed x_t and t into the network and train it to predict the original noise ϵ.

Part D: Generating Recommendations (Inference)

Once the denoising network ϵ_θ is trained, we can generate a new recommendation list for a user.

(1) **Start with Noise:** Begin with a vector of pure Gaussian noise, $x_T \sim \mathcal{N}(0, I)$.

(2) **Iterative Denoising:** Iteratively apply the reverse process for $t = T, T-1, \ldots, 1$. At each step, use the trained network $\epsilon_\theta(x_t, t)$ to predict the noise in the current vector x_t. Then, use this prediction to estimate the slightly less noisy vector from the previous step, x_{t-1}. The formula for one step of this reverse process is:

$$x_{t-1} = \frac{1}{\sqrt{\alpha_t}} \left(x_t - \frac{1 - \alpha_t}{\sqrt{1 - \bar{\alpha}_t}} \epsilon_\theta(x_t, t) \right) + \sigma_t z$$

where $z \sim \mathcal{N}(0, I)$ is newly sampled noise to maintain stochasticity in the generation process, and σ_t is a small constant.

(3) **Final Recommendation:** After T steps, the process yields a clean, generated vector x'_0. The items corresponding to the highest scores in this vector are then presented to the user as the Top-N recommendations.

2.6.7 GFlowNets: GFN4Rec

Key concept — GFN4Rec uses Generative Flow Networks (GFlowNets) to frame recommendation as a sequential decision problem. It learns to construct a *list* of recommended items step-by-step. The model is trained to ensure that the probability of generating a particular list is directly proportional to a predefined **reward** function (e.g., the predicted overall quality or utility of that list).

Key differentiator — Unlike most models that score items individually, GFN4Rec directly optimizes for the utility of an **entire slate of recommendations**. Its training objective inherently promotes **diversity**; if two different lists yield a similar high reward, the GFlowNet learns to assign both a high probability of being generated, rather than collapsing to a single "best" list.

Use cases — GFN4Rec is specifically designed for **listwise recommendation** tasks where both the relevance and diversity of the recommended set are important. It is well-suited for online environments where exploration and the discovery of novel good recommendations are valuable.

When to Consider — Consider GFN4Rec when the business objective is to optimize for the utility of an entire slate, not just individual item clicks. If recommendation diversity is a key performance indicator, GFN4Rec's intrinsic diversity-promoting objective makes it a very compelling choice over models trained with standard cross-entropy loss.

Seminal Paper:

- Liu, J., Jin, Z., Liu, D., He, X., & McAuley, J. (2023). *Generative Flow Network for Listwise Recommendation.* https://arxiv.org/abs/2306.02239.

Mathematical Foundations

GFN4Rec (Generative Flow Network for Recommendation) introduces a novel paradigm that frames recommendation not as a scoring or ranking problem for individual items, but as a sequential **object construction** task. The model learns a policy to build a complete list (or "slate") of recommendations item by item, with the goal of generating lists that are not only relevant but also diverse.

Part A: The Core Idea - Recommendation as a Sequential Construction Process

GFN4Rec models the generation of a recommendation slate as a path through a state space, where states are partial lists and actions involve adding an item to the list.

- **State (s):** A state represents a partial or complete list of recommended items. The process begins at an initial state s_0 (an empty list) and ends at a terminal state s_n (a complete list of n items).
- **Action (a):** An action is the selection of an item to append to the current list.
- **Trajectory (τ):** A trajectory is a complete sequence of states and actions that constructs a final recommendation slate, e.g., $\tau = (s_0 \xrightarrow{a_1} s_1 \xrightarrow{a_2} \dots \xrightarrow{a_n} s_n)$.
- **Reward ($R(\tau)$):** A non-negative reward function assigns a score to a complete trajectory, which is equivalent to scoring the final slate, $R(s_n)$. This reward is flexible and can be designed to capture not just item relevance but also list-level properties like diversity. The model's goal is to generate trajectories (lists) with high rewards.

Part B: The Generative Policy and Flow

The GFlowNet learns a **stochastic policy** to navigate the state space. The central idea is to learn a **flow function** $F(s)$ for each state s, which represents the "total flow" (or unnormalized probability) of all trajectories passing through that state.

The key objective is to train a forward policy $P_F(a|s)$ such that the probability of generating a complete slate s_n is directly proportional to its reward:

$$P(s_n) \propto R(s_n)$$

To achieve this, the model must satisfy a "flow matching" condition

Part C: The Training Objective - The Flow Matching Condition

The training of a GFlowNet is governed by a **detailed balance** or **flow matching** principle. This condition ensures that for any state s that is not the initial state, the total flow coming *into* it from all parent states must equal the total flow going *out of* it to all child states.

Let's define the two policies involved:

- **Forward Policy ($P_F(s'|s)$):** The probability of transitioning from state s to a subsequent state s' by adding an item. This is the policy used at inference time to generate recommendations.
- **Backward Policy ($P_B(s|s')$):** The probability of transitioning "backward" from state s' to a previous state s. This is primarily a theoretical construct used for training.

The flow matching condition for a transition $(s \to s')$ is:

$$F(s) \cdot P_F(s'|s) = F(s') \cdot P_B(s|s')$$

Intuitively, this means the amount of flow moving along a specific edge from s to s' must be consistent in both the forward and backward directions. For terminal states s_n, the flow is defined as the reward, $F(s_n) = R(s_n)$

Part D: The Loss Function (Trajectory Balance)

To enforce the flow matching principle, GFN4Rec can be trained with a **Trajectory Balance (TB)** loss. This loss function is calculated over a complete trajectory $\tau = (s_0, \ldots, s_n)$ and ensures that the total flow is consistent from start to finish.

The Trajectory Balance loss is:

$$\mathcal{L}(\tau) = \left(\log \frac{Z \cdot \prod_{t=0}^{n-1} P_F(s_{t+1}|s_t)}{\prod_{t=0}^{n-1} P_B(s_t|s_{t+1})} - \log R(s_n) \right)^2$$

Let's break down this formula:

- $\log R(s_n)$: This is the logarithm of the **target reward** for the generated list s_n. This is what we want the model's generation probability to match.
- $\prod_{t=0}^{n-1} P_F(s_{t+1}|s_t)$: This is the total forward probability of generating the specific trajectory τ.
- $\prod_{t=0}^{n-1} P_B(s_t|s_{t+1})$: This is the total backward probability of traversing the trajectory in reverse.
- Z: This is the partition function, representing the total flow starting from the initial state, $F(s_0)$.

The loss function trains the model to adjust its forward policy P_F such that the log-ratio of the forward and backward probabilities along any trajectory matches the log-reward of that trajectory's final slate. By minimizing this loss, the GFlowNet learns to generate high-reward slates with high probability and low-reward slates with low probability, directly optimizing for the quality of the entire recommendation list. This structure inherently encourages the model to explore and generate a diverse set of high-reward lists.

2.6.8 Normalizing Flows: IDNP

Key concept — Normalizing Flows are a class of generative models that learn a complex data distribution by applying a series of **invertible and differentiable transformations** to a simple base distribution (e.g., a standard Gaussian). Because every step is perfectly reversible, they can calculate the exact likelihood of any data point, a property not shared by VAEs or GANs.

Key differentiator — The ability to compute the **exact log-likelihood** makes Normalizing Flows a principled and powerful tool for precise density estimation. In the context of recommendation, a related model like **IDNP (Interest Dynamics Neural Process)** uses this concept to model a *distribution over a user's preference function over time*, allowing it to capture uncertainty and generalize from very few data points.

Use cases — In recommendation, Normalizing Flows can learn highly expressive models of user or item embedding distributions. They are particularly promising for few-shot or cold-start sequential recommendation tasks, where modeling the uncertainty in a user's evolving taste is critical.

When to Consider — Normalizing Flows are an advanced generative modeling technique. Consider them for research purposes or in applications where precise density estimation of user preferences is critical. They are generally more complex to implement and train than other generative models.

Seminal Papers:

- **Foundational:** Rezende, D. J., & Mohamed, S. (2015). *Variational Inference with Normalizing Flows.* https://arxiv.org/abs/1505.05770.
- **IDNP:** Du, W., Wang, H., Xu, C., & Zhang, Y. (2023). *Interest Dynamics Modeling with Neural Processes for Sequential Recommendation.* https://arxiv.org/abs/2209.15236.

Python Frameworks

- **IRGAN:** https://github.com/geek-ai/irgan The original implementation is at **geek-ai/irgan** on GitHub. Implementations are typically done from scratch in core deep learning libraries.
- **DiffRec:** https://github.com/YiyanXu/DiffRec Research implementations from the seminal papers are available on GitHub at **YiyanXu/DiffRec** and **WHUIR/DiffuRec**.
- **GFN4Rec:** https://github.com/CharlieMat/GFN4Rec The model whose implementations is primarily found in the authors' research repositories on GitHub.

Production Ready?

- **All Models in this Section: Research Interest.** This entire category represents the frontier of recommendation research.
- **GANs (IRGAN):** While conceptually powerful, they are notoriously difficult to train and stabilize, which has prevented widespread production adoption.
- **Diffusion (DiffRec):** This area is generating significant excitement and strong benchmark results. However, the models are computationally intensive, especially the iterative sampling process at inference time, making low-latency production deployment a major challenge.
- **GFlowNets & Normalizing Flows:** These are highly promising but complex paradigms that are still in the early stages of exploration for recommendation tasks.

Mathematical Foundations

Normalizing Flows are a class of exact-likelihood generative models that learn a complex data distribution by applying a series of **invertible** and **differentiable** transformations to a simple, known base distribution. Unlike VAEs, which learn an approximation, or GANs, which have no explicit likelihood, Normalizing Flows can compute the precise probability of any given data point, making them a principled tool for density estimation

Part A: The Core Idea - Learning a Distribution via Invertible Mappings

The fundamental concept is to learn a highly expressive function, f, that can transform a simple random variable z (with a known probability distribution, like a Gaussian) into a complex random variable x that follows the target data distribution (e.g., the distribution of user preference vectors).

The transformation must have two key properties:

(1) **Invertibility:** The function must be reversible. If we have a data point x, we must be able to compute the unique corresponding point in the simple base distribution, $z = f^{-1}(x)$.

(2) **Efficient Jacobian Determinant:** The determinant of the function's Jacobian matrix must be easy to compute. This is essential for calculating the exact change in probability density caused by the transformation.

Part B: The Mathematical Mechanism - Change of Variables Formula

The ability to compute the exact probability of a data point comes from the **change of variables formula** from probability theory.

Let's start with a simple random variable z from a base distribution with a known probability density function (PDF), $p_Z(z)$. A standard multivariate Gaussian is a common choice, $z \sim \mathcal{N}(0, I)$.

We define an invertible function f that maps from the base space to the data space, so $x = f(z)$. The inverse mapping is $z = f^{-1}(x) = g(x)$. The change of variables formula gives us the exact PDF of the transformed variable x:

$$p_X(x) = p_Z(g(x)) \left|\det\left(\frac{\partial g(x)}{\partial x}\right)\right|$$

- $p_Z(g(x))$: This is the probability density of the corresponding point z in the simple base distribution. Since we know the formula for p_Z (e.g., the Gaussian PDF), this is easy to calculate.
- $\left|\det\left(\frac{\partial g(x)}{\partial x}\right)\right|$: This is the absolute value of the determinant of the **Jacobian matrix** of the inverse function g. This term acts as a correction factor, accounting for how the transformation f stretches or compresses the volume of the space at point x. A major focus of Normalizing Flow research is designing powerful transformations where this determinant is computationally tractable.

Part C: Building Complex Transformations by Stacking

A single, simple transformation is often not expressive enough to model a complex data distribution. Normalizing Flows achieve high expressiveness by **composing** or **stacking** a series of K simpler invertible transformations: $f = f_K \circ \ldots \circ f_2 \circ f_1$.

The model is trained by maximizing the log-likelihood of the observed data. Using the change of variables formula, the log-likelihood of a data point x is:

$$\log p_X(x) = \log p_Z(z_0) - \sum_{k=1}^{K} \log \left| \det \left(\frac{\partial z_k}{\partial z_{k-1}} \right) \right|$$

Where z_0 is the point in the base distribution corresponding to x, and $z_k = f_k(z_{k-1})$ is the output of the k-th transformation. This objective is optimized directly using gradient ascent, which is typically more stable than the training procedures for GANs or VAEs.

Part D: Application in Recommendation (IDNP)

In the context of recommendation, a model like **IDNP (Interest Dynamics Neural Process)** leverages this framework to move beyond learning a single-point estimate for a user's preferences.

Instead of representing a user with a single latent vector (like in Matrix Factorization), a Normalizing Flow can model the user's preference as a **complex probability distribution** in the latent space. This allows the model to capture the **uncertainty** and multi-modal nature of a user's evolving tastes. For example, a user might have strong but distinct interests in both sci-fi films and historical documentaries. A Normalizing Flow can learn a distribution with multiple peaks corresponding to these different interests. This is especially powerful for **few-shot or cold-start sequential recommendation**, where accurately modeling the uncertainty about a new user's preferences from very limited data is critical for making robust predictions.

3 Context-Aware Recommendation Algorithms

While interaction-driven models focus on the user-item matrix, context-aware algorithms achieve higher performance by leveraging additional side features. These models are the workhorses of industrial systems, especially for predicting click-through rates (CTR), as they can incorporate rich information about users, items, and the context of the interaction.

3.1 Factorization Machine Family

Key concept — Factorization Machines (FMs) and their successors are designed to efficiently model feature interactions in high-dimensional sparse data.

- **FM & FFM (Field-aware Factorization Machine):** These classic models extend matrix factorization to work with any real-valued feature vector, making them highly effective for context-rich data.
- **DeepFM & xDeepFM:** These models combine the strengths of FMs for low-order interactions with deep neural networks for high-order interactions, becoming a standard for CTR prediction.
- **NFM & AFM (Neural/Attentional Factorization Machine):** These variants incorporate neural networks and attention mechanisms, respectively, to more powerfully learn the importance of different feature interactions.

3.1.1 Factorization Machines (FM)

Key concept — Factorization Machines (FMs) are a powerful class of models that can work with any real-valued feature vector, making them highly effective for sparse and high-dimensional data common in recommendation tasks. Unlike simpler models, FMs are designed to efficiently capture interactions between features by factorizing them into latent vectors. This allows the model to learn weights for feature combinations it has never even seen in the training data.

Key differentiator — The primary innovation of FMs is their ability to model all second-order (pairwise) feature interactions using factorized parameters. This elegantly solves the data sparsity problem that plagues polynomial regression models. For example, if a model has never seen the combination of a specific user and a specific item, it can still estimate their interaction strength by using the latent factors of the user and the item, which are learned from other interactions.

Use cases — FMs are a general-purpose supervised learning model, but they are particularly famous for their application in **rating prediction** and **Click-Through Rate (CTR) prediction**. They excel in scenarios with sparse categorical features, such as user IDs, item IDs, item categories, and contextual information.

When to Consider — An engineer should consider using a Factorization Machine as a very strong baseline for any context-aware recommendation task. It is more powerful than standard linear models because it captures feature interactions, and it often provides a great balance of performance and efficiency before moving to more complex deep learning architectures like DeepFM.

Seminal Paper:

- Rendle, S. (2010). *Factorization Machines.* https://www.csie.ntu.edu.tw/~b97053/paper/Rendle2010FM.pdf.

Mathematical Foundations

The power of Factorization Machines comes from their model equation, which efficiently incorporates pairwise feature interactions.

Part A: The Model Equation

For a given feature vector $x \in \mathbb{R}^n$ (where n is the number of features), a Factorization Machine of degree 2 estimates the target value $\hat{y}$ with the following formula:

$$\hat{y}(x) = w_0 + \sum_{i=1}^{n} w_i x_i + \sum_{i=1}^{n} \sum_{j=i+1}^{n} \langle v_i, v_j \rangle x_i x_j$$

Let's break down the components:

- w_0: The global bias, similar to an intercept in a linear model.
- $\sum_{i=1}^{n} w_i x_i$: This is the linear regression part of the model, which captures the individual weight of each feature.
- $\sum_{i=1}^{n} \sum_{j=i+1}^{n} \langle v_i, v_j \rangle x_i x_j$: This is the core innovation of FMs. It captures the second-order interactions between every pair of features.
  - x_i and x_j are the values of the i-th and j-th features.

- The interaction weight is not a single parameter but is factorized as the **dot product** of two latent vectors, $\langle v_i, v_j \rangle$.
- Each feature i is associated with a latent vector $v_i \in \mathbb{R}^k$, where k is the dimensionality of the latent space (a hyperparameter).

Part B: Solving the Sparsity Problem

In a standard polynomial regression, the interaction term would have its own independent weight, w_{ij}. In sparse data, most pairs of features (like a specific user and a rare item) never co-occur, so w_{ij} would never be learned.

Factorization Machines solve this by learning the latent vectors v_i and v_j from all the data where features i and j appear, even if they don't appear together. The interaction weight $\langle v_i, v_j \rangle$ can then be estimated even for unseen pairs, allowing the model to generalize to new interactions.

Part C: Efficient Computation

A naive computation of the pairwise interaction term has a complexity of $O(n^2)$. However, the formula can be mathematically reformulated to be computed in linear time, $O(nk)$:

$$\sum_{i=1}^{n} \sum_{j=i+1}^{n} \langle v_i, v_j \rangle x_i x_j = \frac{1}{2} \sum_{f=1}^{k} \left(\left(\sum_{i=1}^{n} v_{i,f} x_i \right)^2 - \sum_{i=1}^{n} v_{i,f}^2 x_i^2 \right)$$

This reformulation makes FMs highly efficient to train and use for prediction, even with millions of features. The model is typically trained using optimization methods like Stochastic Gradient Descent (SGD) to learn the parameters w_0, w_i, and v_i.

3.1.2 AMF (Attentional Factorization Machine)

Key concept — Attentional Factorization Machine (AFM) extends Factorization Machines by incorporating an attention mechanism to weigh the importance of different feature interactions. It learns a sparse, weighted combination of second-order feature interactions, improving both accuracy and interpretability.

Key differentiator — The attention mechanism allows AFM to focus on the most relevant feature interactions, reducing noise from less informative combinations and providing insights into which features drive predictions.

Use cases — Click-through rate (CTR) prediction in online advertising or e-commerce, where high-dimensional, sparse feature sets (e.g., user demographics, item categories) are common, and interpretability is valuable.

When to Consider — Use AFM when you need a context-aware model that balances performance and interpretability for CTR prediction tasks. It is a strong choice when feature interactions are complex but only a subset significantly impacts predictions.

Seminal Paper:

- Xiao, J., Ye, H., He, X., Zhang, H., Wu, F., & Chua, T. S. (2017). *Attentional Factorization Machines: Learning the Weight of Feature Interactions via Attention Networks.* https://arxiv.org/abs/1708.04617.

3.2 Cross-Network Models

Key concept — This family of models focuses on explicitly and automatically learning high-order feature interactions, which is a major challenge in feature-rich recommendation.

- **Wide & Deep:** A pioneering Google model that jointly trains a simple linear model (the "wide" part for memorization) and a deep neural network (the "deep" part for generalization).
- **DCN & DCNv2 (Deep & Cross Network):** This architecture introduces a novel cross-network that is more efficient than a standard MLP for learning explicit feature interactions at each layer.

3.2.1 Wide & Deep

Key concept — A pioneering hybrid architecture from Google that jointly trains two components in a single model: a "wide" linear part for memorization and a "deep" neural network for generalization. The wide component effectively learns the co-occurrence of items or features from historical data using cross-product feature transformations (e.g., "user installed app A" AND "user is shown app B"). The deep component uses dense embeddings to uncover new and less obvious feature combinations, improving the diversity of recommendations.

Key differentiator — Its primary innovation is the joint training of both the wide and deep components toward a single loss function. This is distinct from an ensemble, where models are trained independently. By training them together, the wide part only needs to learn the "exception rules" that the deep part might over-generalize, allowing the model to be both powerful and efficient. This unified approach allows the model to combine the benefits of memorization and generalization for recommender systems.

Use cases — Wide & Deep is a foundational architecture for large-scale industrial recommender systems, especially for Click-Through Rate (CTR) prediction with high-dimensional, sparse inputs. It was famously productionized and evaluated on the Google Play app store, which has over a billion active users.

When to Consider — An engineer should use the Wide & Deep architecture for any feature-rich recommendation task where it's important to balance the ability to learn from frequent, simple rules with the need to discover novel patterns. It's a powerful and scalable choice when you need to handle sparse categorical features and want a model that is both interpretable (the wide part) and capable of deep generalization (the deep part).

Seminal Paper:

- Cheng, H. T., Koc, L., Harmsen, J., et al. (2016). Wide & Deep Learning for Recommender Systems. https://arxiv.org/abs/1606.07792.

3.2.2 Mathematical & Engineering Foundations of Wide & Deep

The Wide & Deep framework is built on a simple yet powerful idea: combining the strengths of a simple linear model with a complex deep neural network. The mathematics define *how* these two parts work, while the engineering pipeline explains how it's implemented at a massive scale.

Mathematical Foundations

The model's final prediction is a combination of the outputs from its "wide" and "deep" components, which are trained jointly.

The Wide Component (Memorization)

The wide component is a **generalized linear model** of the form $y = w^T x + b$. Its purpose is to "memorize" the frequent co-occurrence of features in the historical data.

- **Key Feature: Cross-Product Transformation**. The model's real power for memorization comes from this transformation. It creates new features by combining existing sparse, binary features to capture specific interaction rules. For example, the feature `AND(user_installed_app=netflix, impression_app=pandora)` is 1 only if a user who installed Netflix is later shown Pandora. This explicitly teaches the model the correlation between a pair of features and the target label.

The formal definition is:

$$\phi_k(x) = \prod_{i=1}^{d} x_i^{c_{ki}}, \quad c_{ki} \in \{0, 1\}$$

where $\phi_k(x)$ is the k-th transformation, and c_{ki} is a boolean that is 1 if the i-th feature is part of that transformation.

The Deep Component (Generalization)

The deep component is a standard **feed-forward neural network**. Its goal is to generalize and discover new, previously unseen feature combinations that are predictive of the target.

- **Key Feature: Embeddings**. For sparse categorical features like `language=en`, the model first converts them into a low-dimensional, dense real-valued vector known as an **embedding vector**. These embedding vectors, typically of size O(10) to O(100), are initialized randomly and then trained to minimize the final loss, allowing the model to learn the semantic similarity between features.
- **Hidden Layers**. These dense embeddings are then concatenated and fed through several hidden layers. Each layer performs the computation:

$$a^{(l+1)} = f(W^{(l)}a^{(l)} + b^{(l)})$$

where $a^{(l)}$ is the activation of the l-th layer, $W^{(l)}$ and $b^{(l)}$ are the layer's weights and bias, and f is the activation function, typically **ReLU** (Rectified Linear Units).

Joint Training & Prediction

The wide and deep components are combined for the final prediction, and all model parameters are optimized simultaneously during training.

- **Prediction Formula**. For a logistic regression problem, the final prediction is the output of both components fed through a sigmoid function $\sigma(\cdot)$:

$$P(Y = 1|x) = \sigma(w_{wide}^T[x, \phi(x)] + w_{deep}^T a^{(l_f)} + b)$$

Here, w_{wide} represents the weights of the linear model (including the cross-product features $\phi(x)$), and w_{deep} are the weights applied to the final activations of the neural network $a^{(l_f)}$.

- **Optimization**. The model is trained by back-propagating gradients from the output to both the wide and deep parts simultaneously. In the original paper, the wide part was optimized using the **FTRL** algorithm with L_1 regularization, while the deep part used **AdaGrad**.

Engineering Pipeline

Implementing Wide & Deep in a massive production environment like Google Play required a robust three-stage pipeline.

1. Data Generation

In this stage, training data is prepared from user and app impression logs.

- **Label Creation**: Each example corresponds to one app impression. The label is set to 1 if the app was installed and 0 otherwise.
- **Vocabulary Generation**: Tables are created that map categorical feature strings to unique integer IDs. This is done for all features that appear more than a minimum number of times.
- **Feature Normalization**: Continuous real-valued features are normalized to a range of [0, 1] by mapping them to their quantile.

2. Model Training

This stage involves training the model on over 500 billion examples.

- **Warm-Starting**: To avoid the massive computational expense of retraining the model from scratch every time new data arrives, a **warm-starting** system is used. This system initializes a new model with the embeddings and linear model weights learned from the previous model's training run.

3. Model Serving

Once trained and verified, the model is loaded onto servers to make live predictions.

- **Retrieval and Ranking**: For each user request, a retrieval system first generates a short list of a few hundred candidate apps from the millions available. The Wide & Deep model then scores each of these candidates, and the apps are ranked and shown to the user based on this score.
- **Low-Latency Optimization**: To meet the strict serving latency requirement of around 10 milliseconds per request, the system was optimized for performance. Instead of scoring all candidate apps in a single large batch, the work is split into smaller batches that run in parallel using **multithreading**, which significantly reduced the client-side latency.

3.3 Tree-Based Models for CTR Prediction

While deep learning models excel at learning from dense embeddings, tree-based ensemble models, particularly gradient boosting implementations, remain a powerful and often preferred tool in industrial settings for CTR prediction on tabular data. They are highly efficient, require less feature engineering, and are often more robust out-of-the-box.

3.3.1 LightGBM (Light Gradient Boosting Machine)

Key concept — LightGBM is a high-performance gradient boosting framework that uses tree-based learning algorithms. For recommendation, it's primarily used as a powerful classifier to predict Click-Through Rate (CTR). It takes a wide array of user, item, and contextual features (e.g., user demographics, item category, time of day) as input and builds an ensemble of decision trees to predict the probability of a click. Each subsequent tree is trained to correct the errors of its predecessors, resulting in a highly accurate final model.

Key differentiator — Its primary differentiators are **performance and efficiency**. Unlike other gradient boosting methods that grow trees level-by-level, LightGBM grows trees leaf-by-leaf (**leaf-wise tree growth**). This allows it to converge much faster and often results in lower memory usage and higher accuracy. It also features native handling of categorical features, which is a significant advantage for typical recommendation datasets.

Use cases — LightGBM is a workhorse for large-scale CTR prediction in production systems across online advertising, e-commerce, and feed ranking. It excels at modeling complex, non-linear relationships in sparse, high-dimensional tabular data.

When to Consider — An engineer should consider LightGBM as a first-pass model or a very strong baseline for any feature-rich CTR prediction task. It is often faster to train and tune than deep learning counterparts and can achieve state-of-the-art performance, especially when extensive feature engineering for deep models is not feasible. It is also an excellent candidate for ensembling with deep learning models.

Hyperparameters

- **`n_estimators`**: The number of boosting trees to build. A higher number can lead to better accuracy but also increases the risk of overfitting and longer training times.
- **`learning_rate`**: This parameter, also known as shrinkage, determines the contribution of each tree to the final outcome. A lower learning rate requires a higher `n_estimators` but often leads to better generalization.
- **`num_leaves`**: The maximum number of leaves in one tree. This is the main parameter to control the complexity of the tree model. A higher value can lead to a more accurate model but also increases the risk of overfitting.
- **`max_depth`**: Limits the maximum depth of the tree. This is used to deal with overfitting.
- **`reg_alpha` (L1) & `reg_lambda` (L2)**: Regularization parameters to reduce overfitting by penalizing model complexity.

Production Ready?

- **Absolutely Production-Ready.** LightGBM is one of the most widely used and trusted machine learning libraries in the industry. It is known for its speed, efficiency, and predictive power, making it a go-to choice for production-level CTR prediction and ranking tasks at major tech companies.

Seminal Paper:

- Ke, G., Meng, Q., Finley, T., Wang, T., Chen, W., Ma, W., ... & Liu, T. Y. (2017). *LightGBM: A Highly Efficient Gradient Boosting Decision Tree.* https://papers.nips.cc/paper/2017/hash/6449f44a102fde848669bdd9eb6b76fa-Abstract.html.

Mathematical Foundations

LightGBM is an implementation of the Gradient Boosting Decision Tree (GBDT) algorithm. The core idea is to build an ensemble of weak learners (decision trees) in a sequential manner.

Part A: The GBDT Ensemble Model

The model makes a prediction by summing the outputs of a series of K decision trees. The prediction $\hat{y}_i$ for an input feature vector x_i is given by:

$$\hat{y}_i = \sum_{k=1}^{K} f_k(x_i)$$

where f_k is the k-th decision tree in the ensemble.

Part B: The Additive Training Process

The trees are trained in an additive fashion. Let $\hat{y}_i^{(t)}$ be the prediction for the i-th instance at the t-th iteration. The model is built sequentially:

$$\hat{y}_i^{(t)} = \hat{y}_i^{(t-1)} + f_t(x_i)$$

At each step t, the goal is to find a new tree f_t that best improves the model by minimizing a loss function $\mathcal{L}(y_i, \hat{y}_i)$. The objective function to minimize at step t is:

$$\text{Obj}^{(t)} = \sum_{i=1}^{n} \mathcal{L}(y_i, \hat{y}_i^{(t-1)} + f_t(x_i)) + \Omega(f_t)$$

where n is the number of training samples and $\Omega(f_t)$ is a regularization term that penalizes the complexity of the tree f_t.

Part C: Optimization with Gradient Descent

Instead of optimizing the function directly, which is difficult, GBDT uses a second-order Taylor approximation of the loss function. This allows us to reframe the objective in terms of the first and second-order gradients of the loss function:

Let $g_i = \frac{\partial \mathcal{L}(y_i, \hat{y}_i^{(t-1)})}{\partial \hat{y}_i^{(t-1)}}$ be the first-order gradient (the "residual" or error). Let $h_i = \frac{\partial^2 \mathcal{L}(y_i, \hat{y}_i^{(t-1)})}{(\partial \hat{y}_i^{(t-1)})^2}$ be the second-order gradient.

The objective function can be approximated as:

$$\text{Obj}^{(t)} \approx \sum_{i=1}^{n} [g_i f_t(x_i) + \frac{1}{2} h_i f_t^2(x_i)] + \Omega(f_t)$$

This simplified objective allows the model to find the optimal tree structure f_t by greedily adding splits that maximize the reduction in the loss function. For a given split, the optimal leaf value and the change in loss can be calculated directly from the sums of the gradients g_i and Hessians h_i of the instances in each leaf.

Part D: LightGBM's Innovations

LightGBM's efficiency stems from two main techniques for finding the best splits:

(1) **Gradient-based One-Side Sampling (GOSS):** Instead of using all data instances to calculate the information gain for a split, GOSS keeps all instances with large gradients (i.e., those that are undertrained) and randomly samples from instances with small gradients. This significantly reduces the data volume for computation without sacrificing much accuracy.

(2) **Exclusive Feature Bundling (EFB):** High-dimensional data is often very sparse. EFB bundles mutually exclusive features (i.e., features that rarely take non-zero values simultaneously) into a single feature. This reduces the number of features to consider, speeding up the training process.

Tutorial: LightGBM for CTR Prediction

The tutorial sections in this guide are entirely optional, though they can be extremely valuable for building intuition and a deeper understanding of the algorithms in practice. They assume, however, a basic familiarity with the libraries and frameworks being used. If you are interested in exploring why a particular method, function, or framework class is invoked at a specific point in the code, we encourage you to consult the Appendix, where we provide detailed, line-by-line commentary for selected algorithms from the Tutorial sections.

This tutorial provides a practical, step-by-step implementation of the LightGBM algorithm for Click-Through Rate (CTR) prediction. We will build a recommender that learns to predict the probability of a user clicking on an item, given a set of user, item, and context features.

Step 1. Prepare the Data

First, we need a dataset with user-item interactions and associated features. For this example, we will create a synthetic dataset using pandas and NumPy, where each row represents an impression (a user seeing an item) and includes:

- `user_id`: A unique identifier for the user.
- `item_id`: A unique identifier for the item.
- `user_feature`: A categorical feature for the user (e.g., age group).
- `item_feature`: A categorical feature for the item (e.g., category).
- `clicked`: The target variable (1 if the user clicked, 0 otherwise).

```
import pandas as pd
import numpy as np
import lightgbm as lgb
from sklearn.model_selection import train_test_split
from sklearn.preprocessing import LabelEncoder
from sklearn.metrics import roc_auc_score

# Create a synthetic dataset
np.random.seed(42)
num_samples = 10000
data = {
    'user_id': np.random.randint(1, 1001, num_samples),
    'item_id': np.random.randint(1, 501, num_samples),
    'user_feature': np.random.choice(['A', 'B', 'C'], num_samples),
    'item_feature': np.random.choice(['X', 'Y', 'Z'], num_samples),
}
df = pd.DataFrame(data)

# Simulate clicks based on feature interactions
df['clicked'] = (
```

```
    (df['user_feature'] == 'A') & (df['item_feature'] == 'X') |
    (df['user_feature'] == 'B') & (df['item_feature'] == 'Y') |
    np.random.rand(num_samples) < 0.2
).astype(int)

# Encode categorical features
for col in ['user_id', 'item_id', 'user_feature', 'item_feature']:
    le = LabelEncoder()
    df[col] = le.fit_transform(df[col])

# Split data into training and testing sets
X = df.drop('clicked', axis=1)
y = df['clicked']
X_train, X_test, y_train, y_test = train_test_split(X, y,
                                                    test_size=0.2,
                                                    random_state=42)
```

This code sets up our dataset for training and evaluation. The click simulation is designed to create non-trivial patterns for the model to learn.

Step 2. Define and Train the LightGBM Model

Next, we will define the LightGBM model. LightGBM has a specific data structure, `lgb.Dataset`, that is optimized for performance. We will convert our pandas DataFrames into this format and then train the model.

```
# Create LightGBM datasets
train_data = lgb.Dataset(X_train, label=y_train,
                         categorical_feature=['user_id', 'item_id',
                                              'user_feature',
                                              'item_feature'])
test_data = lgb.Dataset(X_test, label=y_test, reference=train_data)

# Define model parameters
params = {
    'objective': 'binary',
    'metric': 'auc',
    'boosting_type': 'gbdt',
    'num_leaves': 31,
    'learning_rate': 0.05,
    'feature_fraction': 0.9,
    'verbose': -1
```

```
}

# Train the model
model = lgb.train(
    params,
    train_data,
    num_boost_round=100,
    valid_sets=[test_data]
)
```

The categorical_feature parameter is crucial here, as it tells LightGBM to use its efficient built-in algorithms for handling categorical data, which is a key advantage over other gradient boosting libraries.

Step 3. Make Predictions and Evaluate

With the trained model, we can now predict the CTR for the test set and evaluate its performance using the Area Under the ROC Curve (AUC), a standard metric for binary classification tasks.

```
# Make predictions on the test set
y_pred = model.predict(X_test, num_iteration=model.best_iteration)

# Evaluate the model
auc = roc_auc_score(y_test, y_pred)
print(f"Test AUC: {auc:.4f}")
```

The output AUC score will show how well the model was able to distinguish between positive (click) and negative (no click) examples.

Step 4. Putting It All Together: Generating Recommendations

To use this model for recommendations, you would generate a list of candidate items for a user, create a feature matrix for these user-item pairs, and then use the trained model to predict the CTR for each. The items with the highest predicted CTR would then be recommended.

```
# Example: Generate recommendations for a user
user_id_example = X_test['user_id'].iloc[0]
user_feature_example = X_test['user_feature'].iloc[0]

# Create candidate items (e.g., all items the user hasn't seen)
candidate_items = np.unique(df['item_id'])
seen_items = df[df['user_id'] == user_id_example]['item_id'].unique()
unseen_items = np.setdiff1d(candidate_items, seen_items)
```

```
# Create a DataFrame for prediction
candidate_df = pd.DataFrame({
    'user_id': user_id_example,
    'item_id': unseen_items,
    'user_feature': user_feature_example
})

# Get item features for the candidate items
df_r=df[['item_id', 'item_feature']]
item_features_map = df_r.drop_duplicates().set_index('item_id')
candidate_df = candidate_df.join(item_features_map, on='item_id')

# Predict CTR for candidate items
candidate_df['predicted_ctr'] = model.predict(candidate_df,
                                num_iteration=model.best_iteration)

# Get top N recommendations
recommendations = candidate_df.sort_values('predicted_ctr', ascending=False).head(5)

print(f"\nTop recommendations for User {user_id_example}:")
print(recommendations[['item_id', 'predicted_ctr']])
```

This final step demonstrates the end-to-end workflow: from a trained CTR model to a ranked list of personalized recommendations for a specific user.

4 Text-Driven Recommendation Algorithms

This section shifts focus to algorithms that explicitly leverage unstructured text, primarily user reviews and item descriptions. The advent of powerful NLP models, especially Large Language Models, has dramatically expanded the capabilities in this domain.

4.1 Review-Based Models

These models mine user-generated reviews to extract rich, nuanced information about user preferences and item attributes. This helps to alleviate the data sparsity and cold-start problems inherent in interaction-only models. The use of text provides a powerful bridge, improving performance and offering a natural pathway to explainability.

Why read the reviews?

A 5-star rating tells you *what* a user liked, but the review tells you *why*. One user might give a phone 5 stars for its "amazing camera," while another gives the same rating for its "incredible battery life." Review-based models "read" this text to understand these nuances, allowing them to differentiate between users with the same ratings but different preferences, leading to far more personalized recommendations.

4.1.1 DeepCoNN (Deep Cooperative Neural Networks)

Key concept — DeepCoNN uses a dual deep learning architecture. One Convolutional Neural Network (CNN) processes the concatenation of all reviews written *by* a target user to learn a latent user representation. In parallel, a second CNN processes all reviews written *for* a target item to learn a latent item representation. These two vectors are then combined to predict the final rating.

Key differentiator — It was a foundational model demonstrating that user and item profiles could be learned *end-to-end directly from raw text.* Instead of manual feature engineering, it lets the neural networks discover what aspects of language are important for representing users and items.

Use cases — Rating prediction in review-rich environments like Amazon, Yelp, and other e-commerce or content platforms. It is particularly effective at alleviating the cold-start problem, as it can generate meaningful representations from text even when rating data is sparse.

When to Consider — Consider DeepCoNN when you need to leverage review text to improve rating prediction, especially for users or items with few ratings. It is a foundational model that serves as a strong baseline for more advanced text-based models.

Seminal Paper:

- Zheng, L., Noroozi, V., & Yu, P. (2017). *Joint Deep Modeling of Users and Items Using Reviews for Recommendation.* https://arxiv.org/abs/1701.04783.

4.1.2 NARRE (Neural Attentional Rating Regression with Review-level Explanations)

Key concept — NARRE enhances the idea of DeepCoNN by incorporating a dual **attention mechanism**. It learns to identify and assign higher weights to the most useful and informative reviews when constructing the user and item representations, effectively filtering out noisy or irrelevant content.

Key differentiator — The **attention mechanism** is the key innovation. It not only improves prediction accuracy by focusing on what's important but also provides a natural path to **explainability**. The model can highlight the specific reviews that were most influential in making a recommendation, which can significantly increase user trust.

Use cases — NARRE is designed for rating prediction in systems where user reviews are abundant (e-g., e-commerce, service platforms). Its ability to provide explanations makes it valuable for applications where user trust and transparency are important.

When to Consider — Use NARRE when you have a rich dataset of user reviews and want to improve rating prediction accuracy while also generating explanations. It is a powerful tool for building more transparent and trustworthy recommender systems.

Seminal Paper:

- Chen, C., Zhang, M., Liu, Y., & Ma, S. (2018). *Neural Attentional Rating Regression with Review-level Explanations.* https://dl.acm.org/doi/10.1145/3178876.3186070.

4.2 Large Language Model (LLM)-Based Paradigms

The emergence of Large Language Models (LLMs) has created a paradigm shift, reformulating recommendation as a language understanding and generation problem. LLMs can be applied in various ways, from acting as powerful feature extractors to serving as the core recommendation engine itself.

> **The Paradigm Shift: From Pattern Matching to Language Understanding**
>
> Traditional recommenders are expert **pattern matchers**, finding correlations in a huge matrix of clicks and purchases. LLM-based recommenders aim to be **comprehension engines**. They can understand the *semantic meaning* of an item description, infer intent from a user's natural language query, and leverage vast world knowledge (e.g., knowing that "cyberpunk" is a theme connecting *Blade Runner* and *Ghost in the Shell*) to make recommendations based on a deeper level of understanding.

4.2.1 Retrieval-based: Dense Retrieval & Cross-Encoders

Key concept — This paradigm adopts the two-stage "retrieve-then-rank" architecture common in modern information retrieval.

(1) **Dense Retrieval (Bi-Encoder):** A fast "retrieval" stage that uses one model to independently encode the user's query/profile into a vector and another to encode all items in the catalog. It then uses efficient Approximate Nearest Neighbor (ANN) search to find the top-K most similar items from a massive catalog (millions or billions).

(2) **Cross-Encoder:** A slower but more accurate "ranking" stage. It takes the user query and each of the top-K retrieved items *together* as a single input to a more powerful model (like BERT) to produce a highly precise relevance score for re-ranking.

Key differentiator — The **separation of concerns** between a scalable-but-less-precise retriever and a precise-but-less-scalable re-ranker. This hybrid approach allows systems to search over enormous item catalogs with very low latency while ensuring the final results shown to the user are highly accurate.

Use cases — This architecture is the standard for large-scale recommendation and search systems (e.g., Google Search, YouTube recommendations). It is used to retrieve relevant items from massive catalogs in real-time.

When to Consider — This is the go-to architecture for building scalable and high-performance recommender systems. When you need to serve recommendations from a large item corpus with low latency, a bi-encoder for initial retrieval followed by a cross-encoder for re-ranking is a state-of-the-art approach.

Seminal Papers:

- **Dense Retrieval (Foundational):** Karpukhin, V., Oguz, B., Min, S., et al. (2020). *Dense Passage Retrieval for Open-Domain Question Answering.* https://arxiv.org/abs/2004.04906.
- **Cross-Encoders (Foundational):** Nogueira, R., & Cho, K. (2019). *Passage Re-ranking with BERT.* https://arxiv.org/abs/1901.04085.

4.2.2 Generative / Instruction-Tuned

Key concept — This approach reframes recommendation as a text generation problem. An instruction-tuned LLM is given a prompt containing the user's history, profile, and a specific task (e.g., *"Given this user's past movie ratings, recommend 5 new sci-fi movies and explain why they would like each one."*). The LLM then generates the recommendations and explanations as a coherent, natural language response.

Key differentiator — Its **flexibility and zero-shot reasoning ability**. The LLM can leverage its vast pre-trained world knowledge to make novel connections and provide recommendations for queries or user types it has never seen before, complete with human-like justifications.

Use cases — Instruction-tuned LLMs are used for a wide range of tasks, including direct item recommendation, generating explanations, and user profiling. Their flexibility makes them suitable for creating more conversational and multi-task recommendation systems.

When to Consider — Consider this approach when you want to leverage the generative and reasoning power of LLMs. It is particularly promising for cold-start problems and for building systems that can perform multiple recommendation-related tasks within a unified framework.

Need GPU? Any system that uses a Large Language Model for generating or ranking recommendations will almost certainly require a GPU to have acceptable latency.

Seminal Paper:

- Geng, S., Liu, J.,, et al. (2022). *Recommendation as Language Processing (RLP): A Unified Pretrain, Tine-tune, and Prompt Paradigm.* https://arxiv.org/abs/2203.13366.

4.2.3 RAG & Feature Extraction

Key concept — This paradigm uses LLMs as a powerful *component* to enhance other recommender systems in two primary ways:

(1) **LLM as a Feature Enhancer:** Using an LLM as a sophisticated tool to process unstructured text (reviews, item descriptions) and extract high-quality semantic embeddings or structured features (e.g., "user cares about battery life") to feed into any downstream recommendation model.

(2) **Retrieval-Augmented Generation (RAG):** Grounding a generative LLM with real-time, factual information. Before generating a recommendation, the system retrieves relevant documents (e.g., up-to-date product specs, user's recent reviews) and adds them to the LLM's prompt as context.

Key differentiator — RAG's key function is to **mitigate hallucinations** and ensure the LLM's recommendations are factually accurate and based on current information from a trusted knowledge source. Using an LLM for feature extraction is a highly pragmatic way to inject powerful semantic understanding into any existing recommender pipeline.

Use cases — Use **RAG** for building reliable generative recommender systems where factual accuracy is critical (e.g., recommending technical products, academic papers). Use an **LLM as a feature enhancer** to boost the performance of an existing recommendation model by improving its input features.

When to Consider — Use RAG when building a generative recommender to mitigate the risk of the model making things up. Use an LLM as a feature extractor when you have rich textual data and want to create powerful semantic features to boost the performance of an existing model.

- **Seminal Paper (Foundational RAG):** Lewis, P., Perez, E., Piktus, A., et al. (2020). *Retrieval-Augmented Generation for Knowledge-Intensive NLP Tasks.* https://arxiv.org/abs/2005.11401.

4.2.4 LLM Agents & Tool Use

Key concept — This advanced paradigm treats the LLM as a "reasoning engine" or orchestrator that can use external **tools**. The LLM is given access to a set of functions or APIs (e.g., a search API, a database query, a traditional recommender model). For a complex user request, the LLM devises a multi-step plan and decides which tools to call, in what order, to fulfill the request.

Key differentiator — The ability to **autonomously plan, reason, and act**. Unlike other paradigms that perform a single, well-defined task, an LLM agent can decompose a complex goal (e.g., *"Find me a camera with the image quality of a DSLR but lighter than 500g"*) into a sequence of sub-tasks and tool calls.

Use cases — Building next-generation interactive assistants that can handle complex, multi-step goals, where recommendation is just one part of a larger, problem-solving process. The RecMind framework is a concrete example.

When to Consider — This is a frontier area of research and development. Consider building an LLM agent-based system when the user's needs are complex and cannot be met by a single retrieval or ranking call. This is for building sophisticated assistants that help users accomplish complex goals.

Seminal Paper (Example Framework):

- Wang, W., et al. (2024). *RecMind: Large Language Model Powered Agent For Recommendation.* https://arxiv.org/abs/2403.00366.

4.3 Conversational Recommender Systems

This area focuses on creating interactive, multi-turn recommendation experiences, moving beyond the static "recommend and consume" loop.

From Monologue to Dialogue

Traditional recommendation is a monologue: the system presents a list, and the user takes it or leaves it. A conversational recommender turns this into a **dialogue**. It's an interactive back-and-forth where the system can ask clarifying questions and the user can provide nuanced feedback, creating a collaborative process that feels more like talking to a human expert.

4.3.1 Dialogue-based Preference Elicitation

Key concept — This is the process of actively asking a user questions in a multi-turn conversation to learn ("elicit") their needs and preferences, especially when those preferences are unknown (cold-start) or ambiguous. The system maintains an evolving model of the user's preferences that it updates with each turn of the dialogue.

Key differentiator — It is an **interactive and guided** discovery process. Instead of expecting the user to know exactly what they want, the system acts like a helpful sales assistant or concierge, asking clarifying questions to progressively narrow down the options and pinpoint the user's true intent.

Use cases — Conversational recommenders are used in chatbots, voice assistants, and interactive e-commerce platforms where a guided discovery process is beneficial. They are ideal for complex domains with many attributes, like electronics, travel, or real estate.

When to Consider — Implement a dialogue-based system when you need to serve users with no prior history (cold-start) or when the user's intent is ambiguous and requires clarification. It is highly valuable in domains where users may not know exactly what they are looking for.

Key Survey Paper:

- Gao, C., Li, Y., et al. (2021). *A Survey on Conversational Recommender Systems.* https://arxiv.org/abs/2101.06462.

4.3.2 Natural Language Explanation & Critique

Key concept — This focuses on two-way communication *about* the recommendations themselves.

(1) **Explanation:** The system explains *why* an item was recommended in natural language (e.g., *"I'm suggesting this camera because you said you value long battery life."*).

(2) **Critique:** The user can provide feedback on a recommendation in natural language (e.g., *"That's a good start, but can you find something a bit lighter?"*), and the system uses this critique to refine its next suggestion.

Key differentiator — It creates a **collaborative feedback loop**. This empowers the user to iteratively steer the recommendation process, which builds trust and leads to a more satisfying outcome than a static, one-shot recommendation. It transforms the interaction from a simple transaction to a partnership.

Use cases — This is a key feature for advanced conversational agents and recommender systems aiming for a high-quality user experience where building user trust and providing a highly interactive, refined search process is important.

When to Consider — Implement natural language explanation and critique capabilities when the goal is to create a truly interactive and user-centric recommendation experience. If user trust is a key concern, these features are essential.

Key Survey Paper:

- Jannach, D., & Jugovac, M. (2019). *Explainable and Conversational Recommender Systems.* https://arxiv.org/abs/1902.01735.

5 Multimodal Recommendation Algorithms

This section explores models that fuse information from multiple modalities—typically text, images, and video—to build a richer, more comprehensive understanding of items and user preferences. This is particularly crucial in domains like e-commerce, social media, and streaming, where visual content is a primary driver of user choice.

5.1 Contrastive Learning for Multimodal Alignment

A foundational step for effective multimodal reasoning is creating a **shared embedding space** where different modalities of the same concept are mapped to nearby points. For example, the image of a cat and the text "a photo of a cat" should have very similar vector representations. Contrastive learning has emerged as the dominant paradigm for achieving this alignment by training models on massive datasets of paired multimodal data.

What is a Shared Embedding Space?

Think of it as a universal, multilingual dictionary for concepts. In this dictionary, the entry for "cat" is a specific point in a high-dimensional space. The power of a shared embedding space is that the picture of a cat (from the "image language") and the word "cat" (from the "text language") are both translated to that *exact same point*. This allows the model to understand that an image and a piece of text are talking about the same thing, enabling powerful cross-modal search and recommendation.

5.1.1 CLIP (Contrastive Language-Image Pre-Training)

Key concept — CLIP is a powerful model pre-trained on a massive dataset of (image, caption) pairs from the internet. It uses a contrastive objective to learn a shared embedding space where an image and its corresponding text description are mapped to nearby points. For example, a picture of a pair of sneakers and the text "casual shoes" will have very similar vector representations in CLIP's space.

Key differentiator — Its powerful **zero-shot transfer capability**. Because it's trained on such a vast and diverse dataset, a pre-trained CLIP model can understand and classify visual concepts it has never been explicitly fine-tuned on, simply by describing them in text. This makes it an incredibly versatile, out-of-the-box tool for semantic understanding.

Use cases — It's used to generate rich, semantic embeddings for items from their images. These embeddings can then be used for visual search ("find more dresses like this one"), content-based recommendation, and solving the cold-start item problem. It excels in domains where visual aesthetics are key (e.g., fashion, home decor, social media).

When to Consider — An engineer should consider using pre-trained CLIP embeddings whenever items have associated images. It is an extremely effective way to incorporate multimodal content information into any recommender system (from k-NN to DeepFM) with minimal effort and often significant performance gains.

Seminal Paper:

- Radford, A., Kim, J. W., Hallacy, C., Ramesh, A., et al. (2021). *Learning Transferable Visual Models From Natural Language Supervision.* https://arxiv.org/abs/2103.00020.

5.1.2 ALBEF (Align Before Fuse)

Key concept — ALBEF is a multimodal architecture that learns to align image and text representations. Its core principle is to first align the features from unimodal encoders (one for images, one for text) using a contrastive loss, and *then* fuse them using a more complex cross-modal encoder for downstream tasks.

Key differentiator — The **"Align-Before-Fuse"** strategy and its multi-task training objective, which includes image-text contrastive loss, masked language modeling (MLM), and image-text matching (ITM). The MLM and ITM losses, applied after the initial alignment, enable the model to learn much finer-grained interactions between visual regions and words.

Use cases — Like CLIP, ALBEF is used to generate powerful multimodal embeddings. Its strong performance on retrieval and visual question answering (VQA) tasks makes it particularly well-suited for building sophisticated multimodal recommender or search systems that require a deep understanding of the relationship between image and text.

When to Consider — Consider ALBEF or similar models when you need to train a state-of-the-art multimodal encoder from scratch for your specific domain and require top performance on complex multimodal reasoning tasks, rather than just using off-the-shelf embeddings.

Seminal Paper:

- Li, J., Li, D., Xiong, C., & Hoi, S. (2021). *Align before Fuse: Vision and Language Representation Learning with Momentum Distillation.* https://arxiv.org/abs/2107.07651.

5.2 Generative Multimodal Models

These models aim to learn the joint probability distribution of multimodal data, enabling them to generate new, personalized multimodal content or perform complex cross-modal inference.

From Analysis to Synthesis

The models above are primarily for **analysis**—they learn to understand and represent existing content. Generative multimodal models are for **synthesis**—they learn to *create* new content. Instead of just finding an existing product image you might like, a generative model could one day create a brand-new image of a product tailored to your unique style.

5.2.1 Multimodal VAEs

Key concept — Multimodal VAEs extend the Variational Autoencoder framework to handle multiple data types simultaneously (e.g., images and text). They learn a **joint latent probability distribution** that captures the shared underlying factors across different modalities for a given item.

Key differentiator — Their ability to model the joint distribution in a probabilistic way makes them excellent at handling **missing modalities**. If an item has an image but no description, the model can still infer a reasonable joint latent representation from the available data. Their generative nature also allows for cross-modal synthesis (e.g., generating a likely caption for a given image).

Use cases — Multimodal VAEs can be used in recommendation to learn a holistic representation of items from their text, images, and other attributes. This can improve collaborative filtering performance and enable novel applications like generating a textual description for a recommended product image.

When to Consider — Consider Multimodal VAEs when you need a generative model for items with multiple modalities, especially if your dataset has missing data that you need to handle gracefully.

Key Survey Paper:

- Suzuki, M. (2022). *A Survey on Multimodal Deep Learning: From a Recommender Systems Perspective.* https://www.tandfonline.com/doi/abs/10.1080/01691864.2022.2035253.

5.2.2 Multimodal Diffusion

Key concept — This paradigm applies the powerful denoising diffusion process to multimodal data. The model learns to reverse a process where noise is gradually added to data from multiple modalities (e.g., an image and its corresponding text) simultaneously. By learning to denoise them jointly, the model captures their joint distribution with high fidelity.

Key differentiator — Its ability to generate **exceptionally high-quality**, realistic multimodal content. While other generative models can sometimes produce blurry or incoherent outputs, diffusion models have set a new standard for quality in content generation.

Use cases — This is a cutting-edge area. Potential applications include enhancing multimodal recommendations by generating more robust representations or creating highly personalized content for users (e.g., generating a custom image and description for a recommended product *concept*). Frameworks like **CCDRec** use diffusion to guide the recommendation process.

When to Consider — Consider exploring multimodal diffusion models for applications requiring high-fidelity generative capabilities or for improving the robustness of multimodal representations. Given their computational cost, they are best suited for research-focused projects or large-scale industrial labs exploring the next generation of generative recommendation.

Key Survey Paper:

- Wei, T. R., & Fang, Y. (2024). *A Survey on Diffusion Models for Recommender Systems.* https://arxiv.org/abs/2401.10548.

Python Frameworks

- **Contrastive Models (CLIP/ALBEF):**
- **OpenAI CLIP:** The official repository is available at https://github.com/openai/CLIP.
- **OpenCLIP:** A popular, high-performance open-source implementation of CLIP is maintained at https://github.com/mlfoundations/open_clip.
- **Hugging Face Transformers:** Provides easy access to pre-trained CLIP and ALBEF models for integration into pipelines.
- **Generative Models (VAEs/Diffusion):**
- These are typically implemented using core deep learning libraries like **PyTorch** or **TensorFlow**.
- **Hugging Face Diffusers** is a state-of-the-art library for pre-trained diffusion models, which can be adapted for multimodal tasks.

Production Ready?

- **Contrastive Models (CLIP): Production-Ready as a Feature Extractor.** Using pre-trained CLIP embeddings to represent visual content is a powerful, common, and highly effective practice in industrial recommender systems. It is one of the best ways to solve the visual cold-start problem.

- **Generative Models (VAEs/Diffusion): Research Interest.** While generative AI is in production for content creation, its specific application for multimodal *recommendation* (beyond simple data augmentation) is still an emerging and computationally expensive field. The potential is enormous, but practical, low-latency deployment remains a significant challenge.

6 Knowledge-Aware Recommendation Algorithms

These algorithms enhance recommendations by incorporating data from external knowledge graphs (KGs), which provide structured information about items and their relationships (e.g., a movie is directed by a certain director, who also directed other movies).

6.1 Graph Neural Networks for CF: NGCF & LightGCN

This family of models represents a significant conceptual leap, reframing collaborative filtering by treating the entire user-item interaction matrix as a single, large **bipartite graph**. By applying Graph Neural Networks (GNNs), these models learn user and item embeddings by explicitly modeling the high-order connectivity between them. This approach moves beyond direct user-item interactions to capture signals like "users are similar because they interact with similar items, which in turn are liked by other similar users."

6.1.1 NGCF (Neural Graph Collaborative Filtering)

Key concept — NGCF was a pioneering model that applied a standard, powerful GNN architecture directly to the user-item interaction graph. It learns user and item embeddings by iteratively aggregating features from their neighbors. The core idea is that the features from a node's neighborhood can enrich its own representation, and by stacking multiple aggregation layers, the model can capture information from neighbors several "hops" away, thus modeling high-order relationships.

Key differentiator — Its main innovation was the direct application of a full-fledged GNN to collaborative filtering, complete with feature transformation matrices and non-linear activation functions in each layer. This was designed to model complex, high-order interaction patterns in the graph.

Use cases — Top-N recommendation from implicit feedback, especially in scenarios where capturing complex relational signals is believed to be important. It serves as a foundational GNN-based model for CF.

When to Consider — NGCF is best understood as the important conceptual predecessor to LightGCN. While it can achieve strong performance, its complexity makes it slower and harder to train. An engineer should primarily study it to understand the evolution of GNNs in recommendation before moving to its more efficient successor.

Seminal Paper:

- Wang, X., He, X., Wang, M., Feng, F., & Chua, T. S. (2019). *Neural Graph Collaborative Filtering.* https://arxiv.org/abs/1905.08108.

6.1.2 LightGCN (Light Graph Convolution Network)

Key concept — LightGCN is a radical simplification of NGCF. After extensive experiments, its authors found that the two most common components in a standard GNN—the feature transformation matrices and the non-linear activation functions—were not only unnecessary for collaborative filtering but were actually detrimental to its performance. LightGCN removes them entirely, leaving only the core GNN component: **neighborhood aggregation**. It learns user and item embeddings by simply taking the weighted sum of the embeddings of their neighbors from the previous layer.

Key differentiator — Its **extreme simplicity**. By removing all the "heavy" parts of the GNN, LightGCN becomes much more efficient, easier to train, and, most importantly, often achieves significantly better performance than its more complex predecessor. It proved that for CF, the key is to effectively model the graph structure, not to apply complex feature transformations.

Use cases — LightGCN has become a state-of-the-art model for Top-N recommendation from implicit feedback. It is a very strong and often difficult-to-beat baseline for pure collaborative filtering tasks.

When to Consider — An engineer should consider LightGCN as a default, high-performance model for any collaborative filtering task based on implicit feedback. Its combination of top-tier accuracy, simplicity, and efficiency makes it an excellent choice for both research and production environments.

Seminal Paper:

- He, X., Deng, K., Wang, X., Li, Y., Zhang, Y., & Wang, M. (2020). *LightGCN: Simplifying and Powering Graph Convolution Network for Recommendation.* https://arxiv.org/abs/2002.02126.

Mathematical Foundations

The core of both models is the **propagation rule**, which defines how embeddings are refined by aggregating information from graph neighbors.

(1) The User-Item Bipartite Graph

First, we represent the interaction data as a graph where users and items are nodes. An edge exists between user u and item i if an interaction has occurred. The initial embeddings for all users and items, $e_u^{(0)}$ and $e_i^{(0)}$, are stored in an embedding matrix $E^{(0)}$. These are randomly initialized and learned during training.

(2) The NGCF Propagation Layer

NGCF updates a node's embedding by aggregating messages from its neighbors. The embedding for user u at layer $k+1$ is computed as:

$$e_u^{(k+1)} = \sigma\left(W_1 e_u^{(k)} + \sum_{i \in N_u} \frac{1}{\sqrt{|N_u||N_i|}} \left(W_1 e_i^{(k)} + W_2(e_i^{(k)} \odot e_u^{(k)})\right)\right)$$

Let's break this down:

- N_u is the set of items that user u has interacted with (their neighbors).
- The summation $\sum_{i \in N_u}$ aggregates messages from all neighboring items.
- The term $W_1 e_i^{(k)}$ is a standard feature transformation of the neighbor's embedding.
- The term $W_2(e_i^{(k)} \odot e_u^{(k)})$ is a second feature transformation applied to the element-wise product of the neighbor's and the user's embeddings. This is designed to model more explicit interaction information.
- W_1 and W_2 are learnable weight matrices.
- σ is a non-linear activation function (e.g., LeakyReLU).
- The term $\frac{1}{\sqrt{|N_u||N_i|}}$ is a graph Laplacian norm that stabilizes the updates.

This is a complex rule with many learnable parameters, designed to capture intricate patterns.

(3) The LightGCN Propagation Layer

LightGCN's key insight was to remove the complexity. The propagation rule is simplified to a weighted sum of the embeddings from the previous layer:

$$e_u^{(k+1)} = \sum_{i \in N_u} \frac{1}{\sqrt{|N_u||N_i|}} e_i^{(k)}$$

Notice the differences: the weight matrices W_1 and W_2 are gone, the element-wise interaction term is gone, and the non-linear activation function σ is gone. The model only performs normalized neighborhood aggregation. A symmetric rule is used to update item embeddings.

(4) Final Representation and Prediction

After performing K layers of propagation, the final embedding for a user is not just the output of the last layer, but a combination of the embeddings from all layers. A common strategy is a weighted sum:

$$e_u = \sum_{k=0}^{K} \alpha_k e_u^{(k)}$$

where α_k are hyperparameters that weigh the importance of each layer (often set to $\frac{1}{K+1}$). The same is done for items. The final prediction score for a user-item pair is simply the dot product of their final embeddings:

$$\hat{y}_{ui} = e_u^\top e_i$$

The model is then trained using a pairwise loss function like BPR.

Production Ready?

- **Absolutely.** LightGCN, in particular, is a powerful, efficient, and widely adopted model. It often serves as a very strong baseline in industrial settings for collaborative filtering. While NGCF is less common in production due to its higher complexity and often lower performance, its principles are foundational.

Python Frameworks:

- **RecBole**: Provides high-quality, easy-to-use implementations of both NGCF and LightGCN.
- **PyTorch Geometric (PyG)** and **Deep Graph Library (DGL)**: These are general-purpose libraries for GNNs that can be used to build NGCF and LightGCN from scratch.

6.1.3 Self-Supervised Graph Learning for CF: SGL

Self-supervised Graph Learning (SGL) is not a new model architecture, but rather a powerful **training paradigm** that can be applied on top of any GNN-based recommender, such as LightGCN. Its core idea is to improve the quality of user and item embeddings by introducing an auxiliary self-supervised task, which forces the model to learn more robust and generalizable representations. This is especially effective at combating the data sparsity problem, where standard supervised signals (user-item interactions) are limited.

Key concept — SGL enhances a GNN recommender by training it on two tasks simultaneously. The first is the standard recommendation task (e.g., predicting interactions). The second is a self-supervised task based on **contrastive learning**. To achieve this, SGL first creates two alternate, slightly corrupted "views" of the user-item graph through data augmentation (e.g., by randomly dropping some interactions or users). It then trains the GNN to understand that the representation of a specific user (or item) should be very similar across these two different views, while being dissimilar to the representations of all other users in the same batch.

Key differentiator — The introduction of a **contrastive, self-supervised objective** to graph-based collaborative filtering is the key innovation. This objective acts as a powerful regularizer, forcing the model to learn the essential, intrinsic properties of users and items rather than just memorizing the graph's local structure. By learning to be invariant to small structural perturbations (the augmentations), the learned embeddings become more robust and generalize better, especially for users with very few interactions.

Use cases — SGL is used to improve the performance and robustness of any GNN-based model for Top-N recommendation from implicit feedback. It has shown particularly strong results in scenarios with high data sparsity, where it helps alleviate overfitting and improves recommendation quality for long-tail items.

When to Consider — An engineer should consider applying the SGL framework when an existing GNN-based model like LightGCN is underperforming due to sparse data or is showing signs of overfitting. It is an excellent way to boost model performance by improving the quality of the learned representations without changing the core model architecture.

Seminal Paper:

- Wang, X., Jin, H., He, X., Zhang, Y., & Chua, T. S. (2021). *Self-supervised Graph Learning for Recommendation.* https://arxiv.org/abs/2010.10783.

Mathematical Foundations

SGL is a multi-task learning framework that combines a primary supervised loss with an auxiliary self-supervised loss.

(1) The Multi-Task Framework

The final objective function is a weighted sum of two components:

$$\mathcal{L} = \mathcal{L}_{main} + \lambda \mathcal{L}_{SSL}$$

- $\mathcal{L}_{main}$: This is the primary supervised recommendation loss, typically the **BPR loss**, which optimizes for the ranking of items.
- $\mathcal{L}_{SSL}$: This is the auxiliary self-supervised loss, which is based on contrastive learning.
- λ: A hyperparameter that balances the importance of the two tasks.

(2) Graph Data Augmentation

The core of the self-supervised task is creating two correlated "views" of the user-item interaction graph, $G' = (U, I, E')$ and $G'' = (U, I, E'')$, from the original graph $G = (U, I, E)$. This is done using stochastic augmentation operators, such as:

(1) **Node Dropout:** Randomly remove a fraction of user and item nodes and all their associated edges.
(2) **Edge Dropout:** Randomly remove a fraction of the interaction edges E.

These two new graphs, G' and G'', represent slightly different perspectives on the same underlying user preference structure.

(3) The Contrastive Learning Objective (InfoNCE)

Next, the GNN encoder (e.g., LightGCN) is used to generate user and item embeddings based on both augmented graphs, yielding two sets of representations: Z' from G' and Z'' from G''.

The contrastive objective aims to pull the representations of the same node from the two different views together, while pushing them apart from the representations of other nodes. For a given user u, their embeddings from the two views, z'_u and z''_u, form a **positive pair**. For any other user $v \neq u$, the pair (z'_u, z''_v) is a **negative pair**.

The loss function for a single user u is the **InfoNCE loss**:

$$\mathcal{L}_{SSL}^{(u)} = -\log \frac{\exp(\text{sim}(z'_u, z''_u)/\tau)}{\sum_{v \in \mathcal{B}} \exp(\text{sim}(z'_u, z''_v)/\tau)}$$

Let's break this down:

- $\text{sim}(a, b)$ is the cosine similarity between two vectors.
- τ is a **temperature** hyperparameter that controls how sharply the model distinguishes between negative samples. A smaller τ makes the task harder for the model.
- The numerator encourages the similarity of the positive pair to be high.
- The denominator normalizes this score over the similarities of all possible pairs in the current batch $\mathcal{B}$ (one positive, many negatives).

The total self-supervised loss $\mathcal{L}_{SSL}$ is the sum of these individual losses for all users and items in the batch. By minimizing this loss, the model learns embeddings that are robust to the minor structural changes introduced by the augmentations.

Production Ready & Frameworks

Production Ready?

- **Yes**, the principles are production-ready. While deploying a multi-task framework requires more engineering than a standard model, the concept of using self-supervised and contrastive learning to regularize models and improve representation quality is a powerful and increasingly common technique in large-scale industrial systems.

Python Frameworks:

- **RecBole**: Provides a supported implementation of SGL.
- **SELFRec**: A Python library specifically dedicated to self-supervised recommendation models, featuring a high-quality implementation of SGL.

6.2 Embedding-based & Path-based Models

Key concept — Knowledge-aware models leverage the structure and semantics of KGs to enrich item representations and find new recommendation pathways.

- **Embedding-based (CKE, KTUP):** These methods jointly learn embeddings for entities and relations in the KG along with user and item embeddings from interaction data, creating a unified representation space.
- **Path-based (RippleNet):** This model propagates user preferences along paths in the KG, explicitly modeling how interests can spread from one item to another through shared attributes.
- **GNN-based (KGCN, KGAT, KGIN):** These state-of-the-art models apply Graph Neural Networks directly to the knowledge graph, allowing for more powerful and flexible aggregation of neighborhood information to enrich item embeddings.

Python Frameworks

- **TensorFlow** https://github.com/tensorflow/tensorflow: Provides flexible implementations for FM, FFM, DeepFM, and AFM through custom model building.

- **RecBole** https://github.com/RUCAIBox/RecBole: Includes implementations of DeepFM, xDeepFM, and AFM for context-aware recommendation tasks.
- **LibRecommender** https://github.com/massquantity/LibRecommender: Offers a TensorFlow-based implementation of AFM with support for attention mechanisms.

7 Specialized Recommendation Tasks

Beyond standard recommendation accuracy, several critical sub-fields focus on making recommender systems more robust, fair, and practical.

7.1 Debiasing & Fairness

Key concept — Standard recommendation algorithms can inadvertently learn and amplify biases present in historical data (e.g., popularity bias, where popular items get recommended even more). This area develops methods to mitigate these issues.

- **Debiasing (MF-IPS, CausE):** These methods use techniques like inverse propensity scoring (IPS) or causal inference to train models that are less susceptible to biases in the data.
- **Fairness (FairGo):** These algorithms aim to ensure that recommendations are equitable across different groups of users or item producers.

7.2 Cross-Domain Recommendation

Key concept — This task addresses the challenge of providing recommendations in a target domain with sparse data by leveraging knowledge from a source domain with richer data (e.g., using book ratings to improve movie recommendations). Models like **CMF** and **CoNet** learn to transfer user preferences across different domains.

7.3 Meta-Learning for Cold Start

Key concept — The "cold-start" problem—making recommendations for new users or items with no interaction history—is a major challenge. Meta-learning, or "learning to learn," offers a powerful solution.

- Models like **MeLU** and **MAMO** are trained on a variety of tasks in a way that allows them to quickly adapt and make reasonable predictions for a new user with just a few interactions.

Of course. Here is the Markdown content in a code block, detailing the new algorithmic paradigms with clear, understandable explanations for each concept.

8 New Algorithmic Paradigms in Recommender Systems

This document outlines emerging paradigms that extend beyond traditional recommendation algorithms, focusing on long-term value, causality, and transparency.

8.1 Reinforcement Learning (RL) for RecSys

8.1.1 Core Idea

Instead of predicting a static "rating" for an item, RL treats recommendations as a dynamic conversation. The system is an **agent** that takes **actions** (recommending items) in an **environment** (the user). The goal is to learn a **policy**—a strategy for recommending items—that maximizes a long-term **reward**, such as user engagement over an entire session or even their lifetime value.

- **Analogy:** Think of a YouTube algorithm. Its goal isn't just to make you click one video. It wants to recommend a sequence of videos that keeps you watching for as long as possible. It learns that after a science video, you might like another science video, but after three, you might prefer a comedy sketch. That's a learned policy.

8.1.2 Key Concepts & Algorithms

8.1.2.1 Multi-Armed Bandits (MAB) & Contextual Bandits

This is the classic **"explore vs. exploit"** problem.

- **Exploit:** Show the item that has historically performed the best (e.g., the news article with the highest click-through rate). This is a safe bet.
- **Explore:** Show a new or less popular item to gather data on how users react to it. This is risky but necessary for discovering new hits.

Contextual Bandits make this smarter by adding context to the decision. Instead of just knowing the global click-rate of an article, it considers the user's profile, device, and time of day to decide whether to explore or exploit. It answers the question: "What is the best article *for this specific user right now*?"

- **Best for:** News recommendations, advertising, and other domains where content value changes rapidly.

8.1.2.2 Deep Reinforcement Learning (e.g., DQN, Actor-Critic)

This is for optimizing **long-term, sequential interactions**. The system learns the value of recommending an item not just for the immediate click, but for how it sets up future successful recommendations. It models the user's "state" (e.g., what they've just watched or bought) and learns which recommendations will lead to a better future state.

- **Best for:** Video/music streaming services (YouTube, Spotify, Netflix), e-commerce session optimization.

8.2 Causal Inference in Recommender Systems

8.2.1 Core Idea

Causal inference moves beyond correlation to understand **causation**. The key question is not "Do users who see item X buy it?" but rather, "**Does *showing* item X *cause* users to buy it more than they would have otherwise?**"

- **Analogy:** Recommending the new iPhone to everyone will result in a very high conversion rate. But this is a misleading success metric. Most of those people were going to buy it anyway because it's a popular product. A causal approach aims to find users who are on the fence and recommend an item that will actually *persuade* them to buy, thereby generating true "uplift."

8.2.2 Key Concepts & Algorithms

8.2.2.1 Uplift Modeling

The goal is to model the **treatment effect**—the additional value generated by the recommendation. The model segments users into four groups:

1. **Sure Things:** Will buy the item whether it's recommended or not. (Don't waste the recommendation).
2. **Lost Causes:** Will not buy the item, no matter what. (Don't waste the recommendation).
3. **Persuadables:** Will only buy the item *if* it is recommended. (**These are the target users!**).
4. **Sleeping Dogs:** Will be *less* likely to buy if they see the recommendation (e.g., an annoying ad). (Avoid showing it to them).

By estimating the "uplift score" for a user-item pair, the system can prioritize recommendations that have the highest persuasive power, rather than just the highest predicted click probability.

Mathematical Foundations

(Placeholder for formalisms like Potential Outcomes framework (Rubin Causal Model), Propensity Score Matching, and specific uplift modeling techniques.)

8.3 Explainable AI (XAI) for RecSys

8.3.1 Core Idea

XAI focuses on answering the question "**Why was this recommended to me?**" The goal is to make the recommendation process transparent, trustworthy, and controllable for the user. Good explanations can increase user satisfaction and adoption of the system.

- **Analogy:** A helpful friend doesn't just say, "Watch this movie." They say, "You should watch this movie *because* you loved that other sci-fi film and this one is by the same director." This context makes the recommendation more powerful.

8.3.2 Key Concepts & Algorithms

8.3.2.1 Graph-Based Explanations

If the recommender system uses a Knowledge Graph (connecting users, items, genres, actors, etc.), it can generate intuitive explanations by finding the path in the graph that connects a user's past behavior to a recommended item.

- **Example Explanation:** "We recommend **The Mandalorian** because you liked **Star Wars**" (User → Liked → Star Wars → Part of → Star Wars Universe → Contains → The Mandalorian).

8.3.2.2 Feature-Based Explanations

These methods identify the most important user or item features that led to the recommendation.

- **Example Explanation:** "Recommended for you because you often listen to artists in the **Indie Pop** genre." or "Other users who bought **Running Shoes** also bought this."

9 Evaluating Recommender Systems

Evaluating the performance of a recommender system is a critical step in its development lifecycle. The choice of metrics depends heavily on the specific task the system is designed to solve. Broadly, these tasks fall into two categories:

1. **Rating Prediction**: For systems that use **explicit feedback** (e.g., 1-5 star ratings), the goal is to predict the exact rating a user would give to an item. The evaluation measures how close these predicted ratings are to the actual ratings. Models are assessed using error-based metrics like **RMSE** and **MAE**.

2. **Item Ranking**: For systems that use **implicit feedback** (e.g., clicks, views, purchases), predicting an exact score is less important than generating a high-quality, ordered list of items the user is likely to interact with. The evaluation measures the quality of this ranked list using metrics like **Precision@k**, **Recall@k**, and **nDCG**.

This chapter covers the most essential metrics for both tasks, as well as metrics that look beyond simple prediction accuracy.

9.1 Metrics for Rating Prediction

9.1.1 Root Mean Squared Error (RMSE)

RMSE is one of the most widely used metrics for evaluating rating prediction models. It measures the average magnitude of the error between predicted ratings and actual ratings. The "squared" term gives a disproportionately high weight to large errors, meaning that the model is more heavily penalized for being wildly wrong on a few predictions than for being slightly off on many.

How to compute

The RMSE is the square root of the average of the squared differences between the predicted rating ($\hat{r}_{ui}$) and the actual rating (r_{ui}) for all user-item pairs in the test set ($\mathcal{T}$).

$$\text{RMSE} = \sqrt{\frac{1}{|\mathcal{T}|} \sum_{(u,i) \in \mathcal{T}} (r_{ui} - \hat{r}_{ui})^2}$$

```
import numpy as np
from sklearn.metrics import mean_squared_error

# Example actual and predicted ratings
y_true = np.array([5, 4, 3, 5, 2])
y_pred = np.array([4.8, 3.5, 3.2, 4.0, 2.5])

# Using sklearn
rmse = np.sqrt(mean_squared_error(y_true, y_pred))
print(f"RMSE (sklearn): {rmse:.4f}")

# From scratch
rmse_scratch = np.sqrt(np.mean((y_true - y_pred)**2))
print(f"RMSE (scratch): {rmse_scratch:.4f}")

# Output:
# RMSE (sklearn): 0.6197
# RMSE (scratch): 0.6197
```

When to use

Use **RMSE** when you are working with an explicit feedback dataset and your primary goal is to predict ratings as accurately as possible. It became the standard metric during the Netflix Prize competition and remains a benchmark for rating prediction tasks.

However, be mindful of its sensitivity to outliers. If your business case considers a prediction of 1 star for a 5-star item to be significantly worse than two predictions of 4 stars for 5-star items, then RMSE is a suitable choice. If all errors are considered to have a similar business impact regardless of their magnitude, MAE might be more appropriate.

9.1.2 Mean Absolute Error (MAE)

MAE is another common metric for rating prediction tasks. Like RMSE, it measures the average error between predicted and actual ratings. However, by taking the absolute difference instead of the squared difference, MAE treats all errors equally in proportion to their magnitude. It is therefore less sensitive to large, outlier errors than RMSE.

How to compute

MAE is the average of the absolute differences between the predicted rating ($\hat{r}_{ui}$) and the actual rating (r_{ui}) for all user-item pairs in the test set ($\mathcal{T}$).

$$\text{MAE} = \frac{1}{|\mathcal{T}|} \sum_{(u,i)\in\mathcal{T}} |r_{ui} - \hat{r}_{ui}|$$

```
import numpy as np
from sklearn.metrics import mean_absolute_error

# Example actual and predicted ratings
y_true = np.array([5, 4, 3, 5, 2])
y_pred = np.array([4.8, 3.5, 3.2, 4.0, 2.5])

# Using sklearn
mae = mean_absolute_error(y_true, y_pred)
print(f"MAE (sklearn): {mae:.4f}")

# From scratch
mae_scratch = np.mean(np.abs(y_true - y_pred))
print(f"MAE (scratch): {mae_scratch:.4f}")

# Output:
# MAE (sklearn): 0.4800
# MAE (scratch): 0.4800
```

When to use

Use **MAE** for explicit feedback rating prediction tasks when you want a metric that is more robust to outliers and easily interpretable. MAE directly represents the "average error" in rating points. For example, an MAE of 0.5 means that, on average, the model's predictions are off by half a star.

If your dataset contains noisy or unusual ratings that might unfairly skew the evaluation, MAE can provide a more stable and representative measure of overall model performance compared to RMSE. It's often reported alongside RMSE to give a more complete picture of the model's error characteristics.

9.2 Metrics for Top-N Ranking

9.2.1 Precision@k and Recall@k

These are the most fundamental metrics for evaluating the quality of a ranked recommendation list. They are adapted from the field of information retrieval to assess how many relevant items are found within the top-k recommendations.

- **Precision@k**: Answers the question, "Out of the top-k items recommended, what fraction were actually relevant?" It measures the accuracy of the recommendations.
- **Recall@k**: Answers the question, "Out of all the relevant items that exist, what fraction did we recommend in the top-k?" It measures the coverage of the recommendations.

How to compute

Let R_u be the set of items recommended to a user u, and let T_u be the set of test items that are known to be relevant for that user (e.g., items the user interacted with in a hold-out set). For a list of size k:

$$\text{Precision@k} = \frac{|R_u(k) \cap T_u|}{k}$$

$$\text{Recall@k} = \frac{|R_u(k) \cap T_u|}{|T_u|}$$

```
import numpy as np

def precision_recall_at_k(recommended_items, relevant_items, k):
    # Ensure k is not larger than the number of recommended items
    rec_k = recommended_items[:k]

    # Calculate the number of relevant items in the top-k
    hits = len(set(rec_k) & set(relevant_items))

    # Calculate precision and recall
    precision = hits / k if k > 0 else 0
    recall = hits / len(relevant_items) if len(relevant_items) > 0 else 0

    return precision, recall

# Example for a single user
recommended = [101, 203, 105, 401, 502, 303]
```

```
relevant = [105, 303, 404, 501]
k_val = 5

p, r = precision_recall_at_k(recommended, relevant, k_val)
print(f"Precision@{k_val}: {p:.4f}")
print(f"Recall@{k_val}: {r:.4f}")

# Output:
# Precision@5: 0.4000
# Recall@5: 0.5000
```

When to use

Precision@k and **Recall@k** are essential for any Top-N recommendation task, especially with implicit feedback where ranking is the primary goal. **Precision@k** is particularly important when the user-facing interface has limited slots (e.g., a "Top 5 recommendations for you" widget). In this case, ensuring every recommended item is highly relevant is critical, as each irrelevant item wastes a valuable spot.

Recall@k, on the other hand, is important when the goal is to help users discover the full range of relevant items. For example, in an e-commerce search result, maximizing recall ensures that most of the items a user might want to buy appear on the first page. There is a natural trade-off between the two: recommending more items can increase recall but often decreases precision. They are typically reported together to provide a balanced view of performance.

9.2.2 Mean Average Precision (MAP@k)

Mean Average Precision (MAP@k) is a ranking metric that evaluates the quality of an ordered list by considering the precision at the position of each relevant item. It is more sensitive to the entire ordering of the top-k items than Precision@k alone. MAP is the mean of the Average Precision (AP) scores calculated for each user.

Average Precision (AP@k) for a single user rewards a model for placing relevant items higher up in the recommendation list. It's the average of precision values calculated at each point a relevant item is found.

How to compute

First, for a single user, we calculate Average Precision (AP).

$$\text{AP@k} = \frac{1}{|T_u|} \sum_{i=1}^{k} \text{Precision@i} \times \text{rel}(i)$$

where rel(i) is an indicator function that is 1 if the item at rank i is relevant, and 0 otherwise. The MAP is then the average of these AP scores across all users $\mathcal{U}$.

$$\text{MAP@k} = \frac{1}{|\mathcal{U}|} \sum_{u \in \mathcal{U}} \text{AP@k}_u$$

```
import numpy as np

def average_precision_at_k(recommended_items, relevant_items, k):
    rec_k = recommended_items[:k]
    score = 0.0
    num_hits = 0.0

    for i, p in enumerate(rec_k):
        if p in relevant_items:
            num_hits += 1.0
            precision_at_i = num_hits / (i + 1.0)
            score += precision_at_i

    if not relevant_items:
        return 0.0

    return score / len(relevant_items)

# Example for two users
# User 1: Good ranking
rec1 = [101, 102, 201, 103, 301]
rel1 = [101, 102, 103]

# User 2: Poor ranking
rec2 = [201, 301, 101, 102, 103]
rel2 = [101, 102, 103]

k_val = 5
ap1 = average_precision_at_k(rec1, rel1, k_val)
ap2 = average_precision_at_k(rec2, rel2, k_val)
map_score = np.mean([ap1, ap2])

print(f"AP@5 for User 1: {ap1:.4f}")
print(f"AP@5 for User 2: {ap2:.4f}")
print(f"MAP@5 for all users: {map_score:.4f}")
```

```
# Output:
# AP@5 for User 1: 0.9444
# AP@5 for User 2: 0.4556
# MAP@5 for all users: 0.7000
```

When to use

Use **MAP@k** when the order of the entire ranked list matters, not just the number of hits in the top-k. It is a very common metric in information retrieval and provides a single, stable figure that summarizes both precision and the ranking quality. Because it heavily penalizes models that place relevant items late in the list, it's an excellent choice for evaluating systems where users are expected to scan recommendations from top to bottom, such as search engine results or a primary recommendation feed.

Compared to Precision@k, MAP@k provides a more comprehensive assessment of ranking performance. Two models might have the same Precision@5, but the one that places its relevant items at positions 1 and 2 will have a much higher MAP@5 than one that places them at positions 4 and 5.

9.2.3 Normalized Discounted Cumulative Gain (nDCG@k)

Normalized Discounted Cumulative Gain (nDCG@k) is a sophisticated ranking metric that evaluates the quality of a recommendation list based on the graded relevance of the recommended items. It operates on two principles:

1. Highly relevant items are more useful than marginally relevant items.
2. Relevant items are more useful when they appear earlier in the list.

It achieves this by assigning a "gain" for each item based on its relevance and "discounting" that gain based on its position in the list. The final score is normalized by the best possible score, making it comparable across different users or queries.

How to compute

First, **Discounted Cumulative Gain (DCG@k)** is calculated:

$$\text{DCG@k} = \sum_{i=1}^{k} \frac{\text{rel}_i}{\log_2(i+1)}$$

where rel_i is the graded relevance score of the item at position i. To make this score comparable across users, it is normalized by the **Ideal DCG (IDCG@k)**, which is the DCG score of a perfectly ranked list.

$$\text{nDCG@k} = \frac{\text{DCG@k}}{\text{IDCG@k}}$$

```
import numpy as np
from sklearn.metrics import ndcg_score

# Example where relevance is graded (e.g., 0=irrelevant, 3=highly relevant)
# In implicit feedback, this is often binary (0 or 1)
true_relevance = np.asarray([[3, 2, 1, 0, 0]]) # Ideal ranking
predicted_scores = np.asarray([[.5, .2, .8, .1, .3]]) # Model's scores
# The predicted ranking based on scores is: [item 3, item 1, item 5, item 2, item 4]
# Relevance of that ranking is: [1, 3, 0, 2, 0]

# Using sklearn
ndcg = ndcg_score(true_relevance, predicted_scores, k=5)
print(f"nDCG@5 (sklearn): {ndcg:.4f}")

# From scratch
def dcg_at_k(relevance, k):
    relevance = np.asarray(relevance)[:k]
    return np.sum(relevance / np.log2(np.arange(2, relevance.size + 2)))

def ndcg_at_k(relevance, scores, k):
    best_ranking_relevance = sorted(relevance[0], reverse=True)
    current_ranking_indices = np.argsort(scores[0])[::-1]
    current_ranking_relevance = relevance[0][current_ranking_indices]

    actual_dcg = dcg_at_k(current_ranking_relevance, k)
    ideal_dcg = dcg_at_k(best_ranking_relevance, k)

    return actual_dcg / ideal_dcg if ideal_dcg > 0 else 0

ndcg_scratch = ndcg_at_k(true_relevance, predicted_scores, k=5)
print(f"nDCG@5 (scratch): {ndcg_scratch:.4f}")

# Output:
# nDCG@5 (sklearn): 0.6131
# nDCG@5 (scratch): 0.6131
```

When to use

nDCG@k is the gold standard for evaluating ranked lists, especially when you have access to graded relevance judgments (e.g., explicit ratings, or implicit signals that can be tiered, like "purchased", then "added to cart", and then "clicked"). Its logarithmic discount factor means it heavily rewards putting the most relevant items in the top few positions.

Even with binary relevance (relevant=1, not relevant=0), nDCG is a powerful metric that is more sensitive to rank than Precision or Recall. If the exact position of every relevant item matters, and especially if some items are "more" relevant than others, nDCG is the most appropriate and informative metric to use.

9.3 Beyond-Accuracy Metrics

While accuracy and relevance are crucial, a good recommender system must also provide a satisfying user experience. Metrics in this category evaluate other important aspects of recommendation quality, such as novelty, serendipity, and diversity.

9.3.1 Diversity

Diversity measures how different the items in a recommendation list are from one another. A system that only recommends highly similar items (e.g., only sequels to a movie the user just watched) may be accurate but can lead to a boring and monotonous user experience, trapping the user in a "filter bubble." Maximizing diversity aims to broaden the user's discovery of new content.

A common way to measure diversity is by calculating the average dissimilarity of all pairs of items in the recommendation list. This is often framed as **Intra-List Similarity (ILS)**, where diversity is simply $1 - ILS$.

How to compute

Given a recommendation list L for a user, the Intra-List Similarity is the average cosine similarity between the feature vectors of all item pairs in the list.

$$\text{ILS} = \frac{1}{|L|(|L|-1)} \sum_{i \in L} \sum_{j \in L, j \neq i} \text{similarity}(i, j)$$

Diversity can then be defined as $1 - ILS$.

```
import numpy as np
from sklearn.metrics.pairwise import cosine_similarity
import itertools
```

```
# Assume we have feature vectors for a catalog of items
item_features = {
    101: np.array([0.9, 0.1, 0.2]), # Action
    102: np.array([0.8, 0.2, 0.1]), # Action
    201: np.array([0.1, 0.9, 0.8]), # Comedy
    301: np.array([0.1, 0.2, 0.9]), # Drama
}

# Example recommendation list
recommended_ids = [101, 102, 201]

def calculate_ils(item_ids, feature_map):
    if len(item_ids) < 2:
        return 0.0 # Diversity is undefined for lists with less than 2 items

    # Get the feature vectors for the recommended items
    vectors = [feature_map[item_id] for item_id in item_ids]

    # Calculate pairwise cosine similarity
    # itertools.combinations gets all unique pairs
    total_similarity = 0.0
    num_pairs = 0
    for i, j in itertools.combinations(range(len(vectors)), 2):
        sim = cosine_similarity([vectors[i]], [vectors[j]])[0][0]
        total_similarity += sim
        num_pairs += 1

    return total_similarity / num_pairs if num_pairs > 0 else 0

# Low diversity list (mostly action)
list_a = [101, 102]
ils_a = calculate_ils(list_a, item_features)
diversity_a = 1 - ils_a

# High diversity list
list_b = [101, 201, 301]
ils_b = calculate_ils(list_b, item_features)
diversity_b = 1 - ils_b

print(f"List A ILS: {ils_a:.4f}, Diversity: {diversity_a:.4f}")
print(f"List B ILS: {ils_b:.4f}, Diversity: {diversity_b:.4f}")
```

```
# Output:
# List A ILS: 0.9574, Diversity: 0.0426
# List B ILS: 0.2452, Diversity: 0.7548
```

When to use

Use **Diversity** as a key balancing metric alongside accuracy metrics like nDCG or MAP. In many real-world systems, optimizing solely for relevance leads to predictable and uninteresting recommendations. By monitoring diversity, you can tune the recommendation algorithm (or add post-processing steps) to ensure a healthy mix of items.

This metric is particularly important in domains where discovery is a core part of the user experience, such as music streaming, movie recommendations, or e-commerce fashion. A slight decrease in short-term relevance metrics might be an acceptable trade-off for a significant increase in diversity, as this can lead to higher long-term user satisfaction and engagement.

9.4 Metrics for Classification Tasks in Recommendation

Many recommendation tasks, such as Click-Through Rate (CTR) prediction, are fundamentally binary classification problems: will the user interact (1) or not (0)? The following metrics provide a detailed view of a classifier's performance beyond a single accuracy score.

9.4.1 Confusion Matrix

The **Confusion Matrix** is the bedrock of classification evaluation. It is a table that visualizes the performance of an algorithm by breaking down its predictions into four categories. It allows you to see not just *how many* predictions were wrong, but *how* they were wrong.

The four outcomes are:

- **True Positives (TP):** The model correctly predicted the positive class. (e.g., predicted a click, and the user did click).
- **True Negatives (TN):** The model correctly predicted the negative class. (e.g., predicted no click, and the user did not click).
- **False Positives (FP):** The model incorrectly predicted the positive class (a "Type I error"). (e.g., predicted a click, but the user did not click).

- **False Negatives (FN):** The model incorrectly predicted the negative class (a "Type II error"). (e.g., predicted no click, but the user would have clicked).

How to compute

A confusion matrix is typically visualized as a 2x2 table, with the columns "Predicted: Negative" and "Predicted: Positive" and rows "Actual: Negative" and "Actual: Positive" and TNs/FNs in the cells.

```
import numpy as np
from sklearn.metrics import confusion_matrix
import seaborn as sns
import matplotlib.pyplot as plt

# Example ground truth and predictions for a CTR task
y_true = np.array([1, 0, 1, 1, 0, 1, 0, 0, 1, 0]) # 1=Clicked, 0=Not Clicked
y_pred = np.array([1, 1, 1, 0, 0, 1, 0, 0, 1, 0]) # Model's predictions

# Using sklearn
cm = confusion_matrix(y_true, y_pred)
print("Confusion Matrix:\n", cm)

tn, fp, fn, tp = cm.ravel()
print(f"\nTN: {tn}, FP: {fp}, FN: {fn}, TP: {tp}")

# Optional: Visualize the matrix
# sns.heatmap(cm, annot=True, fmt='d', cmap='Blues')
# plt.xlabel('Predicted')
# plt.ylabel('Actual')
# plt.show()
```

Output:

' Confusion Matrix: [[4 1] [1 4]]

TN: 4, FP: 1, FN: 1, TP: 4

When to use

Always use a confusion matrix when evaluating a classifier, especially when the classes are imbalanced (e.g., in CTR prediction, non-clicks vastly outnumber clicks). A simple accuracy score can be misleading. For instance, a model that always predicts "no click" might achieve 99% accuracy if the true click rate is 1%, but it would be a useless model. The confusion matrix exposes this by showing a high number of True Negatives but zero True Positives. It is the starting point for calculating more advanced metrics like Precision, Recall, F1-Score, and MCC.

9.4.2 Matthews Correlation Coefficient (MCC)

The **Matthews Correlation Coefficient (MCC)** is a highly regarded metric for binary classification because it produces a balanced score that takes into account all four values in the confusion matrix (TP, TN, FP, FN). It is particularly useful when the classes are of very different sizes. The score ranges from -1 to +1, where +1 indicates a perfect prediction, 0 represents a random prediction, and -1 indicates a total disagreement between prediction and observation.

How to compute

MCC is calculated directly from the values of the confusion matrix.

$$MCC = \frac{TP \times TN - FP \times FN}{\sqrt{(TP + FP)(TP + FN)(TN + FP)(TN + FN)}}$$

```
import numpy as np
from sklearn.metrics import matthews_corrcoef

# Example ground truth and predictions
y_true = np.array([1, 0, 1, 1, 0, 1, 0, 0, 1, 0])
y_pred = np.array([1, 1, 1, 0, 0, 1, 0, 0, 1, 0])

# Using sklearn
mcc = matthews_corrcoef(y_true, y_pred)
print(f"MCC Score: {mcc:.4f}")

# Output:
# MCC Score: 0.6000
```

When to use

Use **MCC** when you need a single, reliable score that summarizes the performance of a classifier, especially on imbalanced datasets. While the F1 score is also popular for imbalanced data, it ignores the number of True Negatives. MCC, by contrast, incorporates TNs, providing a more complete picture of the model's ability to classify both the positive and negative classes correctly.

If you have a CTR prediction task where correctly identifying non-clicks (TNs) is just as important as identifying clicks (TPs), MCC is an excellent choice. It is considered one of the most robust and informative single-number metrics for binary classification.

9.4.3 Log Loss (Binary Cross-Entropy)

Log Loss, or **Binary Cross-Entropy**, evaluates the performance of a classifier that outputs a probability value between 0 and 1. It measures how close the predicted probability is to the corresponding actual value (0 or 1). Unlike metrics that evaluate the final predicted class, Log Loss heavily penalizes predictions that are confident and wrong. A lower Log Loss value indicates a better-calibrated model.

How to compute

The formula for Log Loss on a single prediction is:

$$-(y\log(p) + (1-y)\log(1-p))$$

where y is the actual label (0 or 1) and p is the predicted probability. The final metric is the average over all N samples.

$$\text{LogLoss} = -\frac{1}{N}\sum_{i=1}^{N}(y_i\log(p_i) + (1-y_i)\log(1-p_i))$$

```
import numpy as np
from sklearn.metrics import log_loss

# Actual labels
y_true = np.array([1, 0, 1, 0])
# Predicted probabilities from the model
y_pred_proba = np.array([0.9, 0.2, 0.8, 0.4])

loss = log_loss(y_true, y_pred_proba)
print(f"Log Loss: {loss:.4f}")
```

```
# Example of a confident but wrong prediction
y_true_bad = np.array([1])
y_pred_bad = np.array([0.01]) # Model is 99% sure it's 0, but it's 1
bad_loss = log_loss(y_true_bad, y_pred_bad)
print(f"Log Loss for a confident, wrong prediction: {bad_loss:.4f}")

# Output:
# Log Loss: 0.2582
# Log Loss for a confident, wrong prediction: 4.6052
```

When to use

Use **Log Loss** when the raw probability scores from your model are important. In many recommendation scenarios, you don't just want a ranked list; you want a well-calibrated estimate of the probability of an event (like a click or purchase). This is crucial for downstream tasks like bidding in online advertising or calculating expected user value.

Log Loss is the standard loss function used to train most probabilistic binary classifiers (e.g., logistic regression, neural networks), and it serves as an excellent evaluation metric for the same reason. It provides a very sensitive measure of model performance that goes beyond simple class assignment and evaluates the model's confidence in its predictions.

9.4.4 ROC Curve and AUC Score

The **Receiver Operating Characteristic (ROC) Curve** is a graphical plot that illustrates the diagnostic ability of a binary classifier as its discrimination threshold is varied. It provides a comprehensive view of a model's performance across all possible thresholds.

The curve plots two parameters:

- **True Positive Rate (TPR)**, also known as Recall or Sensitivity, on the y-axis. This is the proportion of actual positives that are correctly identified.
- **False Positive Rate (FPR)** on the x-axis. This is the proportion of actual negatives that are incorrectly identified as positive.

The **Area Under the Curve (AUC)** summarizes the ROC curve into a single value. It represents the probability that the classifier will rank a randomly chosen positive instance higher than a randomly chosen negative one. An AUC of 1.0 represents a perfect classifier, while an AUC of 0.5 represents a model with no discriminative ability (equivalent to random guessing).

How to compute

The TPR and FPR are calculated from the confusion matrix values:

$$TPR = \frac{TP}{TP + FN}$$

$$FPR = \frac{FP}{FP + TN}$$

The ROC curve is created by plotting TPR vs. FPR at various threshold settings. The AUC is the integral of this curve.

```
import numpy as np
from sklearn.metrics import roc_curve, roc_auc_score
import matplotlib.pyplot as plt

# Actual labels
y_true = np.array([0, 0, 1, 1, 0, 1, 0, 1, 0, 1])
# Predicted probabilities from the model
y_pred_proba = np.array([0.1, 0.4, 0.35, 0.8, 0.2, 0.9, 0.3, 0.5, 0.05, 0.6])

# Calculate AUC
auc = roc_auc_score(y_true, y_pred_proba)
print(f"AUC Score: {auc:.4f}")

# Calculate values for the ROC curve
fpr, tpr, thresholds = roc_curve(y_true, y_pred_proba)

# Plot the ROC Curve
plt.figure(figsize=(8, 6))
plt.plot(fpr, tpr, color='darkorange', lw=2, label=f'ROC curve (area = {auc:.2f})')
plt.plot([0, 1], [0, 1], color='navy', lw=2, linestyle='--')
plt.xlim([0.0, 1.0])
plt.ylim([0.0, 1.05])
plt.xlabel('False Positive Rate (FPR)')
plt.ylabel('True Positive Rate (TPR)')
plt.title('Receiver Operating Characteristic (ROC) Curve')
plt.legend(loc="lower right")
plt.grid(True)
plt.show()
```

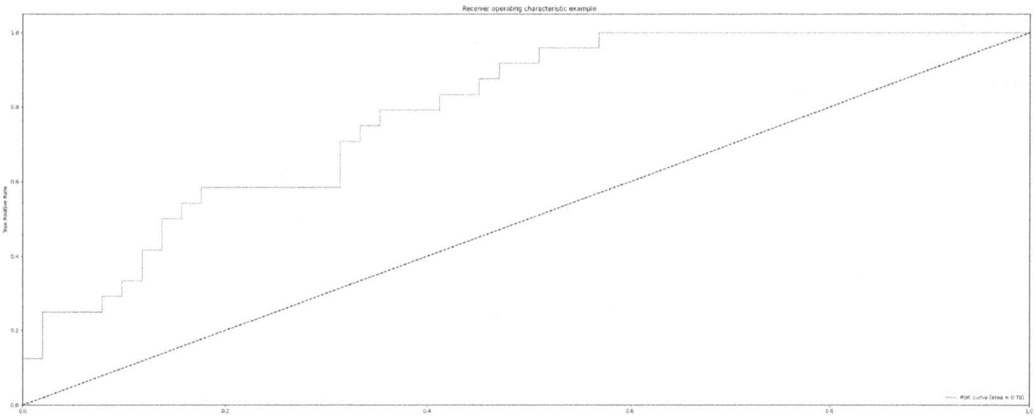

When to use

Use the **ROC curve and AUC score** whenever you are evaluating a probabilistic classifier, especially when the classes are imbalanced. Its key strength is that it is **threshold-invariant**. Metrics like accuracy, precision, and recall depend on a specific classification threshold (e.g., predict "click" if probability \¿ 0.5), but AUC evaluates the model's performance across *all* possible thresholds.

This makes AUC an excellent metric for measuring the intrinsic discriminative power of a model. It helps answer the question: "How good is this model at separating the positive and negative classes?" When comparing different models, the one with the higher AUC is generally considered better at distinguishing between classes, regardless of the final threshold you choose for deployment.

9.4.5 F-beta Score

The **F-beta score** is a generalization of the F1 score that allows you to adjust the balance between precision and recall. While the F1 score gives equal weight to both, the F-beta score introduces a parameter, β, that controls this balance.

- If $\beta < 1$, more weight is given to **precision**.
- If $\beta > 1$, more weight is given to **recall**.
- If $\beta = 1$, it is the standard F1 score.

A common variant is the **F2 score** ($\beta = 2$), which weighs recall twice as heavily as precision.

How to compute

The F-beta score is the weighted harmonic mean of precision and recall.

$$F_\beta = (1 + \beta^2) \cdot \frac{\text{precision} \times \text{recall}}{(\beta^2 \cdot \text{precision}) + \text{recall}}$$

```
import numpy as np
from sklearn.metrics import fbeta_score, precision_score, recall_score

# Example ground truth and predictions
y_true = np.array([1, 0, 1, 1, 0, 1, 0, 0, 1, 1]) # 6 positives, 4 negatives
y_pred = np.array([1, 1, 1, 0, 0, 1, 0, 0, 1, 0]) # 4 TPs, 1 FP, 2 FNs, 3 TNs

# Calculate precision and recall
p = precision_score(y_true, y_pred) # TP / (TP+FP) = 4 / 5 = 0.8
r = recall_score(y_true, y_pred)  # TP / (TP+FN) = 4 / 6 = 0.667

print(f"Precision: {p:.4f}")
print(f"Recall: {r:.4f}")

# F1 Score (beta=1): balances precision and recall
f1 = fbeta_score(y_true, y_pred, beta=1)
print(f"F1 Score (beta=1): {f1:.4f}")

# F2 Score (beta=2): emphasizes recall
f2 = fbeta_score(y_true, y_pred, beta=2)
print(f"F2 Score (beta=2): {f2:.4f}")

# F0.5 Score (beta=0.5): emphasizes precision
f0_5 = fbeta_score(y_true, y_pred, beta=0.5)
print(f"F0.5 Score (beta=0.5): {f0_5:.4f}")
```

Output:

```
Precision: 0.8000
Recall: 0.6667
F1 Score (beta=1): 0.7273
F2 Score (beta=2): 0.6897
F0.5 Score (beta=0.5): 0.7767
```

When to use

Use the **F-beta score** when the business cost of False Positives and False Negatives is unequal. You should choose the value of β based on your specific goal.

- **Use a high β (e.g., F2 score)** when False Negatives are more costly than False Positives. For example, in a medical diagnosis system for a serious disease, failing to identify a sick patient (a False Negative) is much worse than incorrectly flagging a healthy patient for more tests (a False Positive). Here, maximizing **recall** is paramount.
- **Use a low β (e.g., F0.5 score)** when False Positives are more costly than False Negatives. For example, in a system that sends out expensive promotional materials, you want to be very sure the recipient is interested before sending the item. An incorrect prediction (a False Positive) wastes money, so maximizing **precision** is the priority.

9.4.6 Cohen's Kappa

Cohen's Kappa is a statistic that measures how much better a classifier's performance is compared to the performance of a random classifier that makes predictions based on the frequency of each class. It accounts for the possibility of agreement occurring by chance, which makes it a more robust measure than simple accuracy, especially on imbalanced datasets.

The score ranges from -1 to +1. A score of 1 indicates perfect agreement, 0 indicates that the agreement is equivalent to random chance, and a negative score indicates that the agreement is worse than random chance.

How to compute

The formula for Cohen's Kappa is:

$$\kappa = \frac{p_o - p_e}{1 - p_e}$$

where p_o is the observed accuracy of the classifier, and p_e is the expected accuracy of a random classifier.

```
import numpy as np
from sklearn.metrics import cohen_kappa_score, accuracy_score

# Example on a slightly imbalanced dataset
y_true = np.array([1, 0, 0, 0, 0, 0, 0, 0, 1, 0]) # 2 positives, 8 negatives
y_pred = np.array([1, 0, 0, 1, 0, 0, 0, 0, 0, 0]) # 1 TP, 1 FP, 1 FN, 7 TNs
```

```
# Simple accuracy can be misleading here
accuracy = accuracy_score(y_true, y_pred)
print(f"Accuracy: {accuracy:.4f}")

# Cohen's Kappa gives a more nuanced score
kappa = cohen_kappa_score(y_true, y_pred)
print(f"Cohen's Kappa: {kappa:.4f}")

# Output:
# Accuracy: 0.8000
# Cohen's Kappa: 0.3529
```

When to use

Use **Cohen's Kappa** when you need to evaluate a classifier on an imbalanced dataset and want a metric that corrects for the probability of chance agreement. While a model might achieve 95% accuracy on a dataset where 95% of the samples belong to one class simply by always predicting that class, its Kappa score would be close to 0, correctly identifying that it has no real predictive power.

It is also the standard metric for measuring inter-rater reliability, where you want to know if two human judges are agreeing on classifications more than they would by chance. In machine learning, it serves a similar purpose: evaluating if the model's "judgments" (predictions) are significantly better than random guessing.

9.4.7 Brier Score

The **Brier Score** is a metric used to evaluate the accuracy and, more importantly, the **calibration** of a model that produces probabilistic predictions. It is the mean squared error between the predicted probabilities and the actual outcomes.

A model is well-calibrated if its predicted probabilities reflect the true underlying likelihood of the event. For example, for all the times the model predicts a 70% probability of a click, the actual click rate should be approximately 70%. The Brier score measures how well a model achieves this. A lower Brier score is better, with a perfect score being 0.

How to compute

The Brier score for a set of N predictions is:

$$\text{Brier Score} = \frac{1}{N}\sum_{i=1}^{N}(p_i - y_i)^2$$

where p_i is the predicted probability for the i-th instance, and y_i is the actual outcome (0 or 1).

```
import numpy as np
from sklearn.metrics import brier_score_loss

# Actual labels
y_true = np.array([1, 0, 1, 0, 1])
# Predicted probabilities from two different models
model_A_proba = np.array([0.9, 0.2, 0.8, 0.4, 0.6]) # Well-calibrated
model_B_proba = np.array([0.99, 0.01, 0.95, 0.1, 0.9]) # Overconfident

brier_A = brier_score_loss(y_true, model_A_proba)
brier_B = brier_score_loss(y_true, model_B_proba)

print(f"Brier Score (Model A): {brier_A:.4f}")
print(f"Brier Score (Model B): {brier_B:.4f}")

# Output:
# Brier Score (Model A): 0.1140
# Brier Score (Model B): 0.0351
# Note: In this specific case, the more confident model B gets a better score
# because its confident predictions
# happened to be more correct. If it was confidently wrong,
# its score would be much higher.
# Let's add an example of that:
y_true_bad = np.array([0])
y_pred_bad = np.array([0.99]) # Confidently predicts 1, but it's 0
bad_brier = brier_score_loss(y_true_bad, y_pred_bad)
print(f"Brier Score for a confident, wrong prediction: {bad_brier:.4f}")

# Output for the bad prediction:
# Brier Score for a confident, wrong prediction: 0.9801
```

When to use

Use the **Brier score** when the quality and calibration of your model's probability estimates are important. It is a good alternative to Log Loss and is widely used in fields like meteorology for evaluating weather forecasts.

While Log Loss heavily penalizes confident, incorrect predictions due to its logarithmic nature, the Brier score's penalty is quadratic, making it slightly less sensitive to single extreme errors. If your application requires reliable probability scores that can be trusted at face value (e.g., for financial risk modeling or calculating expected values), the Brier score is an excellent way to measure how well-calibrated your model's outputs are.

Conclusion

This survey has charted the expansive and rapidly evolving landscape of recommendation algorithms, organized through the lens of the primary data modalities they employ. The journey from simple neighborhood-based methods to complex, generative large language models reveals several overarching themes that define the field's progress and point toward its future.

First, a persistent and healthy tension exists between model complexity and practical performance. While the field's frontier is constantly pushed by more sophisticated architectures, foundational models like ItemKNN and simple matrix factorization remain remarkably robust baselines. The success of LightGCN, which achieved superior performance by simplifying its more complex predecessor, NGCF, underscores a critical lesson: for the specific task of collaborative filtering, targeted simplicity often trumps general-purpose complexity. For engineers, this highlights the non-negotiable importance of benchmarking against simple, well-understood models before investing in more intricate solutions.

Second, the evolution of the field can be seen as a continuous search for more effective optimization objectives and representation learning techniques. The shift from pointwise rating prediction (optimizing RMSE) to pairwise ranking (optimizing with BPR) was a pivotal moment, aligning the machine learning objective more closely with the user-facing task of creating a useful ranked list. More recently, the widespread adoption of self-supervised contrastive learning in both sequential (CL4SRec) and graph-based (SGL, SimGCL) models has proven to be a powerful technique for learning robust representations from sparse and noisy data, acting as a potent regularizer and helping to mitigate issues like popularity bias.

Third, the convergence of recommender systems with other domains of AI, particularly Natural Language Processing and Computer Vision, has been a primary engine of innovation. The adoption of RNNs, CNNs, and Transformers for sequential recommendation demonstrates a conceptual reframing of user behavior modeling as a language modeling task. Similarly, the use of multimodal models like CLIP, which learn from natural language supervision, shows that the foundation for rich, content-aware recommendation lies in creating well-aligned, shared embedding spaces across different data types.

Finally, the emergence of Large Language Models is not merely an incremental advance but a potential paradigm shift. LLMs are being explored in a multitude of roles: as powerful feature extractors, as zero-shot generative recommenders, as the reasoning engine in RAG-based systems, and as the core of autonomous, tool-using agents. This trajectory points toward a future where the lines between interaction-driven, text-driven, and multimodal recommendation blur. The ultimate recommender system may not be a single model but a sophisticated, conversational agent that can understand multimodal user queries, reason about complex needs, retrieve and synthesize information from diverse external sources, generate personalized and multimodal recommendations, and explain its reasoning in a transparent, interactive dialogue. Navigating this future will require a deep understanding of the foundational principles outlined in this survey—from collaborative filtering to context-aware, knowledge-infused, and fair-minded systems—coupled with a readiness to embrace the new generative and agentic paradigms that are beginning to redefine the field.

Appendix I. Content-Based Similarity with Feature Embeddings

Line-by-Line Explanation of Tutorial #1: Content-Based Similarity with Feature Embeddings

This appendix provides a detailed, line-by-line explanation of the code in Tutorial #1. The tutorial is divided into four steps, and we explain each step's code accordingly. We assume the reader may not be familiar with Python libraries like PyTorch, NumPy, or Pandas, so we describe what each component does. PyTorch is a machine learning framework for building and training neural networks; NumPy is for numerical computations with arrays; Pandas is for data manipulation, like reading and handling tabular data; and collections.defaultdict is a dictionary that provides default values for missing keys. Explanations are provided after each code snippet, grouped where lines are trivial and closely related (e.g., multiple consecutive print statements or simple assignments).

Step 1: Prepare Data from Movie Genres

This step loads movie data, extracts genres as features, builds a vocabulary, generates training pairs, and sets up a data loader for batching during training.

```
import torch
import torch.nn as nn
import torch.optim as optim
import numpy as np
import pandas as pd
from torch.utils.data import Dataset, DataLoader
from collections import defaultdict
```

- These lines import necessary libraries. `torch` is the core PyTorch module for tensors (multi-dimensional arrays) and computations. `torch.nn` provides neural network building blocks like layers. `torch.optim` offers optimizers for training (e.g., updating model weights). `numpy as np` is for efficient array operations. `pandas as pd` is for loading and manipulating structured data like CSV files. `Dataset` and `DataLoader` from `torch.utils.data` help create custom datasets and load data in batches for training. `defaultdict` from `collections` is a dictionary that defaults to a value (here, 0) for missing keys.

```
#  Data Loading and Preparation

movie_df = pd.read_csv(
    'ml-100k/u.item', sep='|', encoding='latin-1', header=None,
    names=['movie_id', 'title'] + list(range(22))
)
```

- This loads the MovieLens dataset file 'u.item' into a Pandas DataFrame (a table-like structure) called `movie_df`. `pd.read_csv` reads the CSV file with a pipe character as separator, 'latin-1' encoding, no header row, and assigns column names: 'movie_id', 'title', and dummy numbers for the remaining 22 columns (which include genres and other metadata).

```
# Extract genres for each movie
genre_cols = movie_df.columns[-19:]
```

- Identifies the last 19 columns as genre indicators (binary flags like 1 for present, 0 otherwise).

```
movie_genres = {}
```

- Creates an empty dictionary `movie_genres` to store lists of genres for each movie.

```
for index, row in movie_df.iterrows():
    genres = [
        genre_cols[i] for i, val in enumerate(row[genre_cols]) if val
    ]
    if genres: # Only include movies with at least one genre
        movie_genres[row['movie_id']] = genres
```

- Loops over each row using `iterrows()` (which yields index and row data). For each movie, collects genre column names where the value is truthy (non-zero) using a list comprehension with `enumerate` to get indices. Stores the list of genres in the dictionary keyed by movie_id, but only if there are genres.

```
#  Vocabulary and Pair Generation

all_genres = sorted(list(set(
    g for genres in movie_genres.values() for g in genres
```

```
)))
```

- Builds a sorted list of unique genres using a set for uniqueness and a generator expression to flatten the genre lists from all movies.

```
genre_to_idx = {genre: i for i, genre in enumerate(all_genres)}
```

- Creates a dictionary `genre_to_idx` mapping each genre to a unique integer index (0 to vocab_size-1) using `enumerate`.

```
vocab_size = len(all_genres)
```

- Sets `vocab_size` to the number of unique genres.

```
print(f"Found {len(movie_genres)} movies and {vocab_size} genres.")
```

- Prints the count of movies with genres and unique genres for logging.

```
# Generate positive pairs from co-occurring genres in the same movie
positive_pairs = []
```

- Initializes an empty list for positive pairs (tuples of co-occurring genre indices).

```
for genres in movie_genres.values():
    if len(genres) >= 2:
        indices = [genre_to_idx[g] for g in genres]
        for i in range(len(indices)):
            for j in range(len(indices)):
                if i != j:
                    positive_pairs.append((indices[i], indices[j]))
```

- Loops over each movie's genres (if at least 2). Converts genres to their indices using a list comprehension. Generates all pairwise combinations (excluding self-pairs) as tuples (center, context) using nested loops and appends to the list.

```
print(f"Generated {len(positive_pairs)} positive genre pairs.")
```

- Prints the number of generated pairs.

```
# Create negative sampling distribution from genre frequency
genre_freq = defaultdict(int)
```

- Uses `defaultdict(int)` to create a frequency counter for genres.

```
for genres in movie_genres.values():
    for g in genres: genre_freq[g] += 1
```

- Loops over all movies and their genres to count occurrences of each genre.

```
freq_list = [genre_freq[g] for g in all_genres]
```

- Creates a list of frequencies in the order of `all_genres` using a list comprehension.

```
prob = np.array(freq_list) ** 0.75
prob /= prob.sum()
```

- Converts frequencies to a NumPy array, raises to the 0.75 power (as per Word2Vec paper to downweight common items), and normalizes to sum to 1 for probabilities using division.

```
prob_tensor = torch.from_numpy(prob).float()
```

- Converts the NumPy array to a PyTorch tensor (float type) for efficient sampling later.

```
# Setup DataLoader for training
class GenrePairsDataset(Dataset):
```

- Begins defining a custom PyTorch Dataset class inheriting from `Dataset` to wrap the positive pairs.

```
    def __len__(self): return len(positive_pairs)
```

- Defines `__len__` method, which returns the total number of pairs in the dataset.

```
    def __getitem__(self, idx): return torch.tensor(positive_pairs[idx])
```

- Defines `__getitem__` method, which returns the pair at index `idx` as a PyTorch tensor (array).

```
dataloader = DataLoader(GenrePairsDataset(), batch_size=1024, shuffle=True)
```

- Creates a DataLoader instance from the dataset, with batch size 1024 (pairs per batch) and shuffling enabled for random training order.

Step 2: Define the SkipGramNS Model

This step defines the neural network model for Skip-gram with Negative Sampling.

```
class SkipGramNS(nn.Module):
```

- Begins defining the PyTorch model class inheriting from `nn.Module` (base class for all neural networks).

```
    def __init__(self, vocab_size, embed_dim):
        super().__init__()
        self.in_embed = nn.Embedding(vocab_size, embed_dim)
        self.out_embed = nn.Embedding(vocab_size, embed_dim)
        self.in_embed.weight.data.uniform_(-1, 1) # Init weights
        self.out_embed.weight.data.uniform_(-1, 1)
```

- Defines the constructor (`__init__`) taking vocabulary size and embedding dimension. Calls `super().__init__()` to initialize the base class. Creates two `nn.Embedding` layers: `in_embed` for center genres and `out_embed` for context genres (separate embeddings improve learning). Initializes their weights uniformly between -1 and 1 using `.uniform_()` on the weight data (tensors).

```
    def forward(self, centers, contexts, negatives):
```

- Defines the forward pass method, which computes the model's output (loss) given input tensors: `centers` (batch of center indices), `contexts` (matching context indices), and `negatives` (batch x k negative indices).

```
        v_c = self.in_embed(centers)
        v_o = self.out_embed(contexts)
        pos_dot = (v_c * v_o).sum(1)
        pos_loss = torch.log(torch.sigmoid(pos_dot))
```

- Looks up embeddings for centers (`v_c`) and contexts (`v_o`). Computes element-wise product and sums along dimension 1 to get dot products for positive pairs (`pos_dot`). Applies sigmoid activation (squashes to 0-1 range) and log to compute the positive pair loss component (`pos_loss`).

```
        v_neg = self.out_embed(negatives)
        v_c_unsq = v_c.unsqueeze(2)
        neg_dot = torch.bmm(v_neg, v_c_unsq).squeeze(2)
        neg_loss = torch.log(torch.sigmoid(-neg_dot)).sum(1)
```

- Looks up embeddings for negatives (`v_neg`). Unsqueezes `v_c` to add a dimension for batch matrix multiplication. Computes dot products between negatives and centers using `torch.bmm` (batch matrix multiply) and squeezes to remove extra dimension (`neg_dot`). Flips sign with `-`, applies sigmoid and log, and sums along dimension 1 for the negative loss component (`neg_loss`).

```
        loss = - (pos_loss + neg_loss).mean()
        return loss
```

- Computes the total loss as the negative mean of positive and negative losses (to maximize similarities for positives and minimize for negatives). Returns the scalar loss value.

Step 3: Train the Model to Learn Genre Embeddings

This step trains the model using the optimizer and data loader.

```
device = torch.device("cuda" if torch.cuda.is_available() else "cpu")
```

- Determines the computation device: GPU ("cuda") if available via `torch.cuda.is_available()`, otherwise CPU.

```
model = SkipGramNS(vocab_size, embed_dim=30).to(device)
```

- Instantiates the model with the vocabulary size and embedding dimension of 30, then moves it to the selected device using `.to(device)`.

```
optimizer = optim.Adam(model.parameters(), lr=0.01)
```

- Creates an Adam optimizer from `torch.optim`, which adapts learning rates during training. It operates on all model parameters (`model.parameters()`) with a learning rate of 0.01.

```
k, epochs = 5, 20
```

- Sets hyperparameters: `k=5` (number of negative samples per positive pair) and `epochs=20` (number of full passes through the data).

```
print("\nStarting training for genre embeddings...")
```

- Prints a message to indicate the start of training, with a newline for formatting.

```
for epoch in range(epochs):
    total_loss = 0
```

- Begins the outer loop over epochs. Initializes `total_loss` to 0 for accumulating loss per epoch.

```
    for batch in dataloader:
        centers, contexts = batch[:, 0].to(device), batch[:, 1].to(device)
```

- Inner loop over batches from the DataLoader. Splits each batch tensor along dimension 0 (columns) to get centers and contexts, then moves them to the device.

```
        # Draw k negative samples for each positive pair
        negs = torch.multinomial(prob_tensor, len(centers) * k, True)
        negs = negs.view(len(centers), k).to(device)
```

- Samples `k` negatives per positive using `torch.multinomial` (draws with replacement `True` from the probability tensor, total samples = batch_size * k). Reshapes the flat tensor to (batch_size, k) using `.view()`, then moves to device.

```
        loss = model(centers, contexts, negs)
```

- Passes the inputs to the model's forward method to compute the loss.

```
        optimizer.zero_grad()
        loss.backward()
        optimizer.step()
```

- Clears old gradients with `zero_grad()`. Computes new gradients via backpropagation with `backward()`. Updates model parameters using the optimizer's `step()` method.

```
        total_loss += loss.item()
```

- Accumulates the scalar loss value (`.item()` extracts it from the tensor) for the batch.

```
    print(f"Epoch {epoch+1}: Loss = {total_loss/len(dataloader):.4f}")
```

- After all batches in the epoch, prints the average loss (total divided by number of batches), formatted to 4 decimal places.

```
# Extract the learned genre embeddings for use in recommendation
genre_embeddings = model.in_embed.weight.data.cpu().numpy()
```

- Extracts the learned input embeddings as a NumPy array: accesses the weight tensor, moves to CPU with `.cpu()`, and converts to NumPy with `.numpy()`.

Step 4: Generate Content-Based Recommendations

This step uses learned embeddings to compute movie vectors and similarities.

```
# Create a vector for each movie by averaging its genre embeddings
movie_vectors = {}
```

- Creates an empty dictionary `movie_vectors` to store averaged embedding vectors for each movie.

```
for movie_id, genres in movie_genres.items():
    if genres:
        genre_indices = [genre_to_idx[g] for g in genres]
        movie_vectors[movie_id] = genre_embeddings[genre_indices].mean(0)
```

- Loops over each movie and its genres (if any). Converts genres to indices using a list comprehension. Averages the corresponding rows from `genre_embeddings` along axis 0 (`.mean(0)`) to get a single vector per movie and stores it.

```
# Convert to a matrix and list for efficient similarity calculation
movie_ids_list = list(movie_vectors.keys())
```

- Creates a list of movie IDs from the dictionary keys for indexing.

```
movie_matrix = np.array([movie_vectors[mid] for mid in movie_ids_list])
```

- Stacks the movie vectors into a NumPy array (rows are movies, columns are embedding dimensions) using a list comprehension.

```
def get_similar_movies(target_title, top_n=5):
```

- Defines a function to find and print the top top_n (default 5) similar movies to a given title.

```
    target_row = movie_df[movie_df['title'] == target_title]
    if target_row.empty:
        print(f"Movie '{target_title}' not found.")
        return
```

- Queries the DataFrame for rows matching the target title using boolean indexing. If no match (empty), prints an error and returns early.

```
    target_id = target_row['movie_id'].iloc[0]
    target_idx = movie_ids_list.index(target_id)
    target_vec = movie_matrix[target_idx]
```

- Extracts the movie_id from the first (and only) matching row using .iloc[0]. Finds its index in movie_ids_list with .index(). Retrieves the corresponding vector from movie_matrix.

```
    # Calculate cosine similarity between the target and all others
    sims = (movie_matrix @ target_vec) / (
        np.linalg.norm(movie_matrix, axis=1) * np.linalg.norm(target_vec)
    )
```

- Computes cosine similarities for all movies: dot products (@ matrix-vector multiply) normalized by the Euclidean norms of movie vectors (.linalg.norm with axis=1 for row-wise norms) and the target vector's norm. The result sims is an array of similarity scores.

```
    # Get top N indices, excluding the first one (the item itself)
    sim_indices = np.argsort(sims)[::-1][1:top_n+1]
```

- Sorts indices by similarity scores in descending order (np.argsort(sims)[::-1] reverses ascending sort). Slices from index 1 (skips self) to top_n+1 for the top N indices.

```
print(f"\nMovies similar to '{target_title}':")
```

- Prints a header with the target title, including a newline for formatting.

```
for idx in sim_indices:
    sim_id = movie_ids_list[idx]
    sim_title = movie_df[movie_df['movie_id']==sim_id]['title'].iloc[0]
    score = sims[idx]
    print(f"- {sim_title}: Sim = {score:.4f}")
```

- Loops over the top indices. Gets the similar movie ID from the list. Queries the DataFrame for the title using boolean indexing and extracts it with `.iloc[0]`. Gets the similarity score. Prints the title and score formatted to 4 decimal places.

```
get_similar_movies('Toy Story (1995)', top_n=5)
get_similar_movies('Star Wars (1977)', top_n=5)
```

- Calls the function twice: once for "Toy Story (1995)" and once for "Star Wars (1977)", each requesting the top 5 similar movies.

ItemKNN Implementation

Line-by-Line Explanation of the `fit` Method for ItemKNN

```
def fit(self, R):
    self.train_data_ = R
    num_items = R.shape[1]
    self.similarity_matrix_ = np.zeros((num_items, num_items))

    # Part A: Adjusted Cosine Similarity
    # Calculate the mean rating for each user
    # who has rated at least one item
    self.user_means_ = np.true_divide(R.sum(axis=1), (R!=0).sum(axis=1))
    # Replace NaN (from users with no ratings) with 0
    self.user_means_[np.isnan(self.user_means_)] = 0

    # Center the ratings by subtracting the user's mean
    R_centered = R - np.where(R != 0, self.user_means_[:, np.newaxis], 0)

    # Calculate cosine similarity on the centered matrix
    from sklearn.metrics.pairwise import cosine_similarity
    self.similarity_matrix_ = cosine_similarity(R_centered.T)

    # Part C: Applying Shrinkage and Min Support
    # Calculate co-rated counts
    mask = (self.train_data_ > 0).astype(float)
    co_rated_counts = mask.T @ mask

    # Apply min_support threshold
    if self.min_support > 0:
        self.similarity_matrix_[co_rated_counts < self.min_support] = 0

    # Apply shrinkage factor
    if self.shrinkage > 0:
```

```
            counts_shrinkage = (co_rated_counts + self.shrinkage)
            shrinkage_factor = co_rated_counts / counts_shrinkage
            self.similarity_matrix_ *= shrinkage_factor

        # An item cannot be its own neighbor
        np.fill_diagonal(self.similarity_matrix_, 0)

        return self
```

This code:

(1) Stores the input data and initializes the similarity matrix.

(2) Computes user mean ratings and centers the rating matrix.

(3) Calculates cosine similarity between items based on the centered data.

(4) Applies a minimum support threshold and shrinkage to improve similarity quality.

(5) Sets diagonal elements to zero to exclude items as their own neighbors.

(6) Returns the object for further use.

This is a detailed explanation of the `fit` method for an ItemKNN (k-nearest neighbors for items) algorithm used in recommender systems. The method takes a rating matrix `R` (where rows are users and columns are items) and computes a similarity matrix between items.

```
def fit(self, R):
```

- Defines the `fit` method of a class (presumably ItemKNN). It takes a rating matrix `R` (where `R[i, j]` is the rating user `i` gave to item `j`) and stores it for further processing.

```
self.train_data_ = R
```

- Saves the input rating matrix `R` into the class attribute `self.train_data_` for later use. This is simply copying the data into the class object.

```
num_items = R.shape[1]
```

- Extracts the number of items (columns) from the matrix `R`. `R.shape` returns a tuple `(number_of_users, number_of_items)`. `R.shape[1]` is the number of columns, i.e., the number of items (e.g., movies or products).

```
self.similarity_matrix_ = np.zeros((num_items, num_items))
```

- Creates a square matrix of zeros with size `num_items × num_items` using `np.zeros`. This matrix (`self.similarity_matrix_`) will store similarity scores between pairs of items (e.g., how similar two movies are).

```
self.user_means_ = np.true_divide(R.sum(axis=1), (R!=0).sum(axis=1))
```

- Computes the average rating for each user, considering only non-zero ratings (where the user actually rated an item).
- `R.sum(axis=1)`: Sums the ratings for each user (across rows of `R`), returning an array where each element is the sum of ratings for a user.
- `(R!=0)`: Creates a matrix of the same size as `R`, with `True` (1) where ratings are non-zero and `False` (0) where ratings are absent.
- `(R!=0).sum(axis=1)`: Counts the number of non-zero ratings for each user.
- `np.true_divide(a, b)`: Divides `a` by `b` element-wise, returning an array of results. Here, it divides the sum of ratings by the count of ratings to get the mean.
- The result is stored in `self.user_means_`, an array of average ratings for each user.

```
self.user_means_[np.isnan(self.user_means_)] = 0
```

- Checks for `NaN` values in `self.user_means_` (which can occur if a user has no ratings, leading to division by zero).
- `np.isnan(self.user_means_)`: Returns a boolean array with `True` where values are `NaN`.
- Replaces such `NaN` values with 0.

```
R_centered = R - np.where(R != 0, self.user_means_[:, np.newaxis], 0)
```

- Centers the rating matrix `R` by subtracting the user's mean rating from each of their non-zero ratings. This is done to compute *adjusted cosine similarity.*
- `self.user_means_[:, np.newaxis]`: Reshapes the `self.user_means_` array into a 2D array of size `[number_of_users, 1]` so it can be subtracted from `R`.

- `np.where(R != 0, self.user_means_[:, np.newaxis], 0)`: Creates a matrix of the same size as `R`. If a rating in `R` is non-zero (`R != 0`), it uses the user's mean rating (`self.user_means_[:, np.newaxis]`); otherwise, it uses 0.
- `R - ...`: Subtracts this matrix from `R` to get a centered matrix `R_centered`, where each non-zero rating is reduced by the user's mean rating.

```
from sklearn.metrics.pairwise import cosine_similarity
```

- Imports the `cosine_similarity` function from the scikit-learn library. This function calculates the cosine similarity between vectors (in this case, between items).

```
self.similarity_matrix_ = cosine_similarity(R_centered.T)
```

- Computes the cosine similarity between items using the centered matrix `R_centered`.
- `R_centered.T`: Transposes `R_centered` so that rows become items and columns become users (needed to compare items).
- `cosine_similarity(R_centered.T)`: Calculates the cosine similarity between all pairs of items (rows of the transposed matrix). The result is a `num_items × num_items` matrix where element `[i, j]` shows how similar items `i` and `j` are.
- The result is stored in `self.similarity_matrix_`.

```
mask = (self.train_data_ > 0).astype(float)
```

- Creates a mask for non-zero ratings in the original matrix `self.train_data_` (i.e., `R`).
- `self.train_data_ > 0`: Returns a boolean matrix where `True` is where ratings are greater than 0, and `False` otherwise.
- `.astype(float)`: Converts `True` to 1.0 and `False` to 0.0, enabling numerical computations with the mask.

```
co_rated_counts = mask.T @ mask
```

- Calculates the number of users who rated both items for each pair of items.
- `mask.T @ mask`: Performs matrix multiplication of the transposed mask with itself. The result is a `num_items × num_items` matrix where element `[i, j]` is the number of users who rated both items `i` and `j`.

```
if self.min_support > 0:
    self.similarity_matrix_[co_rated_counts < self.min_support] = 0
```

- Applies a minimum support threshold (`self.min_support`).
- If the number of users who rated both items (`co_rated_counts[i, j]`) is less than `self.min_support`, the similarity between those items (`self.similarity_matrix_[i, j]`) is set to 0.
- This ignores item pairs rated by too few users to avoid unreliable similarity scores.

```
if self.shrinkage > 0:
    counts_shrinkage = (co_rated_counts + self.shrinkage)
    shrinkage_factor = co_rated_counts / counts_shrinkage
    self.similarity_matrix_ *= shrinkage_factor
```

- Applies shrinkage to the similarity matrix to reduce the influence of item pairs with few co-ratings.
- `counts_shrinkage = (co_rated_counts + self.shrinkage)`: Adds a constant `self.shrinkage` (a hyperparameter) to the co-rating counts to smooth the values.
- `shrinkage_factor = co_rated_counts / counts_shrinkage`: Computes a shrinkage factor for each pair of items. If `co_rated_counts` is small, the factor will be less than 1, reducing the similarity score.
- `self.similarity_matrix_ *= shrinkage_factor`: Multiplies the similarity matrix by this factor, reducing similarity scores for pairs with few co-ratings.

```
np.fill_diagonal(self.similarity_matrix_, 0)
```

- Sets the main diagonal of the similarity matrix (`self.similarity_matrix_`) to zeros. This ensures an item is not considered its own neighbor (an item's similarity to itself is not used in recommendations).

```
return self
```

- Returns the object itself (`self`), allowing method chaining (e.g., `model.fit(R).predict(...)`).

Line-by-Line Explanation of the predict_for_user Method for ItemKNN

```
def predict_for_user(self, user_ratings):
    predictions = np.zeros_like(user_ratings, dtype=float)

    # Find items the user has already rated
    rated_inds = np.where(user_ratings > 0)[0]

    # Iterate over all items to predict scores for unrated ones
    for item2pdct in range(len(user_ratings)):
        if user_ratings[item2pdct] == 0:
            # Get similarities between the target item and
            # all items the user has rated
            sims2rtd_itms = self.similarity_matrix_[item2pdct, rated_inds]

            # Get the user's ratings for those items
            ratings_of_rated = user_ratings[rated_inds]

            # Select the top K nearest neighbors
            if self.k > 0 and len(sims2rtd_itms) > self.k:
                # Find indices of the top-k absolute similarities
                top_neighbors = np.argsort(-np.abs(sims2rtd_itms))[:self.k]

                # Filter down to only the top-k neighbors
                sims2rtd_itms = sims2rtd_itms[top_neighbors]
                ratings_of_rated = ratings_of_rated[top_neighbors]

            # Calculate the weighted average
            numerator = sims2rtd_itms @ ratings_of_rated
            denominator = np.sum(np.abs(sims2rtd_itms))

            if denominator > 1e-8: # Add a small epsilon to avoid division by 0
                predictions[item2pdct] = numerator / denominator

    return predictions
```

This code:

(1) Initializes a predictions array to store predicted ratings.

(2) Identifies items the user has rated.

(3) For each unrated item, computes a predicted rating using a weighted average of the user's ratings for similar items.

(4) Optionally limits the computation to the top `k` most similar items (neighbors).

(5) Uses similarity scores from the similarity matrix (from `fit`) as weights.

(6) Ensures numerical stability by checking for a non-zero denominator.

(7) Returns the array of predicted ratings for all items.

Below is a detailed explanation of the `predict_for_user` method for an ItemKNN (k-nearest neighbors for items) algorithm used in recommender systems. The method takes a vector of user ratings (`user_ratings`) for all items and predicts ratings for items the user has not rated, using the similarity matrix computed in the `fit` method.

```
def predict_for_user(self, user_ratings):
```

- Defines the `predict_for_user` method of a class (presumably ItemKNN). It takes a vector `user_ratings`, where `user_ratings[i]` is the rating the user gave to item `i` (or 0 if the item is unrated), and predicts ratings for unrated items.

```
predictions = np.zeros_like(user_ratings, dtype=float)
```

- Creates an array `predictions` of the same shape as `user_ratings`, filled with zeros, to store predicted ratings. `np.zeros_like` ensures the array matches the input's shape and sets the data type to `float` for storing decimal predictions.

```
rated_inds = np.where(user_ratings > 0)[0]
```

- Identifies the indices of items the user has rated. `np.where(user_ratings > 0)` returns a tuple of arrays with indices where the condition is true. `[0]` extracts the array of indices for items where `user_ratings[i] > 0` (i.e., items the user has rated).

```
for item2pdct in range(len(user_ratings)):
```

- Iterates over all items (indices from 0 to the length of `user_ratings`) to predict ratings for each item. `item2pdct` represents the index of the item for which a rating is being predicted.

```
if user_ratings[item2pdct] == 0:
```

- Checks if the current item (`item2pdct`) is unrated by the user (i.e., `user_ratings[item2pdct] == 0`). Predictions are only computed for unrated items, as rated items already have known values.

```
sims2rtd_itms = self.similarity_matrix_[item2pdct, rated_inds]
```

- Retrieves the similarity scores between the target item (`item2pdct`) and all items the user has rated. `self.similarity_matrix_[item2pdct, rated_inds]` extracts a subset of the similarity matrix (computed in `fit`), giving similarities between `item2pdct` and the indices in `rated_inds`.

```
ratings_of_rated = user_ratings[rated_inds]
```

- Gets the user's ratings for the items they have rated. `user_ratings[rated_inds]` extracts the ratings corresponding to the indices in `rated_inds` (i.e., the ratings for items the user has previously rated).

```
if self.k > 0 and len(sims2rtd_itms) > self.k:
```

- Checks if the number of nearest neighbors (`self.k`) is specified and if the number of rated items (`len(sims2rtd_itms)`) exceeds `self.k`. If true, only the top `k` most similar items will be used for prediction to limit the number of neighbors.

```
top_neighbors = np.argsort(-np.abs(sims2rtd_itms))[:self.k]
```

- Finds the indices of the top `k` items with the highest absolute similarity to the target item. `np.abs(sims2rtd_itms)` takes the absolute value of similarities (to handle negative similarities), `-np.abs(sims2rtd_itms)` negates them for descending order sorting, and np.argsort(...)\[0:self.k\] selects the indices of the top `k` values.

```
sims2rtd_itms = sims2rtd_itms[top_neighbors]
```

- Filters the similarity scores to include only those of the top `k` neighbors, using the indices in `top_neighbors`.

```
ratings_of_rated = ratings_of_rated[top_neighbors]
```

- Filters the user's ratings to include only those for the top `k` neighbors, using the same `top_neighbors` indices.

```
numerator = sims2rtd_itms @ ratings_of_rated
```

- Computes the numerator for the weighted average prediction. `sims2rtd_itms @ ratings_of_rated` performs a dot product, multiplying each similarity score by the corresponding rating and summing the results. This gives a weighted sum of ratings, where weights are the similarity scores.

```
denominator = np.sum(np.abs(sims2rtd_itms))
```

- Computes the denominator for the weighted average by summing the absolute values of the similarity scores (`np.abs(sims2rtd_itms)`). This normalizes the prediction to account for the magnitude of similarities.

```
if denominator > 1e-8:
```

- Checks if the denominator is greater than a small threshold (`1e-8`) to avoid division by zero. This ensures numerical stability when similarities are very small or zero.

```
predictions[item2pdct] = numerator / denominator
```

- Calculates the predicted rating for the target item (`item2pdct`) as the weighted average: `numerator / denominator`. The result is stored in the `predictions` array at the corresponding index.

```
return predictions
```

- Returns the `predictions` array containing predicted ratings for all items. For rated items, the prediction remains 0 (as no prediction is computed), and for unrated items, it contains the predicted rating based on the weighted average of similar items.

Line-by-Line Explanation of ItemKNNRecommender Usage

```
# 1. Instantiate the recommender with hyperparameters
item_knn = ItemKNNRecommender(k=2, min_support=1, shrinkage=1.0)

# 2. Train the model on the rating data
item_knn.fit(R)

# 3. Get recommendations for a specific user (e.g., user 0)
```

```
target_user_ratings = R[0, :]
predicted_scores = item_knn.predict_for_user(target_user_ratings)

# 4. Generate the final ranked list
# Create a list of (item_id, score) for unrated items
unrated_items = np.where(target_user_ratings == 0)[0]
recommendations = sorted(
    zip(unrated_items, predicted_scores[unrated_items]),
    key=lambda x: x[1],
    reverse=True
)

print(f"Original ratings for User 0: {target_user_ratings}")
print(f"Predicted scores for User 0: {np.round(predicted_scores, 2)}")
print("\nTop recommendations for User 0:")
for item_id, score in recommendations:
    print(f"  Item {item_id}: Predicted Score = {score:.4f}")
```

This code:

(1) Initializes an `ItemKNNRecommender` with specified hyperparameters (`k`, `min_support`, `shrinkage`).

(2) Trains the model on a rating matrix `R` to compute item similarities.

(3) Extracts ratings for a specific user (user 0) and predicts ratings for all items.

(4) Generates a ranked list of unrated items based on predicted scores.

(5) Prints the user's original ratings, predicted scores, and top recommendations.

Below is a detailed explanation of a code snippet that demonstrates how to use the `ItemKNNRecommender` class to train a model on rating data and generate recommendations for a specific user. The code assumes a rating matrix `R` (where rows are users and columns are items) and uses the `ItemKNNRecommender` to predict ratings and recommend items.

Line-by-Line Explanation of ItemKNNRecommender Usage

This is a detailed explanation of a code snippet that demonstrates how to use the `ItemKNNRecommender` class to train a model on rating data and generate recommendations for a specific user. The code assumes a rating matrix `R` (where rows are users and columns are items) and uses the `ItemKNNRecommender` to predict ratings and recommend items.

```
# 1. Instantiate the recommender with hyperparameters
item_knn = ItemKNNRecommender(k=2, min_support=1, shrinkage=1.0)
```

- Creates an instance of the `ItemKNNRecommender` class, initializing it with hyperparameters:
  - `k=2`: Specifies that the top 2 most similar items (neighbors) will be used when predicting ratings.
  - `min_support=1`: Sets the minimum number of users who must have rated both items for their similarity to be considered non-zero.
  - `shrinkage=1.0`: Applies a shrinkage factor to reduce the influence of item pairs with few co-ratings, improving similarity reliability.
- The instance is stored in the variable `item_knn`.

```
# 2. Train the model on the rating data
item_knn.fit(R)
```

- Trains the `ItemKNNRecommender` model by calling its `fit` method with the rating matrix `R`.
- `R` is a matrix where `R[i, j]` represents the rating user `i` gave to item `j` (0 if unrated).
- The `fit` method computes the similarity matrix between items based on adjusted cosine similarity, applying the specified `min_support` and `shrinkage` parameters.

```
# 3. Get recommendations for a specific user (e.g., user 0)
target_user_ratings = R[0, :]
```

- Extracts the ratings for user 0 from the rating matrix `R`. `R[0, :]` selects the first row of `R`, which is a vector of ratings for all items by user 0 (e.g., `[3, 0, 4, 0]` if user 0 rated item 0 as 3, item 2 as 4, and left others unrated).
- Stores this vector in `target_user_ratings`.

```
predicted_scores = item_knn.predict_for_user(target_user_ratings)
```

- Calls the `predict_for_user` method of `item_knn` to predict ratings for user 0 for all items, based on their existing ratings in `target_user_ratings`.
- The method uses the similarity matrix (from `fit`) to compute weighted averages of ratings for unrated items, considering the top `k` similar items.
- The result, `predicted_scores`, is an array of predicted ratings for all items (0 for rated items, predicted values for unrated items).

```
# 4. Generate the final ranked list
# Create a list of (item_id, score) for unrated items
unrated_items = np.where(target_user_ratings == 0)[0]
```

- Identifies the indices of items that user 0 has not rated. `np.where(target_user_ratings == 0)` returns a tuple of arrays with indices where the condition is true. `[0]` extracts the array of indices for items where `target_user_ratings[i] == 0` (i.e., unrated items).
- Stores these indices in `unrated_items`.

```
recommendations = sorted(
    zip(unrated_items, predicted_scores[unrated_items]),
    key=lambda x: x[1],
    reverse=True
)
```

- Creates a ranked list of recommendations for unrated items.
- `zip(unrated_items, predicted_scores[unrated_items])`: Pairs each unrated item's index with its predicted score from `predicted_scores`.

- `sorted(..., key=lambda x: x[1], reverse=True)`: Sorts the pairs by the predicted score (`x[1]`) in descending order (`reverse=True`) to rank items from highest to lowest predicted rating.
- The result, `recommendations`, is a list of tuples `(item_id, predicted_score)` for unrated items, sorted by score.

```
print(f"Original ratings for User 0: {target_user_ratings}")
```

- Prints the original ratings for user 0, stored in `target_user_ratings`. This shows the user's actual ratings for all items (including zeros for unrated items).

```
print(f"Predicted scores for User 0: {np.round(predicted_scores, 2)}")
```

- Prints the predicted scores for user 0, rounded to 2 decimal places using np.round(predicted_scores, 2). This displays the predicted ratings for all items, with zeros for rated items and predicted values for unrated items.

```
print("\nTop recommendations for User 0:")
```

- Prints a header for the list of top recommendations for user 0, adding a newline (\n) for formatting.

```
for item_id, score in recommendations:
    print(f"  Item {item_id}: Predicted Score = {score:.4f}")
```

- Iterates over the `recommendations` list, where each element is a tuple `(item_id, predicted_score)`.
- Prints each recommendation in the format `Item {item_id}: Predicted Score = {score:.4f}`, showing the item index and its predicted score rounded to 4 decimal places for clarity.

UserKNN Implementation

This section provides a line-by-line explanation of the `UserKNNRecommender` class, which implements a user-based k-nearest neighbors (UserKNN) algorithm for recommender systems. Unlike `ItemKNNRecommender`, which computes similarities between items, `UserKNNRecommender` computes similarities between users to predict ratings. The code assumes a rating matrix `R` (where rows are users and columns are items). Where the implementation mirrors `ItemKNNRecommender`, references are made to avoid repetition.

Line-by-Line Explanation of the `fit` Method for UserKNN

The full code of the `fit` method:

```
def fit(self, R):
    self.train_data = R

    # Part A: Adjusted Cosine Similarity (Pearson Correlation)
    # Calculate the mean rating for each user.
    # np.true_divide handles division by zero for users with no ratings.
    self.user_means = np.true_divide(self.train_data.sum(axis=1),
                                     (self.train_data != 0).sum(axis=1))
    # Replace any resulting NaNs (from users with no ratings) with 0.
    self.user_means[np.isnan(self.user_means)] = 0

    # Center the ratings by subtracting the user's mean
    # from each of their non-zero ratings.
    R_centered = self.train_data - np.where(self.train_data != 0,
                                            self.user_means[:, np.newaxis], 0)

    # Calculate cosine similarity on the centered user-rating vectors.
    self.similarity_matrix = cosine_similarity(R_centered)

    # A user cannot be their own neighbor, so we set their self-similarity to 0.
    np.fill_diagonal(self.similarity_matrix, 0)

    return self
```

This code:

(1) Stores the input data and initializes the similarity matrix for users (not items, unlike `ItemKNN`).

(2) Computes user mean ratings and centers the rating matrix, as in `ItemKNN`.

(3) Calculates cosine similarity between users (not items) based on centered data.

(4) Sets diagonal elements to zero to exclude users as their own neighbors.

(5) Returns the object for further use.

The `fit` method for `UserKNNRecommender` is very similar to that of `ItemKNNRecommender` (see the `fit` explanation in the ItemKNN section). Below, we highlight differences and explain each line, avoiding repetition where possible.

```
def fit(self, R):
```

- Defines the `fit` method, taking a rating matrix `R` (where `R[i, j]` is the rating user `i` gave to item `j`). This is identical to `ItemKNN`'s `fit` method (see ItemKNN section).

```
self.train_data = R
```

- Saves the rating matrix `R` into `self.train_data`, similar to `self.train_data_ = R` in `ItemKNN` (see ItemKNN section). Note the slight naming difference (`train_data` vs. `train_data_`).

```
self.user_means = np.true_divide(self.train_data.sum(axis=1),
                                 (self.train_data != 0).sum(axis=1))
```

- Computes the mean rating for each user, identical to `ItemKNN`'s `self.user_means_` computation (see ItemKNN section for details). Stored in `self.user_means` (no underscore).

```
self.user_means[np.isnan(self.user_means)] = 0
```

- Replaces `NaN` values in `self.user_means` with 0, as in `ItemKNN` (see ItemKNN section).

```
R_centered = self.train_data - np.where(self.train_data != 0,
                                        self.user_means[:, np.newaxis], 0)
```

- Centers the rating matrix by subtracting each user's mean rating from their non-zero ratings, identical to `ItemKNN`'s centering process (see ItemKNN section).

```
self.similarity_matrix = cosine_similarity(R_centered)
```

- Computes cosine similarity between users using `cosine_similarity` from scikit-learn. Unlike `ItemKNN`, which transposes `R_centered` (`R_centered.T`) to compare items, here `R_centered` is used directly to compare users (rows of `R_centered` are user rating vectors). The result is a `num_users × num_users` similarity matrix stored in `self.similarity_matrix`.

```
np.fill_diagonal(self.similarity_matrix, 0)
```

- Sets the diagonal of `self.similarity_matrix` to zero, ensuring a user is not their own neighbor, as in `ItemKNN` (see ItemKNN section).

```
return self
```

- Returns the object for method chaining, identical to `ItemKNN` (see ItemKNN section).

Key Difference from ItemKNN: The `UserKNN fit` method computes similarities between users (rows of `R`) rather than items (columns of `R`). It omits `min_support` and `shrinkage` adjustments present in `ItemKNN`, making the similarity computation simpler.

Line-by-Line Explanation of the `predict` Method for UserKNN

The full code of the `predict` method:

```
def predict(self):
    num_users, num_items = self.train_data.shape
    predictions = np.zeros_like(self.train_data, dtype=float)
    # Iterate over each user to make predictions
    for u in range(num_users):
        # Get indices of most similar users
        neighbor_indices = np.argsort(-self.similarity_matrix[u, :])
        # Predict scores for each unrated item
        for i in range(num_items):
            if self.train_data[u, i] != 0:
                continue
            numerator = 0
            denominator = 0
            neighbor_count = 0
            # Calculate weighted average from the k-nearest neighbors
            for neighbor_idx in neighbor_indices:
                if neighbor_count >= self.k:
                    break
                # Ensure the neighbor has rated the item
                if self.train_data[neighbor_idx, i] > 0:
                    sim = self.similarity_matrix[u, neighbor_idx]
                    neighbor_rating = self.train_data[neighbor_idx, i]
                    neighbor_mean = self.user_means[neighbor_idx]
                    # Add the weighted rating deviation to the totals
                    numerator += sim * (neighbor_rating - neighbor_mean)
                    denominator += np.abs(sim)
                    neighbor_count += 1
            # Calculate the final prediction
            if denominator > 0:
```

```
                pred = self.user_means[u] + (numerator / denominator)
                # Clip the score to be within the valid rating range
                predictions[u, i] = np.clip(pred, 1, 5)
            else:
                # Use the user's average as a fallback
                predictions[u, i] = self.user_means[u]
    # Combine original ratings with the new predictions
    self.R_predicted = np.where(
        self.train_data > 0,
        self.train_data,
        predictions
    )
    return self.R_predicted
```

This code:

(1) Initializes a predictions matrix for all users and items.

(2) For each user, identifies the `k` most similar users and predicts ratings for unrated items.

(3) Uses a weighted average of rating deviations from similar users, adjusted by the target user's mean.

(4) Clips predictions to a valid range (1 to 5) and uses the user's mean as a fallback if no neighbors have rated an item.

(5) Combines original ratings with predictions and returns the full matrix.

```
def predict(self):
```

- Defines the `predict` method, which predicts ratings for all users and items, returning a full matrix of predictions. Unlike `ItemKNN`'s `predict_for_user`, which predicts for a single user, this method computes predictions for all users.

```
num_users, num_items = self.train_data.shape
```

- Extracts the dimensions of the rating matrix `self.train_data`: `num_users` (number of rows) and `num_items` (number of columns).

```
predictions = np.zeros_like(self.train_data, dtype=float)
```

- Creates a matrix predictions of the same shape as self.train_data (i.e., num_users × num_items), filled with zeros, to store predicted ratings. np.zeros_like ensures matching shape, and dtype=float allows decimal predictions.

```
for u in range(num_users):
```

- Iterates over all users (indices from 0 to num_users - 1) to compute predictions for each user.

```
neighbor_indices = np.argsort(-self.similarity_matrix[u, :])
```

- Finds the indices of users sorted by their similarity to user u. self.similarity_matrix[u, :] gives similarities between user u and all users. -self.similarity_matrix[u, :] negates the values for descending order sorting, and np.argsort returns indices of users from most to least similar.

```
for i in range(num_items):
```

- Iterates over all items (indices from 0 to num_items - 1) to predict ratings for each item for user u.

```
if self.train_data[u, i] != 0:
    continue
```

- Skips prediction if user u has already rated item i (i.e., self.train_data[u, i] != 0), as predictions are only needed for unrated items.

```
numerator = 0
denominator = 0
neighbor_count = 0
```

- Initializes variables for computing the weighted average prediction: numerator (sum of weighted rating deviations), denominator (sum of absolute similarities), and neighbor_count (tracks the number of neighbors used).

```
for neighbor_idx in neighbor_indices:
```

- Iterates over the indices of similar users (neighbor_indices), starting with the most similar.

```
if neighbor_count >= self.k:
    break
```

- Stops after considering `self.k` neighbors (the `k` most similar users who rated the item), ensuring only the top `k` neighbors contribute to the prediction.

```
if self.train_data[neighbor_idx, i] > 0:
```

- Checks if the neighbor (`neighbor_idx`) has rated item `i`. Only neighbors who rated the item contribute to the prediction.

```
sim = self.similarity_matrix[u, neighbor_idx]
```

- Retrieves the similarity score between user `u` and the neighbor (`neighbor_idx`) from the similarity matrix.

```
neighbor_rating = self.train_data[neighbor_idx, i]
```

- Gets the neighbor's rating for item `i` from `self.train_data`.

```
neighbor_mean = self.user_means[neighbor_idx]
```

- Retrieves the neighbor's mean rating from `self.user_means`.

```
numerator += sim * (neighbor_rating - neighbor_mean)
```

- Adds the weighted rating deviation to the numerator. The deviation (`neighbor_rating - neighbor_mean`) is the neighbor's rating for item `i` minus their mean rating, weighted by the similarity score `sim`.

```
denominator += np.abs(sim)
```

- Adds the absolute value of the similarity score to the denominator to normalize the prediction.

```
neighbor_count += 1
```

- Increments the count of neighbors used for the prediction.

```
if denominator > 0:
```

- Checks if the denominator is positive to avoid division by zero (i.e., ensures at least one neighbor contributed a rating).

```
pred = self.user_means[u] + (numerator / denominator)
```

- Computes the predicted rating for user `u` and item `i` as the user's mean rating (`self.user_means[u]`) plus the weighted average of rating deviations (`numerator / denominator`).

```
predictions[u, i] = np.clip(pred, 1, 5)
```

- Clips the predicted rating to the valid range [1, 5] using `np.clip` to ensure ratings are realistic (assuming a 1–5 rating scale). Stores the result in `predictions[u, i]`.

```
else:
    predictions[u, i] = self.user_means[u]
```

- If no neighbors rated the item (`denominator == 0`), uses the user's mean rating (`self.user_means[u]`) as a fallback prediction.

```
self.R_predicted = np.where(self.train_data > 0,
                            self.train_data, predictions)
```

- Creates a final matrix `self.R_predicted` combining original ratings and predictions. np.where(self.train_data \¿ 0, self.train_data, predictions) keeps original ratings where self.train_data \¿ 0 and uses predicted ratings elsewhere.

```
return self.R_predicted
```

- Returns the `self.R_predicted` matrix containing original ratings for rated items and predicted ratings for unrated items.

Key Difference from ItemKNN: The `predict` method computes ratings for all users and items, using similarities between users rather than items. It incorporates the target user's mean rating and clips predictions to a valid range, unlike `ItemKNN`, which predicts for a single user and does not clip ratings.

Line-by-Line Explanation of UserKNNRecommender Usage

The full code for using `UserKNNRecommender`:

```
# 1. Instantiate the recommender with a neighborhood size k=2.
user_knn = UserKNNRecommender(k=2)

# 2. Train the model on the rating data to build the similarity matrix.
user_knn.fit(R)

# 3. Generate the full matrix of predicted ratings.
R_predicted = user_knn.predict()

# 4. Examine the recommendations for a specific user (e.g., user 0).
target_user_ratings = R[0, :]
predicted_ratings_for_user = R_predicted[0, :]

# Create a ranked list of recommendations for unrated items.
unrated_items = np.where(target_user_ratings == 0)[0]
recommendations = sorted(
    zip(unrated_items, predicted_ratings_for_user[unrated_items]),
    key=lambda x: x[1],
    reverse=True
)

print(f"Original ratings for User 0: {target_user_ratings}")
print(f"Predicted ratings (U0): {np.round(predicted_ratings_for_user, 2)}")
print("\nTop recommendations for User 0:")
for item_id, score in recommendations:
    print(f"  Item {item_id}: Predicted Score = {score:.4f}")
```

This code:

(1) Initializes a `UserKNNRecommender` with a specified number of neighbors (`k`).

(2) Trains the model on a rating matrix `R` to compute user similarities.

(3) Generates a full matrix of predicted ratings for all users and items.

(4) Extracts and ranks recommendations for a specific user (user 0).

(5) Prints the user's original ratings, predicted ratings, and top recommendations.

```
# 1. Instantiate the recommender with a neighborhood size k=2.
user_knn = UserKNNRecommender(k=2)
```

- Creates an instance of `UserKNNRecommender` with `k=2`, specifying that predictions use the 2 most similar users. Unlike `ItemKNN`, which also sets `min_support` and `shrinkage`, only `k` is specified here.

```
# 2. Train the model on the rating data to build the similarity matrix.
user_knn.fit(R)
```

- Trains the model by calling `fit` with the rating matrix `R`, computing user similarities (see `fit` explanation above). This is similar to `ItemKNN`'s training step (see ItemKNN usage section).

```
# 3. Generate the full matrix of predicted ratings.
R_predicted = user_knn.predict()
```

- Calls the `predict` method to generate a full `num_users × num_items` matrix of predicted ratings, stored in `R_predicted`. Unlike `ItemKNN`'s `predict_for_user`, which predicts for one user, this predicts for all users.

```
# 4. Examine the recommendations for a specific user (e.g., user 0).
target_user_ratings = R[0, :]
```

- Extracts user 0's ratings from `R` (`R[0, :]`), identical to `ItemKNN` usage (see ItemKNN usage section).

```
predicted_ratings_for_user = R_predicted[0, :]
```

- Extracts predicted ratings for user 0 from `R_predicted` (`R_predicted[0, :]`), giving a vector of ratings (original for rated items, predicted for unrated items).

```
unrated_items = np.where(target_user_ratings == 0)[0]
```

- Identifies indices of items user 0 has not rated, identical to ItemKNN usage (see ItemKNN usage section).

```
recommendations = sorted(
    zip(unrated_items, predicted_ratings_for_user[unrated_items]),
```

```
    key=lambda x: x[1],
    reverse=True
)
```

- Creates a ranked list of recommendations for unrated items, identical to `ItemKNN` usage (see ItemKNN usage section).

```
print(f"Original ratings for User 0: {target_user_ratings}")
```

- Prints user 0's original ratings, identical to `ItemKNN` usage (see ItemKNN usage section).

```
print(f"Predicted ratings (U0): {np.round(predicted_ratings_for_user, 2)}")
```

- Prints user 0's predicted ratings, rounded to 2 decimal places. Unlike `ItemKNN`, which labels this as "Predicted scores," this uses "Predicted ratings" to reflect the inclusion of original ratings for rated items.

```
print("\nTop recommendations for User 0:")
```

- Prints a header for the recommendations, identical to `ItemKNN` usage (see ItemKNN usage section).

```
for item_id, score in recommendations:
    print(f"  Item {item_id}: Predicted Score = {score:.4f}")
```

- Prints each recommendation, identical to `ItemKNN` usage (see ItemKNN usage section).

Key Difference from ItemKNN: The usage code predicts ratings for all users at once (`predict`) rather than for a single user (`predict_for_user`). The recommendation ranking and printing steps are nearly identical, but `UserKNN`'s predictions incorporate original ratings in the output matrix.

SLIM Implementation

This section provides a line-by-line explanation of the `SLIMRecommender` class, which implements the Sparse Linear Methods (SLIM) algorithm for Top-N item ranking from implicit feedback data. Unlike `ItemKNNRecommender` and `UserKNNRecommender`, which use predefined similarity metrics (cosine similarity), SLIM learns a sparse item-item similarity matrix by solving regression problems with ElasticNet regularization. The code assumes a binary user-item interaction matrix `R` (where rows are users, columns are items, 1 indicates interaction, and 0 indicates no interaction). Where the implementation mirrors ItemKNN or UserKNN, references are made to avoid repetition.

Line-by-Line Explanation of the fit Method for SLIM

The full code of the fit method:

```
def fit(self, R):
    self.train_data_ = R
    num_items = R.shape[1]
    self.similarity_matrix_ = np.zeros((num_items, num_items))

    # We use ElasticNet which combines L1 and L2 penalties.
    alpha = self.l1_reg + self.l2_reg
    l1_ratio = self.l1_reg / alpha if alpha > 0 else 0

    model = ElasticNet(
        alpha=alpha,
        l1_ratio=l1_ratio,
        positive=True, # Enforce non-negative similarity coefficients
        fit_intercept=False,
        copy_X=False,
        max_iter=1000
    )

    warnings.filterwarnings("ignore", category=ConvergenceWarning)

    # Train a model for each item
    for j in range(num_items):
        y = R[:, j]
        X = np.delete(R, j, axis=1)
        model.fit(X, y)
        self.similarity_matrix_[j, :] = np.insert(model.coef_, j, 0)

    warnings.resetwarnings()
    return self
```

This code:

(1) Stores the input data and initializes an item-item similarity matrix.

(2) Configures an ElasticNet model with L1 and L2 regularization for sparsity and stability.

(3) Trains a regression model for each item to predict its interactions using other items as features.

(4) Constructs the similarity matrix from the learned regression coefficients.

(5) Returns the object for further use.

```
def fit(self, R):
```

- Defines the `fit` method, taking a binary interaction matrix `R` (where `R[i, j] = 1` if user `i` interacted with item `j`, else `0`). This is similar to `ItemKNN` and `UserKNN` (see their `fit` sections).

```
self.train_data_ = R
```

- Saves the input matrix `R` into `self.train_data_`, identical to `ItemKNN` (see ItemKNN `fit` section).

```
num_items = R.shape[1]
```

- Extracts the number of items (columns) from `R`, identical to `ItemKNN` (see ItemKNN `fit` section).

```
self.similarity_matrix_ = np.zeros((num_items, num_items))
```

- Initializes a `num_items × num_items` matrix of zeros for storing item-item similarities, identical to `ItemKNN` (see ItemKNN `fit` section).

```
alpha = self.l1_reg + self.l2_reg
```

- Computes the total regularization strength `alpha` by summing the L1 (`self.l1_reg`) and L2 (`self.l2_reg`) regularization parameters, which control sparsity and coefficient magnitude in the ElasticNet model.

```
l1_ratio = self.l1_reg / alpha if alpha > 0 else 0
```

- Calculates the L1 ratio for ElasticNet, which is the proportion of L1 regularization (`self.l1_reg / alpha`). If `alpha` is 0, sets `l1_ratio` to 0 to avoid division by zero.

```
model = ElasticNet(
    alpha=alpha,
    l1_ratio=l1_ratio,
    positive=True, # Enforce non-negative similarity coefficients
```

```
    fit_intercept=False,
    copy_X=False,
    max_iter=1000
)
```

- Initializes an `ElasticNet` model from scikit-learn with:
  - `alpha`: Total regularization strength.
  - `l1_ratio`: Proportion of L1 regularization.
  - `positive=True`: Ensures learned coefficients (similarities) are non-negative, as negative similarities are not meaningful for item recommendation.
  - `fit_intercept=False`: Excludes an intercept term, as the model predicts interactions directly from other items.
  - `copy_X=False`: Optimizes memory by not copying input data.
  - `max_iter=1000`: Sets maximum iterations for optimization.

```
warnings.filterwarnings("ignore", category=ConvergenceWarning)
```

- Suppresses `ConvergenceWarning` messages from scikit-learn, which may occur if the ElasticNet model does not fully converge within `max_iter` iterations.

```
for j in range(num_items):
```

- Iterates over each item (index `j`) to learn its similarity coefficients.

```
y = R[:, j]
```

- Sets the target vector `y` as the interaction column for item `j` (`R[:, j]`), representing which users interacted with item `j` (1 or 0).

```
X = np.delete(R, j, axis=1)
```

- Creates the feature matrix `X` by removing column `j` from `R` (using `np.delete`), so the model predicts item `j`'s interactions using all other items as features.

```
model.fit(X, y)
```

- Trains the `ElasticNet` model to predict `y` (interactions for item `j`) using `X` (interactions for all other items). The learned coefficients represent similarities between item `j` and other items.

```
self.similarity_matrix_[j, :] = np.insert(model.coef_, j, 0)
```

- Stores the learned coefficients in row `j` of `self.similarity_matrix_`. `model.coef_` contains coefficients for all items except `j`. `np.insert(model.coef_, j, 0)` inserts a 0 at index `j` (ensuring an item is not its own neighbor) and assigns the result to the row.

```
warnings.resetwarnings()
```

- Restores default warning behavior after suppressing `ConvergenceWarning`.

```
return self
```

- Returns the object for method chaining, identical to `ItemKNN` and `UserKNN` (see their `fit` sections).

Key Difference from ItemKNN/UserKNN: Unlike `ItemKNN` and `UserKNN`, which use cosine similarity, SLIM learns the similarity matrix via ElasticNet regression, optimizing for sparsity and non-negative coefficients. It does not center ratings or apply `min_support/shrinkage`, as it works with implicit (binary) data.

Line-by-Line Explanation of the `predict` Method for SLIM

The full code of the `predict` method:

```
def predict(self, R_input):
    # Prediction is a matrix multiplication of user interactions
    # and the learned similarity matrix.
    R_scores = R_input @ self.similarity_matrix_

    # We only care about scores for items the user has NOT seen.
    # Set scores for already-seen items to 0.
    return np.where(R_input > 0, 0, R_scores)
```

This code:

(1) Computes ranking scores for all users and items via matrix multiplication.

(2) Sets scores for already-interacted items to 0 to focus on recommendations for unseen items.

(3) Returns the score matrix for ranking.

```
def predict(self, R_input):
```

- Defines the `predict` method, taking an input interaction matrix `R_input`. It predicts ranking scores for all users and items, similar to `UserKNN`'s `predict` (which returns a full matrix) but different from `ItemKNN`'s `predict_for_user` (single user).

```
R_scores = R_input @ self.similarity_matrix_
```

- Computes ranking scores via matrix multiplication of `R_input` (user-item interactions) and `self.similarity_matrix_` (item-item similarities). The result, `R_scores`, is a `num_users` × `num_items` matrix where `R_scores[i, j]` is the score for user `i` and item `j`, based on interactions with similar items.

```
return np.where(R_input > 0, 0, R_scores)
```

- Sets scores for items the user has already interacted with (`R_input > 0`) to 0, ensuring recommendations focus on unseen items. `np.where` returns `0` where `R_input > 0` and `R_scores` otherwise. The output is a matrix of scores for ranking.

Key Difference from ItemKNN/UserKNN: SLIM's predictions are simpler, using direct matrix multiplication without weighted averages or clipping. Scores are not ratings but ranking values, and the method focuses on implicit feedback, unlike `ItemKNN/UserKNN`, which handle explicit ratings.

Line-by-Line Explanation of SLIMRecommender Usage

The full code for using `SLIMRecommender`:

```
# 1. Instantiate the recommender with hyperparameters
slim_rec = SLIMRecommender(l1_reg=0.01, l2_reg=0.01)

# 2. Train the model on the implicit interaction data
slim_rec.fit(R_implicit)
```

```
# 3. Generate the full matrix of ranking scores
R_scores = slim_rec.predict(R_implicit)

# 4. Get recommendations for a specific user (e.g., user 0)
target_user_interactions = R_implicit[0, :]
scores_for_user = R_scores[0, :]

# 5. Generate the final ranked list of items the user has not seen
unseen_items = np.where(target_user_interactions == 0)[0]
recommendations = sorted(
    zip(unseen_items, scores_for_user[unseen_items]),
    key=lambda x: x[1],
    reverse=True
)
u0=np.where(target_user_interactions > 0)[0]
rs=np.round(scores_for_user[unseen_items], 4)
print(f"User 0 interacted with items: {u0}")
print(f"Ranking scores for unseen items: {rs}")
print("\nTop recommendations for User 0:")
for item_id, score in recommendations:
    # Only show recommendations with a positive score
    if score > 0:
        print(f"  Item {item_id}: Ranking Score = {score:.4f}")
```

This code:

(1) Initializes a `SLIMRecommender` with L1 and L2 regularization parameters.

(2) Trains the model on a binary interaction matrix to learn item similarities.

(3) Generates a full matrix of ranking scores for all users and items.

(4) Extracts and ranks recommendations for a specific user (user 0).

(5) Prints the user's interactions, scores for unseen items, and top recommendations.

```
# 1. Instantiate the recommender with hyperparameters
slim_rec = SLIMRecommender(l1_reg=0.01, l2_reg=0.01)
```

- Creates an instance of `SLIMRecommender` with `l1_reg=0.01` and `l2_reg=0.01` for ElasticNet regularization, controlling sparsity and coefficient magnitude. Unlike `ItemKNN` (which uses `k`, `min_support`, `shrinkage`) or `UserKNN` (which uses `k`), SLIM uses regularization parameters.

```
# 2. Train the model on the implicit interaction data
slim_rec.fit(R_implicit)
```

- Trains the model by calling `fit` with the binary interaction matrix `R_implicit`, learning the item-item similarity matrix (see SLIM `fit` section). This is similar to `ItemKNN` and `UserKNN` training (see their usage sections).

```
# 3. Generate the full matrix of ranking scores
R_scores = slim_rec.predict(R_implicit)
```

- Calls `predict` to generate a `num_users × num_items` matrix of ranking scores, stored in `R_scores`. Like `UserKNN`'s `predict`, it computes scores for all users, unlike `ItemKNN`'s single-user prediction.

```
# 4. Get recommendations for a specific user (e.g., user 0)
target_user_interactions = R_implicit[0, :]
```

- Extracts user 0's interactions from R_implicit (R_implicit[0, :]), similar to target_user_ratings in ItemKNN/UserKNN (see their usage sections). Here, it's binary (1 for interaction, 0 otherwise).

```
scores_for_user = R_scores[0, :]
```

- Extracts ranking scores for user 0 from `R_scores`, similar to `predicted_ratings_for_user` in `UserKNN` or `predicted_scores` in `ItemKNN` (see their usage sections).

```
# 5. Generate the final ranked list of items the user has not seen
unseen_items = np.where(target_user_interactions == 0)[0]
```

- Identifies indices of items user 0 has not interacted with, identical to unrated_items in ItemKNN / UserKNN (see their usage sections).

```
recommendations = sorted(
    zip(unseen_items, scores_for_user[unseen_items]),
    key=lambda x: x[1],
    reverse=True
)
```

- Creates a ranked list of recommendations for unseen items, identical to `ItemKNN`/`UserKNN` (see their usage sections).

```
print(f"User 0 interacted with items: {np.where(target_user_interactions > 0)[0]}")
```

- Prints the indices of items user 0 interacted with, differing from `ItemKNN/UserKNN`'s "Original ratings" by focusing on binary interactions (not ratings).

```
scores=np.round(scores_for_user[unseen_items], 4)
print(f"Ranking scores for unseen items: {scores}")
```

- Prints ranking scores for unseen items, rounded to 4 decimal places. This is similar to ItemKNN / UserKNN 's predicted scores/ratings but emphasizes "ranking scores" for implicit feedback.

```
print("\nTop recommendations for User 0:")
```

- Prints a header for recommendations, identical to ItemKNN / UserKNN (see their usage sections).

```
for item_id, score in recommendations:
    # Only show recommendations with a positive score
    if score > 0:
        print(f"  Item {item_id}: Ranking Score = {score:.4f}")
```

- Prints recommendations with positive scores, similar to ItemKNN / UserKNN but filters for score \¿ 0 to ensure meaningful recommendations, as SLIM scores are not bounded like ratings.

Key Difference from ItemKNN/UserKNN: SLIM works with implicit feedback (binary interactions) rather than explicit ratings, uses regression to learn similarities, and produces ranking scores rather than predicted ratings. The usage is similar to `UserKNN` (full matrix prediction) but differs in terminology ("interactions" vs. "ratings," "ranking scores" vs. "predicted ratings").

SVD++ Implementation

This section provides a line-by-line explanation of the `SVDPlusPlusRecommender` class, which implements the SVD++ algorithm for rating prediction. SVD++ extends basic matrix factorization by incorporating implicit feedback, modeling both explicit ratings and implicit user-item interactions (e.g., whether a user interacted with an item, regardless of the rating). The code assumes a rating matrix `R` (where rows are users, columns are items, and values are explicit ratings; 0 indicates no rating but can imply implicit non-interaction). Where the implementation mirrors other algorithms like `ItemKNN` or `UserKNN`, references are made to avoid repetition.

Line-by-Line Explanation of the fit Method for SVD++

The full code of the `fit` method:

```
def fit(self, R):
    self.train_data = R
    num_users, num_items = R.shape
    self.mu = np.mean(R[R > 0])  # Global mean rating

    # Initialize biases and factors
    self.user_biases = np.zeros(num_users)
    self.item_biases = np.zeros(num_items)
    self.user_factors = np.random.normal(0, 0.1, (num_users, self.num_factors))
    self.item_factors = np.random.normal(0, 0.1, (num_items, self.num_factors))
    self.implicit_factors = np.random.normal(0, 0.1, (num_items, self.num_factors))

    # Identify implicit interactions (non-zero entries imply interaction)
    implicit_mask = (R > 0).astype(float)

    # SGD training loop
    for epoch in range(self.epochs):
      for u in range(num_users):
        # Get items rated by user u (explicit + implicit)
        rated_items = np.where(R[u, :] > 0)[0]
        if len(rated_items) == 0:
            continue
        sqrt_num_rated = np.sqrt(len(rated_items))

        # Compute implicit user representation
        implicit_sum = np.sum(self.implicit_factors[rated_items, :], axis=0)
        implicit_sum = implicit_sum / sqrt_num_rated
        effective_user_factor = self.user_factors[u, :] + implicit_sum

        for i in rated_items:
          # Prediction
          pred = (self.mu + self.user_biases[u] + self.item_biases[i] +
                  np.dot(effective_user_factor, self.item_factors[i, :]))
          err = R[u, i] - pred

          # Update biases
          c1 = (err - self.reg * self.user_biases[u])
          c2 = (err - self.reg * self.item_biases[i])
```

```
            self.user_biases[u] += self.learning_rate * c1
            self.item_biases[i] += self.learning_rate * c2

            # Update factors
            c3 = (err*self.item_factors[i, :]-self.reg*self.user_factors[u, :])
            c4 = (err*effective_user_factor-self.reg*self.item_factors[i, :])
            self.user_factors[u, :] += self.learning_rate * c3
            self.item_factors[i, :] += self.learning_rate * c4

            # Update implicit factors
            for j in rated_items:
                self.implicit_factors[j, :] += self.learning_rate * (
                    (err * self.item_factors[i, :] / sqrt_num_rated)
                    - self.reg * self.implicit_factors[j, :]
                )

    return sel
```

This code:

(1) Stores the input data and computes the global mean rating.

(2) Initializes user/item biases, latent factors, and implicit factors.

(3) Identifies implicit interactions via a mask.

(4) Performs SGD over epochs, updating parameters based on prediction errors.

(5) Returns the object for further use.

```
def fit(self, R):
```

- Defines the `fit` method, taking a rating matrix `R` (explicit ratings).

```
self.train_data = R
num_users, num_items = R.shape
```

- Extracts the number of users and items from `R`

```
self.mu = np.mean(R[R > 0])
```

- Computes the global mean rating `self.mu` from all non-zero ratings in `R` using `np.mean(R[R > 0])`.

```
self.user_biases = np.zeros(num_users)
```

- Initializes user biases as a zero array of size `num_users`.

```
self.item_biases = np.zeros(num_items)
```

- Initializes item biases as a zero array of size `num_items`.

```
self.user_factors = np.random.normal(0, 0.1, (num_users, self.num_factors))
self.item_factors = np.random.normal(0, 0.1, (num_items, self.num_factors))
self.implicit_factors = np.random.normal(0, 0.1, (num_items, self.num_factors))
```

- Initializes user latent factors as a `num_users × num_factors` matrix with random normal values (mean 0, std 0.1).
- Initializes item latent factors similarly for `num_items × num_factors`.
- Initializes implicit factors (y_j) for items, a `num_items × num_factors` matrix.

```
implicit_mask = (R > 0).astype(float)
```

- Creates a binary mask for implicit interactions (1 where R ¿ 0)

```
for epoch in range(self.epochs):
  for u in range(num_users):
    rated_items = np.where(R[u, :] > 0)[0]
```

- Finds indices of items rated by user `u`.

```
if len(rated_items) == 0:
    continue
```

- Skips users with no ratings.

```
sqrt_num_rated = np.sqrt(len(rated_items))
```

- Computes the square root of the number of rated items for normalization.

```
implicit_sum = np.sum(self.implicit_factors[rated_items, :], axis=0) / sqrt_num_rated
```

- Computes the summed implicit factors normalized by sqrt(—N(u)—).

```
effective_user_factor = self.user_factors[u, :] + implicit_sum
```

- Adds the implicit sum to the user's explicit factors.

```
for i in rated_items:
```

- Iterates over each rated item `i` for user `u`.

```
pred = (self.mu + self.user_biases[u] + self.item_biases[i] +
        np.dot(effective_user_factor, self.item_factors[i, :]))
```

- Computes the predicted rating using SVD++ formula.

```
err = R[u, i] - pred
```

- Calculates the prediction error.

```
c2=(err - self.reg * self.user_biases[u])
self.user_biases[u] += self.learning_rate * c2
```

- Updates user bias with gradient descent.

```
c1=(err - self.reg * self.item_biases[i])
self.item_biases[i] += self.learning_rate * c1
```

- Updates item bias.

```
c3=(err * self.item_factors[i, :] - self.reg * self.user_factors[u, :])
self.user_factors[u, :] += self.learning_rate * c3
```

- Updates user factors.

```
c4=(err * effective_user_factor - self.reg * self.item_factors[i, :])
self.item_factors[i, :] += self.learning_rate * c4
```

- Updates item factors.

```
for j in rated_items:
    m=(err * self.item_factors[i, :] / sqrt_num_rated)
    self.implicit_factors[j, :] += self.learning_rate * (
        m - self.reg * self.implicit_factors[j, :]
    )
```

- Updates all implicit factors for rated items.

```
return self
```

Line-by-Line Explanation of the `predict` Method for SVD++

The full code of the `predict` method:

```
def predict(self):
    num_users, num_items = self.train_data.shape
    predictions = np.zeros((num_users, num_items))
    for u in range(num_users):
        rated_items = np.where(self.train_data[u, :] > 0)[0]
        sqrt_num_rated = np.sqrt(len(rated_items)) if len(rated_items) > 0 else 1
        implicit_sum = np.sum(
          self.implicit_factors[rated_items, :],
          axis=0) / sqrt_num_rated
        effective_user_factor = self.user_factors[u, :] + implicit_sum
        for i in range(num_items):
            if self.train_data[u, i] == 0:
                predictions[u, i] = (
                        self.mu + self.user_biases[u] +
                           self.item_biases[i] +
                        np.dot(effective_user_factor,
                               self.item_factors[i, :]))
    return predictions
```

This code:

(1) Initializes a predictions matrix.

(2) For each user, computes effective user factors and predicts ratings for unrated items.

(3) Returns the predictions matrix.

```
def predict(self):
```

- Defines the `predict` method to compute ratings for unrated items

```
num_users, num_items = self.train_data.shape
```

- Extracts dimensions

```
predictions = np.zeros((num_users, num_items))
```

- Initializes predictions matrix.

```
for u in range(num_users):
```

- Iterates over users.

```
rated_items = np.where(self.train_data[u, :] > 0)[0]
```

- Finds rated items.

```
sqrt_num_rated = np.sqrt(len(rated_items)) if len(rated_items) > 0 else 1
```

- Computes normalization, with fallback to 1.

```
implicit_sum = np.sum(self.implicit_factors[rated_items, :], axis=0) / sqrt_num_rated
```

- Computes implicit sum.

```
effective_user_factor = self.user_factors[u, :] + implicit_sum
```

- Effective user factor.

```
for i in range(num_items):
```

- Iterates over items.

```
if self.train_data[u, i] == 0:
```

- Predicts only for unrated items.

```
predictions[u, i] = (self.mu + self.user_biases[u] + self.item_biases[i] +
                     np.dot(effective_user_factor, self.item_factors[i, :]))
```

- Computes prediction.

```
return predictions
```

Line-by-Line Explanation of SVDPlusPlusRecommender Usage

The full code for using `SVDPlusPlusRecommender`:

```
# 1. Instantiate the recommender with hyperparameters
svd_pp = SVDPlusPlusRecommender(num_factors=20,
                                learning_rate=0.005,
                                reg=0.02, epochs=10)

# 2. Train the model on the rating data
svd_pp.fit(R)

# 3. Generate the matrix of predicted ratings for unrated items
predictions = svd_pp.predict()

# 4. Get recommendations for a specific user (e.g., user 0)
target_user_ratings = R[0, :]
predicted_scores_for_user = predictions[0, :]

# Create a ranked list of recommendations for unrated items
unrated_items = np.where(target_user_ratings == 0)[0]
recommendations = sorted(
    zip(unrated_items, predicted_scores_for_user[unrated_items]),
```

```
    key=lambda x: x[1],
    reverse=True
)

print(f"Original ratings for User 0: {target_user_ratings}")
print(f"Predicted scores for User 0: {np.round(predicted_scores_for_user, 2)}")
print("\nTop recommendations for User 0:")
for item_id, score in recommendations:
    print(f"  Item {item_id}: Predicted Score = {score:.4f}")
```

This code:

(1) Initializes a `SVDPlusPlusRecommender` with factors, learning rate, regularization, and epochs.

(2) Trains the model on the rating matrix.

(3) Generates predictions for unrated items.

(4) Ranks and prints recommendations for a user.

```
# 1. Instantiate the recommender with hyperparameters
svd_pp = SVDPlusPlusRecommender(num_factors=20,
                                learning_rate=0.005,
                                reg=0.02, epochs=10)
```

- Creates instance with SVD++ hyperparameters.

```
# 2. Train the model on the rating data
svd_pp.fit(R)
```

- Trains model

```
# 3. Generate the matrix of predicted ratings for unrated items
predictions = svd_pp.predict()
```

- Gets predictions

```
# 4. Get recommendations for a specific user (e.g., user 0)
target_user_ratings = R[0, :]
```

- Extracts ratings

```
predicted_scores_for_user = predictions[0, :]
```

- Extracts scores.

```
unrated_items = np.where(target_user_ratings == 0)[0]
```

- Finds unrated items.

```
recommendations = sorted(
    zip(unrated_items, predicted_scores_for_user[unrated_items]),
    key=lambda x: x[1],
    reverse=True
)
```

- Ranks recommendations.

```
print(f"Original ratings for User 0: {target_user_ratings}")
print(f"Predicted scores for User 0: {np.round(predicted_scores_for_user, 2)}")
print("\nTop recommendations for User 0:")
for item_id, score in recommendations:
    print(f"  Item {item_id}: Predicted Score = {score:.4f}")
```

- Prints recommendations.

www.ingramcontent.com/pod-product-compliance
Lightning Source LLC
LaVergne TN
LVHW060028210926
848481LV00013B/3812